A Short Course in the Philosophy of Religion

George Pattison

scm press

© George Pattison 2001

British Library Cataloguing in Publication data

A catalogue record of this book is available
from the British Library

0 334 028345

First published in 2001 by SCM Press
9–17 St Albans Place London N1 0NX

SCM Press is a division of
SCM-Canterbury Press Ltd

Typeset by Regent Typesetting, London
Printed in Great Britain by
Biddles Ltd, Guildford and King's Lynn

Contents

Acknowledgements

I would like to thank the staff and students of the St. Andrew's Biblical-Theological Institute in Moscow for the invitation to give the lectures that constitute the core of this book. Through the religious philosophers of the late nineteenth and early twentieth century – as well, of course, as through its literature – Russia provided a model of how it is possible to live religiously on the basis of a philosophically articulated faith. It is good to be able to honour that contribution. At the same time much of what is contained here reflects my own day-to-day teaching in Cambridge, and has been moulded by the needs, reactions and insights of many students and I am indebted also to them.

I should like specifically to thank those individuals who have looked through the manuscript and offered comments: Hugh Rayment-Pickard, Don Cupitt, Geoffrey Price and Neil Pattison. Less specifically, there are many friends, colleagues and occasional acquaintances with whom I have discussed many of the issues dealt with here and to whom I owe either insight or the turn of a phrase. Disliking sentimental and pretentious 'acknowledgements', however, I'll stop there.

Introduction

This 'short course' began as just that, a short course of six lectures on the philosophy of religion given to students of the St Andrew's Biblical-Theological Institute in Moscow (and perhaps a trace of its 'Russian' origin lingers on in the final text). These lectures constitute the core of the first six chapters, although each has been expanded and extensively revised. At the same time the argument developed here can be read as drawing out some of the implications of the position sketched in my *The End of Theology and the Task of Thinking about God*. Perhaps unsurprisingly a number of readers have latched on to the first half of that title 'The End of Theology' and construed my argument there as being essentially negative. Undoubtedly, there was a negative element in it, and it does seem to me that a long tradition of theologizing is coming to an end in our time, though like the shadow of the Buddha alluded to by Nietzsche, 'theology' may continue to enjoy a kind of shadowy half-life for many centuries to come. However, the second half of the title was no less important, because it does not seem to me that the possibilities for thinking about God (not even the possibilities for thinking about God within the Christian tradition) are exhausted by the winding-down of the particular intellectual tradition identified by the term 'theology'. The title of that earlier book itself contains an allusion to an essay by Heidegger, 'The End of Philosophy and the Task of Thinking' and the pattern of end/new-beginning that is so characteristic of the later Heidegger is crucial both for what I was attempting there and am offering here. This time, however, the emphasis falls more on what might be seen as the positive element, the possibility of a 'new beginning' of thinking about God, albeit a 'new beginning' that carries forward impulses found throughout the history of humanity's attempts to think about God. Yet perhaps this contrast between 'negative' and 'positive' is not itself very helpful – is not our life in time a matter of ever repeated endings and beginnings, and are not the endings no less necessary for life than the beginnings, and where is truth to be found outside the movement between the two, the 'between'? The 'end of theology' is not, then, a matter for mourning but simply a part of the situation in which God is to be thought about today, and if that doesn't make thinking about God any easier it doesn't necessarily make it more difficult than it always was.

Another problem some reviewers found with the earlier book was that it contained no footnotes. At one level, this is rather amusing, and suggests the extent to which the task of thinking about God has been subsumed under a certain model of academic writing. Challenging the assumption that one can only think about God with the aid of a battery of footnotes was, indeed, part of the point of broaching 'the end of theology'. The issue there was not 'who has already said this' but the kind of orientation in thought appropriate to contemporary religious reflection, i.e. thinking out of our contemporary situation rather than engaging in a literary exchange. I do have to acknowledge, though, that precisely the hermeneutic approach adopted both there and here means accepting that we do not think in a vacuum but through dialogue with the thought of others and, for us, this means the literary remains of those who have thought before us. In order fully to follow my argument, then, readers have a justifiable claim to have set out for them the literary voices with whom, through whom or against whom I am developing my own position. The present work therefore sets out to start to make good the deficit of its predecessor, and to give colour and mass to what was there sketched only in the merest outline. Even so, as an introductory work it only gives a part of the picture, and those who are particularly interested in how I reached this position must follow up the more specialist studies presented in, e.g. my work on Kierkegaard, Heidegger and religious existentialism.[1]

At the same time I have to admit that like *The End of Theology and the Task of Thinking about God* this short course (and especially the first seven chapters) is largely formal in its approach. In other words, I do not really offer much in the way of actual thinking about God. Rather, I am attempting only to illuminate something of the context that makes the task of thinking about God at all meaningful. Even the last three chapters, which offer an extended essay on the problem of evil and are therefore much more concrete, cannot claim to be more than a beginning and do not constitute anything like a conclusion. In more vernacular terms, this is a 'Let's-get-the-ball-rolling' rather than a 'This-is-how-it-is' sort of work. Perhaps, then, Socratic rather than Platonic.

This reflects not only my conception of the subject but also my practice as a teacher. Theologians (not, of course, unlike historians, literary critics and other academic animals) are easily tempted by the prospect of founding a school, a movement, an axis, or inaugurating a 'project'. My idea of teaching, however, is that it is not a matter of telling the student what I think, but of helping the student to think for him or herself. This demands a certain reticence or withdrawal on the part of the teacher. Managing this in a written text is, however, a different matter from doing it in the context of a 'live' and ongoing relationship. Possibly this present work holds too closely to certain idioms of 'live' speech, but I am unapologetic about the fact that it is intended not to present a rounded or complete position but to stimulate, help or otherwise enter into the process of actual, lived 'thinking about God'.

One thing that has surprised me about the book is the extent to which the kinds of issues usually associated with religious pluralism do not appear directly in it. Although I assert that the practice of thinking about God must be contextualized today in a situation of religious pluralism, there is no discussion of, e.g. Hindu or Islamic points of view on the various theoretical issues discussed. Despite the importance in my own development of the encounter with Buddhism[2] and Judaism, this will read as a book framed by the assumptions of a very particular Western and, largely, Christian discourse. This is probably a shortcoming, but perhaps it also reflects something of the subject itself. For whilst philosophical reflections on religious topics have been a feature of Abrahamic, Indic and other religious traditions for many centuries, the idea of the philosophy of religion in the sense in which that is understood today and is explored here is something that took shape in the West, in the context of the Enlightenment, but also in relation to a specific constellation of questions that, historically, belonged to Christianity and, to a lesser (but perhaps only a slightly lesser) extent to Judaism. This has not prevented this kind of philosophy from impacting on other religious traditions – in the Neo-Hinduism of the nineteenth century or in the Kyoto School of Buddhist philosophers – but it has done so precisely by providing a new context in which the experiences, symbols and beliefs of those religions are to be thought. Here as elsewhere, globalization is for good or ill largely Western in its origins and even when it undergoes radical cultural transformations that apparently remove it from these origins I suggest that its genetic imprint is still discernible – and needs to be discerned if we are fully to understand its meaning for our time. This point is different from that of Hegel or Heidegger, whose insistence on the exclusively Western origin of philosophy is tied up with their view concerning the distinctive role of ancient

Greek thought. However, the philosophy of religion, as I understand it, is not so much distinctively Greek as distinctively modern, and the way in which a Plato or an Augustine thinks about God is as much transformed by being filtered through the media of history, subjectivity and language as is the thought of a Shankara or a Lao Tse. Moreover, if it was indeed the specific historical phenomenon of Enlightenment Christianity that generated the philosophy of religion as we know it, the subject no longer belongs to the West or to Christianity in any exclusive sense. There is no copyright and there are no royalties. This philosophy is what it is only by being practised, and that means only in and as thinking – really thinking.

1

What is Philosophy of Religion?

First, what is philosophy?

The form of words 'philosophy of religion' suggests that in the question 'what is philosophy of religion?' what is at issue is, in the first instance, a kind of philosophy. This further suggests that if we want to understand what is going on in the philosophy of religion we must first understand what is meant by philosophy.

This is not so simple. There are so many different kinds of philosophy around that it might appear almost impossible to find a definition that every philosopher (or even a two-thirds majority of philosophers) would agree to. In Britain today we are witnessing a continuing struggle between, on the one hand, what has been called Anglo-Saxon or analytic philosophy and, on the other, what has been called European or continental philosophy. Each of these, in turn, has its own subdivisions and (sometimes bitter) internal quarrels. So, within the analytic tradition, it might broadly be true to say that the aim of philosophy is to subject language to a rigorous logical analysis that would purge it of all ambiguity and metaphor, and that would, it is claimed, approximate to the rigour of natural science. On the other hand, the analytic tradition also embraces those who might look to the later rather than to the earlier Wittgenstein, who are willing to accept the variety of language games being played and who, consequently, do not so much seek to correct the existing language as to clarify what is going on in it, who see 'ordinary language' as the solution, not the problem. Analogously, the continental tradition would include those like Habermas who still hold on to the Enlightenment ideal of a universal rational discourse, whereas the equally continental philosophers who follow Derrida and Foucault would claim that such a discourse is neither achievable nor desirable. In the last few years, it is true, there have been signs of a less adversarial approach. Some analytic philosophers have started to take some continental philosophers seriously – compared, for example, with the famous essay in which Rudolf Carnap subjected a passage from Heidegger's *Being and Time* to logical analysis in order to expose what Carnap regarded as 'metaphysical pseudostatements' that 'violate' logical syntax.[1] Equally, continental philosophers are beginning to take a more positive interest in the natural sciences. Nevertheless, despite such signs of détente it remains the case that many philosophy departments in Britain and America today follow completely different curricula, reading different texts and addressing different questions. For the Anglo-Saxons, Kant is the last continental philosopher to be taken seriously, whilst for the continentals Kant is when it all begins to get interesting. These same differences affect the philosophy of religion no less than other areas of philosophy. When I recently gave a seminar paper on Heidegger, I was asked by a colleague who stands in the analytic tradition 'That's all very interesting, but what's it got to do with philosophy? What is philosophy for you?'

It is also important to take into account the fact that for much of the twentieth century the map of philosophy was further complicated by the massive presence of Marxism-Leninism. Many (though by no means all[2]) of the major figures of modern continental philosophy were left-oriented, and their thinking was given a certain direction by Hegel and Marx, albeit developed in a different way from official communist doctrine. This not only applies to secular thinkers and movements like Sartre, Adorno, Horkheimer and the whole Frankfurt School, but to several of the significant figures of the philosophy of religion, amongst them Buber, Berdyaev and Tillich.

So, to repeat the question with which I began, if the philosophy of religion is a form of philosophy, what is philosophy?

Clearly, we will get very different answers to this question according as to whom we ask. So, instead of trying to find an agreed definition, let's look at an example of philosophizing, and let's look at one whose claim to be a genuine work of philosophy is, relatively, uncontroversial: Plato's *Republic*. This dialogue is largely concerned with the question as to the definition of justice. The discussion gets going with a saying, attributed to Simonides, that justice is to render every man his due. But what does this mean? As Socrates reveals, what it seems to mean is that we should do good to our friends and harm to our enemies. Harming enemies, however, would not seem to contribute much to the advancement of justice: in fact, Socrates suggests, this kind of definition 'must be due to some despot, so rich and powerful that he thought he could do as he liked'.[3] The next definition is offered by Thrasymachus, who asserts that to say '"just" or "right" means nothing but what is to the interest of the stronger party'.[4] At first this seems to mean simply that whatever the dominant ruler or class says is to be obeyed. However, Socrates points out that such rulers do not always know what is in their own best interests, so that we may actually do more to further the interests of the rulers by disobeying at least some of their commands than by obeying them. Thrasymachus then quickly reworks his definition so as to claim that the 'ruler, in so far as he is acting as ruler, makes no mistakes', i.e. 'as ruler' he is able to rise above the partial or ignorant views and passions that he may have as a private individual: part of being a ruler is having the knowledge that enables you to rule. Socrates next shows that, if being a ruler thus involves skill in what we may call 'statecraft', the ruler will not in fact rule in such a way as to advance his own interest solely or even primarily: like the doctor who exercises his art for the good of the patient, so the ruler will exercise his art for the good of society as a whole . . . and so the argument continues.

Now this may not give us enough to arrive at a definition of philosophy, but it does show us a piece of philosophizing, and it shows us the kind of thing that is typically involved in this activity. One of those with whom Socrates is speaking offers a definition, saying what he takes a particular word or term, in this case 'justice', to mean. Socrates then proceeds to ask them what is implied in this definition and, characteristically, demonstrates that it is self-contradictory, or leads to results that were not intended by the person offering it. What Socrates does, then, is to question assumptions; to question whether we really do know what we think or believe we know; to question whether we really understand what we are saying. In this way philosophy exposes the presuppositions that are embedded in our normal habits of speech and thought. Now, its aims in doing this may be varied. It may, for example, be aiming to get rid of confused and misleading assumptions in order to clear the ground for erecting the edifice of knowledge on a new basis – like Descartes, who spoke of his programme of doubt as being like clearing away the winding streets and ramshackle buildings of an old medieval town in order to make way for building an orderly new city. Or the aim of the philosopher may simply be to clarify what we are thinking and saying without any intention of fundamentally changing or renovating our existing knowledge or practices – perhaps like the later Wittgenstein, who declined to tell us what language games we should be playing, but said we should simply accept that 'this language game is being played'.

Nevertheless, whether the philosopher goes to work with the

positive aim of improving our language and our knowledge, or whether he promises to leave our existing language and knowledge intact, the early stages of philosophizing are usually experienced as rather uncomfortable. It's somewhat humiliating to discover that we don't really know what we're talking about, or that the implications of some of our most cherished views are self-contradictory or even unpleasant. It's no wonder that so many of Socrates' interlocutors became angry or confused. He himself spoke of himself variously as being like a stingray, a gadfly or a midwife. The first numbs its victim, making him lose confidence in what, till he began philosophizing, he had taken for granted. The second stings him, shaking him out of his complacency, his easy acceptance of the prevailing views of his society, his thoughtless participation in the common, everyday discourse of his circle. The midwife, to be sure, drags forth a new life: but even though the midwife's aim is to minimize the discomfort of the woman giving birth, giving birth remains a painful and sometimes protracted business. Moreover, Socrates himself was unable to lead the conversation further than to the point where it became clear that existing beliefs were untenable, and beyond that were only further questions – or the ambiguous, hinting language of myths. It is no wonder that Kierkegaard, who, despite insisting on the dissimilarity between Socrates and Christ remained a great admirer of the one he called 'a simple wise man of old', defined Socrates' position (in contrast to that of Plato) as 'infinite absolute negativity'.[5] Even though Socrates' work was powered by ethical passion, its results, according to Kierkegaard, were consistently negative. Socrates never showed us what we should believe or should do: he only demonstrated the impossibility or the incoherence of what we believed we already knew or practised.

This sense of 'negativity' is likely to be experienced by any beginner in philosophy. As one of my students put it 'it really does my head in'. It should. The way of philosophy makes things more difficult. It shows us that things are not what we thought they were.

However, the motivation of philosophy is not just to be awkward for the sake of it, nor will niggling away at trivial inconsistencies make good the claim implied by its etymology that 'philosophy' is a love of wisdom. Even when characterizing Socrates' standpoint as infinite absolute negativity Kierkegaard concedes that this negativity is not indulged in simply for its own sake but with a view to a better ethical practice. It is, after all, midwifery, not irritability. Hegel was to claim that 'the True is the whole'[6] and that what philosophy ultimately seeks is to overcome the partiality and provisionality of the local and limited viewpoints that most of us start with as inhabitants of the world of everyday talk, chock-full of unexamined presuppositions of every kind. Hegel, too, embraced the negative, but as a means for arriving at a higher, better secured positivity. Very few of his philosophical heirs have shared this optimism, however. The view onto the whole remains elusive, and any claim to have reached a final stopping point in the quest for knowledge immediately arouses the suspicion of the philosophical community. But this does not necessarily mean rejecting the movement towards the whole. For in seeking to draw out the presuppositions that underlie our everyday discourse, philosophy simultaneously performs two quite distinct operations. On the one hand it breaks each proffered statement analytically down into its simplest and most perspicuous form, making plain just what is or isn't being said in any given utterance. On the other hand – but inseparable from the analytic process – it shows that large areas of discourse that appear quite heterogeneous in the everyday perspective actually share certain common assumptions. There are certain bedrock convictions that turn out to shape the way in which I understand whole ranges of topics. Take the simple case of asking the reason for something.

I can ask about the reasons for things in all sorts of diverse contexts: why my cat refuses to come into the house, why a new light has appeared in the night sky, why I keep getting the wrong answer to a mathematical problem, or why I feel so irritable all the time. In our society we believe that each of these questions can be answered in terms of a rational explanation: my cat is angry with me for having dusted her down with flea powder and is fearful that I might do it again; the new light is a comet, that is itself the product of a sequence of distant cosmic events governed by strict mechanical laws; I feel irritated because of a vitamin deficiency or because of some diagnosable psychological syndrome. But different societies and different cultures have different ideas as to what might count as a good reason. In other societies people might appeal to the influence of the gods or witchcraft or spiritual states as the ultimate reasons for things.

Even within our own society we all know that the question 'why?' can mean different things in different contexts. But, quite remarkably, we usually have an unerring sense for the kind of answer that's being sought in any particular case. In most situations when I ask someone the reason for something – 'why are you doing this?' or 'what is the explanation for that?' – the person I'm asking knows spontaneously the kind of answer I'm looking for. In other words, we share certain assumptions as to what counts as a good reason. If someone asked me why I'm so irritable and I say 'because Zeus is angry with me' they'd think that I was either winding them up or else that I was losing it, because that just doesn't count as a good reason in contemporary Britain. Of course, there are all sorts of ways of answering this question that we do regard as legitimate: I could talk about my vitamin deficiency, my failure to resolve an urgent moral dilemma, the row I'd just had with my wife or my gloom at the recent turn of events in political life. Still, we'd agree without having to discuss it that any of these would count as possible reasons, and even if what I regarded as politically disastrous was regarded by my questioner as a new dawn, they'd recognize that my answer made sense. So, although – as in this last case – there is usually scope for arguing about what is, actually, the right answer to any given question, most human discourse relies upon there being prior, unspoken agreement as to the kind of answer that is worth taking seriously.

In seeking to expose the hidden assumptions behind our everyday talk, however, philosophy doesn't – and can't – rule out questioning even these assumptions, and therefore finds itself asking about the basic rules of any discourse whatsoever, i.e. about what makes any particular discourse possible at all. Philosophy might therefore even ask about the justification (is there any justification?) for believing that there must be a reason for every event and every assertion. And: what is the justification for believing that there is only one kind of 'reason' operative across the whole realm of experience and knowledge? Indeed, is there any such justification?

This last question may initially seem simply to reinforce the view that the kind of philosophy being embraced here is ultimately sceptical, since this might appear to throw open the door to a complete relativism. On this view we would not be justified in holding to a belief in any general or all-encompassing framework of truth or reason. All truth would be a matter of cultural conditioning, and appealing to Zeus as the explanation for certain events taking place in the world would, though less common, be no less justifiable than looking to the kind of explanation offered by natural science.[7] The privilege we give to science is not itself scientifically grounded but reflects the metaphysical prejudice that the world is exhaustively knowable in the light of human reason or, more cynically, provides a back-up for the political and economic interests of international capitalism and the global hegemony of the West. However, in terms of the kind of questioning being advocated here, the relativistic view must itself be open to questioning no less than any other. I personally may think the earth goes round the sun *just because* I am the beneficiary of a modern education (since I haven't myself undertaken the observations or calculations that would prove this to be so), but it does not follow that there is no issue of simple fact here. Even in the more complex field of cultural values and attitudes, it is not clear that there are no grounds for preferring democracy (with all its flaws) to military dictatorship as a means of governing a modern industrialized state, or for denying the validity of all judgments of quality in relation to art. If the relativist hypothesis can alert us to the extraordinarily wide range of pre-reflective prejudices at work in us – and thus far serve a useful philosophical role – it does not of itself answer the question it raises, nor indeed show the necessity, depth or scope of that question. Of itself, relativism leads simply to an over-abrupt foreclosing of the path of philosophical questioning. The philosopher is not like the child who keeps on asking 'why?' even when a point has been reached at which such a question is no longer relevant. Philosophical questioning is not questioning for questioning's sake, but for the sake of what is sought in questioning. In the traditional language of philosophy, it is a matter of seeking truth. However, what counts as truth is itself a matter of argument and debate. This may seem perilously close to a vicious circularity, but with just a slight shift in perspective it makes a kind of sense that the pursuit of truth should be inseparable from the question concerning the nature of truth itself.

Acknowledging relativism, but maintaining a certain caution in relation to it, philosophy is led towards ever more general, ever more fundamental questions about knowledge. In setting out to talk about justice, Socrates and his interlocutors are led on to consider the nature of knowledge, the structure of the soul and the nature of Being. Whether, in any given enquiry, it is possible to arrive at or to secure a definitive result with regard to such global questions is, as I have suggested in relation to Hegel, a whole other issue. Plato's own intentions, it should be said, are for the most part harder to decipher in this respect than Hegel's, and many of the ideas that hardened into doctrine in Platonism are presented in the dialogues themselves with great temerity and a deliberate adversion to their difficulty and uncertainty. In any case, having perhaps shown that the thought of such-and-such a thinker is dominated by the assumption that everything human, animal, vegetable and mineral is rationally explicable in terms of a mathematical model of rationality, I have then to question whether this assumption itself is justifiable, and whether there may not be domains of experience or action where such a model is highly inappropriate. The impetus towards generality, then, can by no means break loose from the practice of critical questioning. Heidegger put the point well in asserting that whilst philosophy must, as philosophy, direct its questioning to Being as a whole, it does so precisely with regard to the *questionableness* of such Being,[8] a questionableness that culminates in a sense for the insolubility of the ultimate questions of philosophy: Why is there something rather than nothing? What is it for any being to be at all? What does it mean for our understanding of our own being that we are able to ask such questions at all? The philosopher works to keep open and to deepen the questionableness of such questions, and, as the logical positivists argued, when the questionableness of these questions is forgotten and they are treated as if they might have answers analogous to the answers to the questions as to why trees cannot grow above a certain altitude or why we can be certain that the earth goes round the sun and not vice versa, then what we have is only pseudo-philosophy and pseudo-metaphysics.

And what is religion?

In the light of these preliminary comments we can see that, quite apart from all the particular objections that various schools of philosophy have brought against religion, there is something about philosophy that would seem to set it on an inevitable collision course with religion since religion, as popularly represented, is about providing answers, not asking or deepening questions.

The popular idea of religion is, of course, itself an assumption that the philosopher of religion will want to question, and it is not hard to guess that defining religion will prove no less easy than defining philosophy. Even if we limit ourselves to Christianity, it is hard to find a definition of the essence of Christianity that everyone would agree to. Such basic lack of agreement is eloquently, perhaps also tragically, witnessed by the divisions between the churches of Christendom and the tensions and differences within the various churches. If we extend our perspective to religion as a whole the difficulties can only be compounded.

Again, however, I shall not attempt a definition: instead I shall take a phrase which, whilst not an exact quote from the New Testament, condenses the message of a number of New Testament passages and which, I think, is generally characteristic of a widespread religious orientation: 'Believe and be saved'. Belief and salvation are, it seems, integral to the religious life. This does not, of course, exclude ethics. But, repeatedly, Christian thinkers have argued that an 'ethics' or a morality that is not based on belief, or that occludes the hope of salvation falls short of the fullness of Christian faith. 'Believe and be saved.'

But what does believing mean? Surely one aspect of belief is taking something – or some one – on trust. 'Blessed are those who have not seen and yet believe' (John 20.29). Belief accepts that some things cannot be known with absolute clarity. Faith leaps in where knowledge is lacking. But this is not just a negative thing, as if we were to say 'As I cannot, as a matter of fact, know this, I will have to make do with believing it.' Instead, the expression 'believe and be saved' points to the fact that belief is positive: it is the condition, the ground of salvation. Belief is not second-class knowledge as in Plato's opposition of *doxa* to *episteme*. Belief is the chief thing, what we must have if we are to be saved.

Religion, then, at least in this Christian form, would seem to be set on a collision course with philosophy, for if it is necessary to believe in order to be saved, that means that there are some assumptions, some presuppositions that we just shouldn't question. No matter how liberal we are in allowing philosophical questioning to tackle a thousand and one other issues, 'believing' would seem to be something that is independent from and that cannot be further improved or helped by such questioning. The basics of Christian faith, it seems, are non-negotiable – and this would seem to be equally true whether we understand this bedrock in terms of credal doctrines or as fundamental experiences and commitments on the part of the soul or self.

If that is so, then a philosophy of religion, Anglo-Saxon or continental as the case may be, is going to be experienced by religious believers as hostile. Even if the philosopher claims that he does not want to intrude upon the proper domain of religion and that he is happy for people to go on believing what they like, there would seem to be something about the very process of philosophizing that goes against the grain of religious life. The philosopher may go so far as to declare himself a friend of religion, but the believer will still have his suspicions. He does not want to be numbed, or driven mad or forced to endure birth-pains other than those of which Paul speaks when he speaks of the birth-pains of the new creation. The best we can arrive at, it might seem, is a state of armed neutrality, a cold war, in which each allows the other to have its own spheres of influence. Putting it crudely, 'philosophy of religion' would be what philosophers do in the privacy of their philosophy faculties, whilst theologians get on with their separate business in their seminaries and theology faculties.

Such a stand-off, however, is institutionally and intellectually unsatisfying. Is there a way forward? Can we bridge the gap?

Let us look again at religion, specifically at Christianity (although it may well turn out that analogous processes are going on in other religious traditions also).

If we do indeed take a second look, it would seem that, despite everything I have just said, there is something a bit like philosophizing going on in the history of Christianity itself. In fact, it would seem that there has to be something like philosophizing in religion itself. If I simply say 'Believe and be saved!' I will immediately, and properly, be asked 'Believe what?' For Christian belief, whatever it is in a positive sense, is not just any belief, it is not believing for its own sake. People have believed in many false and many evil things. Some people believe themselves to have been abducted by aliens. Others believe Adolf Hitler to have been a great and admirable man. Many believed so greatly in him that they were prepared to die for him. So the Christian must go beyond saying 'Believe'. The Christian must be able to say what or who is to be believed. 'I know whom I have believed' (2 Tim. 1.12). Even if belief is understood not so much in terms of objective doctrine as of a certain kind of subjective state, *the faith that believes* as opposed to *the faith that is believed in*, the Christian must be able to say what sort of subjective passion this is, and how it differs from the kind of passionate belief that some people have in Hitler, for example, or their football team. Belief and believing are not encountered as a raw, solid, undifferentiated mass: they are specific. Belief is belief in this and not that, in this person and not the other, and believing is a passion of a very particular kind.

From the very earliest days, then, whether in the ministry of Jesus or that of Paul, the content of belief was explained and expanded, and such explanation and expansion is a natural and necessary accompaniment of the process of discipleship, whether it is a matter of initiating the converted into the life of faith or of educating children into it. We need to know what we are to believe and how we are to go about believing it. And this process already contains something a bit like philosophizing. The parables of Jesus and the letters of Paul repeatedly bring to the fore misconceptions of the life of faith, they show what belief is not like, what it excludes, in order to advance what it really is.

However, not even in its earliest days – *especially* not in its earliest days – the church was never a self-contained institution. Belief was never explained in a vacuum. It was explained in relation to the existing beliefs and expectations, the existing 'world-view' of the recipient of the message. Clearly the earliest mission of the church, primarily directed at 'the lost sheep of the house of Israel' (Matt. 15.24), was able to make certain assumptions, to argue on the basis of scriptural texts that the listeners already accepted, and to appeal to certain beliefs and practices – the fatherhood of God, the resurrection of the dead, the practice of prayer, for example – that evangelists and evangelized shared. Yet not even the Jewish community of the early first century was a completely homogenous body. Jews like Paul had already internalized elements of Hellenistic or Graeco-Roman culture. And it was the encounter with this culture that perhaps proved decisive for the development of Christianity as a world religion, moving it beyond the limits of a reform movement within Judaism.

The point I am making here is not simply an historical one. Because the encounter with the Hellenistic world was an encounter with a world shaped in part by philosophy, the encounter necessarily involved a mutual reckoning between faith and philosophy. Of course, it has been to the Bible that many Christian writers have appealed for proof texts attacking the claims of human reason to pass judgment on divine truth. Yet it has been from the same Bible that others have taken exhortations to seek wisdom, pursue truth, to regard nature as a coherent and law-bound whole, to free our minds from the fear of demigods and demonic forces and in thinking to be mature, to regard God as Logos – both Word and Reason. Paul, especially perhaps in the Protestant world, has repeatedly been taken as the pre-eminent representative of faith versus reason, and it is Paul who proclaims that God has chosen the foolish things of this world to bring to nothing the wisdom of men. Yet Acts 17 tells, famously, of Paul's encounter with the philosophers of Athens at the Areopagus, and if that meeting ended without agreement, Paul is clearly represented as seeking common ground and acknowledging a shared element in the concept of God to which he can appeal – indeed, revealing his own familiarity with Hellenistic culture, for he even quotes a pagan poet in support of his argument. The discussion ends in some confusion. When Paul mentions the resurrection, some of the philosophers sneer. Others, however, it is reported, express a wish to continue the discussion at a later date.

Whether or not the philosophers ever got a chance to continue the discussion with Paul we do not know, but undoubtedly the debate described in Acts became the archetype for a major strand in the Christian strategy vis-à-vis the Graeco-Roman world. For what we see here is perhaps the first example of what came to be known as apologetics, i.e. the branch of Christian theology that seeks to defend and to promote the Christian faith in terms that are accepted by and comprehensible to the person being addressed.

From what has been said so far we can see that there was a certain inevitability about the rise of apologetics. It is extremely implausible that Christianity would ever have made the quantitative progress it did in the ancient world if it had not attempted to establish a shared horizon or common ground with educated pagans. Its message was not simply 'Believe and be saved . . .' but 'Believe and be saved *because* . . .'

One of the first great apologists was Justin known as 'Martyr'. Justin himself was born about 100 AD, in a pagan family, and passed through a number of philosophical schools, Stoicism, Aristotelianism, Pythagoreanism and Platonism, before accepting Christianity. Justin's 'First Apology' is addressed to the Emperor Antoninus Pius and to his two sons, described in the dedication as 'philosophers'. However, the apology is not a work of disinterested philosophy. It is a response to the persecution of the Christians and, in this context, an attempt to argue that these persecutions are not justified. The grounds on which this argument is to be conducted are indicated at the very beginning: reason, the love of truth, 'what is right', 'accurate and searching investigation' – versus 'the opinions of the ancients', 'prejudice', the 'desire of pleasing superstitious men', 'irrational impulse' and 'evil rumours'.[9] In other words, Justin is not claiming any special privileges for Christians, he is not saying that they are above or outside the law, but that they should indeed be judged by the same standards used to judge others. Christianity, he expects, will be vindicated by the fact that there is nothing in it that is offensive to reason, truth and the well-being of the state. If the Christians are charged with atheism, Justin reminds his readers that similar charges were levelled against Socrates. Now, however, we can see that Socrates was unjustly put to death, and that Socratic philosophy was intended to put to flight the demons of moral and intellectual corruption. The Christians believe in a God who is 'the Father and Creator of all', who rewards virtue and punishes vice, which, as Justin claims, Plato also taught. I shall not follow further the details of Justin's defence of Christian teachings or his exposition of Christian criticisms of idolatry or his insistence that Christians are committed to obedience to the Emperor and are, indeed, likely to prove model citizens, except to emphasize that, again and again, he insists on the analogies between Christian teaching and that of the best of pagan philosophy and mythology. 'For while we say that all things have been produced and arranged into a world by God, we shall seem to utter the doctrine of Plato; and while we say that there will be a burning up of all, we shall seem to utter the doctrine of the Stoics; and while we affirm that the souls of the wicked, being endowed with sensation even after death, are punished, and that those of the good being delivered from punishment spend a blessed existence, we shall seem to say the same things as the poets and philosophers; and while we maintain that men ought not to worship the works of their hands, we say the very things which have been said by the comic poet Menander, and other similar writers, for they have declared that the workman is greater than the work'.[10]

In his 'Second Apology', Justin makes what is perhaps an even stronger point, in discussing the relationship between Christ and Socrates. For, he says, Christ was 'partially known even by Socrates (For He was and is the Word who is in every man . . .)'.[11]

So, then, Christian doctrine does not just fall into the world like a stone into water: it identifies itself by means of analogies, like-nesses and, in the light of these last words of Justin's, the essential correspondence between Christian truth and all other forms or expressions of truth.

Moreover, although this is not a point I can develop here, I would suggest that it is probably a mistake to represent the apologists and the discipline of apologetics, as if it were simply a matter of what Buddhists call 'skilful means', i.e. of making a doctrine that is already complete within itself understandable to those 'outside'. Rather, I would claim, apologetics was internal to the process by which doctrine came to be defined. By the way in which it defined its rela-tion, first, to Judaism and, second, to paganism, the church estab-lished the basic parameters within which its own proper doctrine was to be formulated: the unity and fatherhood of God, human moral failure and the need for redemption, the messianic hope and the prophetic anticipation of final fulfilment are fundamental to the full articulation of Christian faith, and they were all points that the apolo-gists could connect either to Jewish or to pagan precedents.

In the theology of Athanasius, a church father who played a crucial role in the defining of Christian orthodoxy, we can see that his account of the Fall, for example, builds on the common ground estab-lished by earlier thinkers like Justin. In his depiction of the Fall Athanasius portrays Adam's turning away from the noetic contem-plation of God towards the passions of the body, an interpretation very much in keeping with the world-view of Hellenistic philosophy. However, Athanasius himself characteristically played down such affinities, arguing for the sole sufficiency of Scripture, but it is hard to see his version of the Fall as bearing any real relation to the biblical text as that would be understood by contemporary Hebrew Bible scholarship.

A more positive view is found in Augustine, whose *Confessions* candidly tells the story of his progress through various pagan schools, including Manichaeism and Platonism, before he arrived at Christianity. Both there and in *The City of God* he acknowledges what he regards as the truth to be found in Platonism, despite its distortions in popular Platonism. Especially important for him is the Platonic conception of God as Spirit, a doctrine that, he admits, helped to rescue him from the quasi-materialistic conception of God held by the Manichees. The tension between positive and negative elements in his relation to paganism is nicely summed up in two images he uses in the *Confessions*. In the first, he recalls how, when the Israelites were leaving Egypt, they were told to take with them the gold and jewels of the Egyptians: these, says Augustine, symbolize those positive things in pagan culture from which Christians can learn and that they can incorporate into their Christian lives. In the second, he says that the Platonist's view of truth is indeed a view of the promised land, but it is a view as from a great distance – and, he adds, it is one thing to see the promised land from a distance, and another to know how to find the way to it through the wilderness that lies between us and our goal.

In the wake of the modernist revolution and the rise of religious pluralism it may have become a problem that Christian doctrine came to be tied so closely to the presuppositions of Hellenistic and Graeco-Roman thought. And perhaps many of the problems that have arisen for the church in the situation of modernity have at least as much to do with the clash between the modern and the Hellenistic world-views as they do with the clash between the gospel and the world. This, certainly, has been a question for Protestant theology since the nineteenth century.

Interestingly, in terms of how topics such as 'doctrine' and 'apologetics' are often seen as representing the 'internal' and the 'external' expressions of faith respectively, a modern Catholic encyclopaedia of theology defines what it calls 'fundamental theology' as 'what used to be called apologetics'. And what is this 'fundamental theology'? It is the study and defining of the most fundamental principles of theology, the being, unity and identity of God: precisely the points that the apologists believed it was possible to see as common ground between Christianity and the best of the pagan world.

The development of the relationship between Christian theology and classical thought did not, curiously, end with the Roman Empire. When, in the Middle Ages, Aristotle was rediscovered in the West, many Christian thinkers, of whom the best known was, of course, Thomas Aquinas, were eager to integrate what they experienced as a 'new' body of knowledge into their theological work. Aquinas, famously, provided a model by which to understand the relationship between the Aristotelian philosophy and Christian doctrine that is summed up in his words that 'grace does not destroy but perfects nature'. Philosophy – Aristotle – represents the best achievement of the 'natural' reason. It can offer a 'theology' of a limited, but true kind. An example of this is in what are known as the 'five ways' by which, Thomas said, it is possible to establish the existence of God on the basis of human reason. These arguments are largely couched in terms of Aristotelian concepts and categories. Thus the first is the argument from motion, the second from causality, the third from contingency and necessity, the fourth from gradation, the fifth from design. In each case it is a matter of establishing certain general principles that hold for all beings as beings, and showing how these principles are unsustainable unless they are grounded in what is respectively described as a first mover, a first cause, an absolutely necessary being, the highest being and the designer of all beings – and, in each case, Aquinas comments 'and this everyone understands to be God'. There are, however, other teachings about God that reason, unaided, cannot supply. Reason alone cannot lead us to knowledge of the Incarnation, the Trinity, the Resurrection or salvation through Christ's atoning and substitutionary death. These 'higher' truths, however, complement or perfect the more general philosophical truths, just as Christian charity complements and perfects Aristotelian natural law and virtue.

In some respects Thomas Aquinas reflected the earlier practice of the apologists. However, he also gave authority to two further developments. The first was the development of what has come to be called philosophical theology, i.e. the use of philosophical reason in the clarification of doctrinal issues. Take, for example, a doctrinal issue such as the Incarnation. Now, according to Thomas' own teaching, philosophy, natural reason alone, would never be able to come up with such a doctrine. Its existence presupposes revelation. Nevertheless, once the doctrine is there, it is perfectly legitimate to use reason in clarifying and expounding it, in demonstrating its connection with other doctrines and the consequences that flow from holding it. Scripture and the authority of the church are, he states, incontrovertible. Yet, 'Sacred Doctrine makes use also of the authority of philosophers in those questions in which they were able to know the truth by natural reason'.[12] This 'also' is perhaps the key to Thomas' whole method. We see it again, for example, in his understanding of religious language and his justification of the doctrine of analogy: that words used of God and of created beings respectively are neither completely equivocal, nor univocal: they are used differently in relation to God and to creatures but they also have a shared, analogous meaning and, against extreme versions of negative or apophatic theology, it is meaningful to say that God is good or great or a father or beautiful. These words are, of course, human words, but they *also* have a divine meaning.

The other development that we do not exactly see in Thomas himself, but which his model of nature/grace anticipates is the rise of natural theology in the period of the early scientific revolution. Obviously the impact of the scientific revolution on Christian belief was powerful from the very beginning, as the case of Galileo made clear. The new discoveries were seen as threatening to a faith that had tied itself to a Hellenistic or Aristotelian cosmology. Worse was to follow. Not only did it turn out that the earth went round the sun, but it became increasingly difficult to maintain the biblical chronology or, more generally, the biblical explanation for the origins of the earth (and, later) of human beings – except perhaps as an imaginative, moral or mystical gloss on the story told by science. Nevertheless, there were many, especially in England (where, from Richard Hooker through the Cambridge Platonists and beyond, belief in reason remained a powerful theological thread[13]), who felt able to use the new knowledge in a manner analogous to Thomas's use of Aristotle. The study of nature, as they saw it, need not lead to materialism, but could reveal the evidences of a benign deity to those who knew how to study it aright. Perhaps the most successful of such natural theologians was William Paley, 1743–1805, who, despite writing after David Hume had issued his blistering attack on all forms of natural theology, produced a number of works in this genre, including his *Natural Theology or Evidences of the Existence and Attributes of the Deity collected from the Appearances of Nature*. Paley's argument was not particularly new. Basically it was that the complexity and purposiveness of the natural world were such that the world could not have come about just by chance but had to be the product of intelligent and benevolent design. Now it has become customary amongst modern philosophers of religion and philosophical theologians to scorn what is seen as Paley's naivety. After all, it was only a couple of generations later that

Darwin's account of the origin of the species was to show nature in a very different light, as an arena in which nature, 'red in tooth and claw', conducted an endless struggle for the survival of the fittest. Yet if the general outline of Paley's argument is simple, its beauty was in the detail. Paley was a first-rate naturalist, and his observations of what we would now call the ecological interdependence of natural processes were elegantly and carefully drawn. Indeed, Darwin's own undergraduate education was under the Cambridge naturalist and clergyman J. S. Henslow, a follower of Paley, who believed that it was precisely scientific research into the ordered processes of nature that would provide the best evidence for the existence of God. And such a line of argument has continued to appeal not only to liberal theologians in the Anglican tradition, but also to many scientists.[14]

And so to the philosophy of religion

Let us take stock. We have, in a very broad and general way, followed some of the historical interactions between faith and philosophy, or faith and reason. We have considered the rise of apologetics, and its modern descendant, fundamental theology; we have touched on philosophical theology as that is encountered in the Thomist tradition, and on the natural theology of the British empirical school. However, we must remember that we started out by asking about the philosophy of religion and, particularly, by seeking to understand that specifically as a form of philosophy. We were led, via a brief encounter with Plato, to think of philosophizing as involving the exposing and questioning of assumptions and presuppositions that mostly lie hidden in everyday speaking and thinking and it was suggested that something like this was going on in apologetics. However, in apologetics itself and in the other varieties of theology that seem to welcome natural reason, it is clear that the aim is not, as it seemed to be for Socrates, purely negative: to call these presuppositions into question. Instead the aim has been to establish the more firmly a truth already given, or to establish a truth as given, in order that theology may build upon it. In other words, what we have been examining here – apologetics, philosophical theology and natural theology – are all essentially forms of theology. As such they are perfectly justified, perhaps, in making assumptions about the viability of the fundamental concepts of theology and in understanding their task as contributing to the justification of belief. However, we have already seen that the claim that philosophy can issue in 'results' is highly problematic, and that any presumed 'results' cannot be separated from the process of philosophiz*ing*, in other words from repeatedly calling into question the assumptions we make with regard to the subject in question, in this case religion. Philosophy as doctrine can never finally separate itself from philosophy as critical practice.

If these comments have any force, then the philosophy of religion, *qua* philosophical practice, is going to look very different from even the most 'reasonable' form of theology.[15] Philosophy of religion does not and cannot make any pre-judgment in favour of the object of its enquiry. Its task is simply to bring that object into question, to expose, to undermine, to challenge any vestige or aura of self-evidence. In doing so, it will, like Socrates' practice of dialectic, stun and madden those engaged in it. But it may also help them to bring something new to birth – albeit it itself can only ever be the midwife, not the baby.

A further comment about philosophical method may be in order at this point. In asking about the kind of thing that philosophy is, we took as our starting point Plato's *Republic* and drew attention to the way in which Socrates repeatedly called into question the unexamined presuppositions of his interlocutor. It is also worth noting, however, that here, as in many other dialogues, Plato shows Socrates doing this by means of a methodical dialogue, a talking through of the issue, with a sequence of interlocutors. Sometimes, it strikes many readers, these interlocutors become little more than foils for Socrates' own development of the argument. Nevertheless, in principle, Plato's Socrates illustrates the fundamental and continuing importance of dialogue in philosophy. The matrix of philosophy was, in its beginnings, the freedom of personal conversation, directed towards the illumination of a topic agreed by the participants, and philosophy has continued as a serial conversation to which it is hard to imagine a conclusion ever being drawn. If, on the basis of an agreement as to that which is to be discussed, the personal interests of the participants are surrendered for the sake of the subject itself, if, that is, dialogue is refined into dialectic, dialectic itself will and must always return to the dialogical situation of embodied voices, whose philosophizing must be incorporated into those further dimensions of their lives that lie outside philosophy in the narrow sense. That philosophy arises from and returns to a continuing conversation in which questions arise on the basis of the concrete concerns of the participants suggests another reason, over and above the purely theoretical problems of any claim to absolute knowledge, why philosophizing is neverending. Even if a particular result is secured or a position reached behind which it is not possible to return, the forward flow of time and the inevitable advent of new voices means that unforeseen contextualizations and unguessed-at developments on the basis of that result are always possible. Philosophy as human practice cannot but share the historicality and the continuing openness of the human condition itself, as well as the obligation on all who participate in that condition both to speak and to listen to each other. Producing forward-moving dialogue (or: talking to each other endlessly) is what we humans do best, and the maximum openness to welcome the maximum number of participants must provide the optimum conditions for philosophy's flourishing.

The dialogical character of philosophy is, it should be added, inseparable from two further features. The first we have already considered: that philosophy's manner of questioning is not aimless or arbitrary but is directed towards bringing into view the questionableness of beings-as-a-whole. Even if we can never finally arrive at a point at which we can say 'This is it! The end of all our enquiring!', we are, alongside a maximum openness, also committed to a maximally holistic vision. The second is that the questions of philosophy are questions that, in the context of dialogue, necessarily concern who we ourselves are, and what our quest for knowledge means for us as concrete, existing historical beings. The matter of philosophy is, in other words, a matter of self-knowledge – even if, as Socrates discovered, such 'self-knowledge' might take the form of having to confess one's ignorance. The intimate connection between the dialogical and the personal character of philosophy is exemplified in Plato's dialogues themselves by the way in which those whose views are subjected to criticism respond. Thrasymachus, the proponent of 'might is right' simply stumps off in pique when the incoherence of his position is exposed – itself a telling comment on what it might mean to hold such a position! It is not just a question of knowledge about the world in a detached, neutral sense, but, as Kierkegaard put it, the thinker asks 'about what meaning the world has for him and he for the world …'[16] Although Kierkegaard himself refused to allow that philosophy as such could be 'interested', in the sense of requiring the existential commitment of the philosopher (since he reserved interest of this kind to ethical and religious questions), we may say that if philosophy really is concerned with what the world and my knowledge of it means to me and me to it, then it cannot easily dispense with such interest. As an individual (and, for that matter, as a member of a particular society) the philosopher is personally implicated in the posing of the question, and is personally answerable for the matter of his philosophy.

In this way we can see that philosophy does not merely press towards bringing the questionableness of beings-as-a-whole into view on the theoretical level but, as Heidegger also claimed, in doing so confronts us with the question of our comportment towards beings-as-a-whole and the possibility of our making a free and responsible decision regarding this comportment. For the very possibility of coming to an understanding of our deepest and most pervasive presuppositions invites the further question as to whether we are in fact bound by some kind of necessity to them, or whether things might be otherwise – if only in terms, as Nietzsche put it, of freely choosing the standpoint that the world has bestowed on us. The question of some such basic decision concerning our self-relation to the knowledge that is now ours is, for Heidegger, especially sharp in connection with the question (some would say, the crisis) of contemporary science and technology, a question raised by the fact that the knowledge and the powers bestowed upon humanity by the ever-accelerating expansion of scientific knowledge and its technological applications have themselves provoked new questions as to the nature, the scope and the meaning of our very humanity. For although we know so much, and have in view the prospect of coming to know even more, it remains far from clear whether this knowledge is necessarily, in its present form, for our good. Although we shall not extensively touch on such questions in the remainder of this book, they remain a constitutive part of the horizon within which it operates, as they must do for any serious engagement with the state of contemporary knowledge in any field.[17] Self-knowledge is not just a matter of gazing into the hidden depths of our private consciousness but of coming to face the decisions that make us the human beings that we collectively are.

There is one further point. Most of the positions we have examined have been primarily concerned with the conceptual dimension of belief. Philosophy of religion on the other hand does not (or need not) confine itself to the conceptual aspect of belief, enlarging its view to take in the wider phenomenon of *religion*. In so far as its object is 'religion', and not simply 'theology', it may indeed take in concepts of God, the soul, immortality, etc. for these are a part of religion, but it may also concern itself with forms and aspects of religion that are not limited to the conceptual plane, e.g. the meaning of worship, of sacrifice or prayer, or the role of art or of asceticism in the religious life. All of these reveal assumptions about what it is to be religious that sometimes complement but sometimes perhaps contradict the 'official' pronouncements of doctrine and theory.

This concern with the whole phenomenon of religion is, arguably, one of the reasons why the philosophy of religion is a relatively late arrival in the intellectual field. It has been argued that the very concept of religion and of 'religions' as unitary composite phenomena combining in a single whole doctrine, liturgy, moral codes, cultural traditions, etc. is a modern post-Enlightenment concept, emerging for the first time in such texts as David Hume's critical *Natural History of Religion*.[18] Certainly the argument should be taken seriously. It would be foolish to set out on a path of philosophizing about religion, i.e. questioning the assumptions we make in the field of religion, if we allowed the basic term 'religion' itself to escape scrutiny. Is there any such thing as 'religion'? Is Orthodoxy, for example, or Protestantism '*a* religion'? Or is Christianity in general the kind of thing we mean by 'a religion'? But, then, where do we draw the boundaries, and for what reasons? Is theism a genus of 'religion' alongside polytheism, pantheism and deism?

However, the fact that this key term can and should be questioned, and may be of a relatively modern vintage, does not mean that it is merely an artificial construct. It may be that it was a positive achievement of the early modern period to allow the phenomenon of religion to be seen and to establish itself as a bona fide phenomenon in its own right, in its distinctiveness from, e.g. politics or ethics or science, though it may have important connections with all of these.

Expanding our topic from theology to religion has important methodological implications, for it means that the philosophy of religion will, minimally, need to take account of other disciplines above and beyond theology and 'philosophy' in the narrow sense (i.e. as a set of questions and doctrines about epistemology, logic, etc.). Anthropology, psychology, social science, literary, historical and cultural studies may have important contributions to make. In fact, it is hard to see in advance where we might set the possible limits for a philosophical enquiry into the whole phenomenon of religion.

Modern Trends (i): History

In the last chapter I referred to the long-standing intellectual quarrel between Anglo-Saxon and continental philosophy, a quarrel with implications for the philosophy of religion as much as for any other branch of the subject. For all their differences, however, each of these traditions of philosophy manifests what I claimed was a decisive characteristic of all philosophizing, namely, the attempt to bring into the open the hidden assumptions behind what we think or say or do and challenge those assumptions to see whether they can be justified. Now whether or not it is possible for such critical philosophy to issue in anything like results is another matter. Some would claim that it is: in their very different ways both Descartes and Hegel believed that a programme of systematic doubt could lead to the establishment or at least the clarification of basic principles of knowledge that could not be shaken, and that could therefore be used to provide secure foundations for reconstructing the edifice of science. Others, however, have seen philosophy as an exclusively critical and formal enterprise, which, if it involves any positive content at all, does so by virtue of its involvement in other disciplines or areas of knowledge or practice (in the sense that one can talk about the formal or logical correctness of a line of argument irrespective of the data fed into it). This difference, interestingly, cuts across both Anglo-Saxon and continental traditions. However, I do not want to pursue that question immediately. Instead, I want to ask about what sort of thing is being looked for when we talk about seeking out the presuppositions undergirding language, thought and practice. And here we do hit upon something that very clearly distinguishes the Anglo-Saxon from the continental tradition.

It was also said in the last chapter that perhaps the last continental philosopher to be taken seriously by Anglo-Saxon philosophers was Kant. This is no accident, because it is immediately after Kant that European philosophy takes a radical new turn: beginning with the post-Kantian idealists in Germany (and, above all, Hegel), philosophy starts to understand itself as decisively historical, and the history of mind, the history of ideas and the history of philosophy itself come to be seen as amongst the most important factors conditioning our current understanding of the world and ourselves. In analytic philosophy, by way of contrast, the attempt is made to arrive at a way of assessing the truth of propositions that does not depend on their historical context or genealogy. The calculus of logic is as indifferent to history as is mathematics. Since Hegel, however, the majority view of continental philosophy has been that propositions do not stand or fall on their own, as if timeless, but are embedded in complex historical, social and psychological contexts.

In this chapter, then, I shall look at Hegel's historicization of knowledge and the implications of this for the philosophy of religion. In doing so, we should not imagine that we are merely looking at one issue amongst others. It is no coincidence that Hegel not only marks a watershed in the development of a historical approach to philosophy but is also often spoken of as the founder of the philosophy of religion. Whether that is strictly true or not is not perhaps important. What is important is that it is in this period that we first begin to encounter the expression 'philosophy of religion' as a regular feature of the philosophical landscape.[1] Of course, philosophers from Plato onwards (or even earlier) had had things to say about religion, and topics such as the nature and existence of God (or the gods), the immortality of the soul and so on had been part of the agenda of philosophy. But religion as a whole had not been thematized as a philosophical problem. What I should like to suggest is that the rise of the modern historical consciousness is a necessary step towards such thematization. In other words, it is only when we understand the human situation historically that religion is able to appear as a phenomenon, as a unitary whole, and it is only when it is seen in that way, as a distinctive phenomenon, that philosophical questioning as to its presuppositions can arise at all. In this way I would argue that although the concept of 'religion' may indeed be of relatively recent origin, it is not a mere theoretical construct, nor merely arbitrary, but reflects and is required by a historical understanding of human existence. And such a historical understanding, I should add, is an achievement in the history of science as decisive as Galileo's repudiation of geocentrism. There are, of course, many different schools of historical thought, and these comments are not intended to promote any one of them in particular: they are, instead, simply made in order to underline the epochal significance of the historical view as such.

Hegel's revolution was not, of course, unprepared, and the historical consciousness can be traced back through such thinkers of the

Enlightenment era as Vico, Lessing and Herder, and historians like Gibbon (*Decline and Fall of the Roman Empire*). What is crucial in this period is the gradual bringing together of two distinct currents: on the one hand the development of history itself as an academic study, and, on the other, philosophical reflection on the meaning of history and on the implications of history for philosophy itself. It is particularly with regard to this latter point that Hegel's thought was to prove paradigmatic. Kant's philosophy had not been totally devoid of all historical perspective – on the contrary, Kant had a keen interest in questions of meta-history, such as how the historical process connected with the aim of realizing the community of moral agents, his version of the kingdom of God. Nevertheless, it is plausible (even if not necessarily correct) to see Kant's historical and political writings as ancillary or supplementary to his system as a whole, whereas it would be completely impossible even to begin to understand Hegel without taking into account the historical dimension of his thought. For, in Hegel, philosophy itself has become historicized, and is not understood as conceivable apart from reflection on its own historicality.

Many would want to argue that, in fact, the roots of modern historical thought go much further back than the Enlightenment – back to the Bible itself and to the biblical view that (in opposition to Platonism) saw life in time as decisive for the fate of human beings. It was as historical agents, as actors in the story of a particular people interacting with its surrounding nations, that the people of Israel achieved or lost fellowship with God. And, equally, it was through historical events, the Exodus, the occupation of Canaan, the Exile and the Restoration, that God proved himself to be indeed God. Possibly for some strata in the Hebrew Bible, there was not even any significant expectation of life beyond this world, and the achievement of a Davidic kingdom of peace and justice on this earth was the best humanity could hope for. Nevertheless, it is on the basis of the historical hope for Israel that the eschatological hope for a resurrection of the dead and a cosmic transformation of all things took the form in which it was incorporated into the life and teaching of the early church. That time is a one-way, linear movement towards a final fulfilment would seem to be an important factor in the rise of a historical sense.

Nevertheless, for much of Christian history this strongly historical view was combined with other, chiefly Graeco-Roman, views in such a way as to underplay the significance of history. Augustine's *City of God* did take history sufficiently seriously to argue that the rise and fall of nations is indeed part of God's overall plan for history and that, as the arena in which the struggle between the City of God and the City of Man takes place, history is integral to the working out of God's design. Nevertheless, the continuing presence of Platonic, mystical elements in Augustine, and his insistence on the essential timelessness of God and the essential nullity of time itself, meant that the movement of history was, as it were, suspended within the medium of a larger, all-encompassing timelessness. To put it in the Aristotelian terms adopted into Western theology by Thomas Aquinas, there was indeed movement in history, but behind that movement was an essentially unmoved mover.

Now, of course, throughout the centuries leading up to Hegel, people of all levels of education and of various kinds of culture knew that there was such a thing as the past. The church itself appealed continually to the example of saints of previous ages and, beyond that, to the history told in the Scriptures. But that is not the same as a historical sense in the strong understanding of the term. In literature and art we can see repeatedly how the past was simply portrayed as an earlier version of the present. Artists depicted biblical and classical scenes as if they were contemporary events, clothing their figures in the costumes of their own time. A striking example is provided by the stained glass window that I see every day while conducting services in King's College Chapel. It dates from the early sixteenth century and shows the temptation of Christ in the wilderness. However, the wilderness is not shown as a desert, bare, rocky place. Instead it is represented as a great forest – because this was what 'wilderness' meant to the artist who created that window. Compare this with the work of the nineteenth-century British painter, Henry Holman Hunt, who travelled to Palestine and undertook extensive historical research in order to paint biblical scenes as they would have looked to those who were contemporary with them. This is not to say that one or the other is 'better' as art, but that these two approaches represent the enormous gulf between the two world-views within which the artists operated and that the rise of history is central to the development of the later, historical view.[2]

Symptomatic of the new understanding of history that emerged in the Enlightenment period (and of the implications this could have for the interpretation of religion) was Lessing's seminal essay *The Education of the Human Race*. This provided what can almost be seen as a sketch for the larger and fuller historical understanding of religion that Hegel was to provide. Lessing's essay highlighted the tension between this new historical view and the older theological view of things. A crucial issue was that of the Fall. According to the dominant Christian tradition humanity was created perfect, 'in the image of God'. Adam, however, misused his freedom and threw away that perfection, sinking down into a state of sin, in which human beings have remained ever since. Even those who have found salvation through faith in Christ have to live with the consequences of sin, and will not be fully restored to their original perfection until the end of all things. As Lessing sees it, however, it is a mistake to think of the original state of the first human beings as having been one of perfection, in relation to which everything since has been a falling-away. A better model, he suggests, is to think of history as analogous to that of the education of an individual human being, so that through history the human race actually advances from a primitive, inferior state to a better, more enlightened rational state of things. Divine revelation, according to Lessing, is chiefly the method by which that educative process is carried out. And like all good methods of education, it adapts itself to the needs of those to be educated. Thus the polytheism and idolatry of early societies is not to be seen as the result of rebellion against an original monotheism, but as a form of religion appropriate to the conditions of primitive human society. The miracles, physical rewards and punishments of Old Testament religion are likewise seen not so much as expressive of God's nature in itself, but as means adapted to the capacities of the Israelites at that stage in their history (an idea already suggested by Spinoza). Nevertheless, Lessing could still speak of timeless truths of reason, truths that were not changed in themselves by the fact that they could only be revealed in a gradual, progressive way.

With Hegel, however, things appear quite differently.

Hegel's earliest writings have been published in English as *Early Theological Writings*,[3] although many have commented that they actually read more like anti-theological writings in that Hegel appears to be attacking Christianity in the cause of a religion of pure reason and morality *à la* Kant. In these writings he draws a strong distinction between what he calls 'positive' religion on the one hand and the religion of moral reason on the other. Hegel sets this distinction in the context of a discussion of the origins of Christianity. In this context positive religion is represented by Judaism: such a religion bases its claims on authority; it is a matter of law not morality, of doctrine not reason, of believing not doing, of receiving the truth passively not actively and autonomously legislating; it is marked by a faith in miracles, by a zeal for proselytizing, and by intolerance.[4] By way of contrast, Jesus is represented (in Hegel's earliest writings) as a teacher of what are essentially Kantian ethics, directed at promoting the rational moral capacities of the individual.

However, Hegel soon discovered that there was a problem with presenting Jesus as no more than a moral teacher of this kind. Such a teacher could indeed teach commandments based on universal morality – but could he inspire his disciples to want to follow them, could he move hearts as well as minds? Thus, in the second phase in Hegel's early writing about Christianity, Jesus became a virtually anarchic individualist, someone who represented the spirit of subjectivity in its purest form, who put even the most arbitrary individual act (such as plucking grains of corn on the Sabbath day) above the commandments of the law. Over against the commandments of positive religion, then, Jesus represented the freedom of the individual. However, such a Jesus has some fairly obvious limitations, as Hegel soon came to realize. How could such a happy-go-lucky anarchist ever come to be the founder of a great historical movement, the centre of a community that survived his own death?

If we are really to do justice to the rise of Christianity, then, we have not only to take account of reason and morality: we have to consider experience, life, and love.

With the concept of 'love' Hegel found a key that not only enabled him to see the continuity between the earthly life of Jesus and the christological and trinitarian doctrine by which the church was to interpret the meaning of that life, he was also able to break through a more purely philosophical problem that had been troubling him. How was this?

Following Kant, Hegel had drawn a strong distinction between 'understanding' and 'reason'. Very crudely, 'understanding' is concerned with the outward appearances of things, with empirical objects and the connections between empirical objects. The understanding looks at things in isolation from each other, and sees them as mutually exclusive. It is the standpoint of Enlightenment empiricism and rationality. Reason on the other hand sees the ideas, it looks to the whole, to the final goals that give sense, meaning and purpose to the world and experience. Except that, often, the ideals of reason don't seem to connect with the detail of empirical experience or historical events. So for Kant, it was never really possible for us to know that God existed, that the world would really arrive at the realization of the kingdom of God, that the soul was immortal or even that the world really constituted a single unitary whole. We have to assume all these things, Kant claimed. But, as he put it, they can only ever function regulatively, not constitutively, that is to say, we can use them in regulating and managing our ideas, but we cannot regard them simply as fundamental facts about the world. There is, we may say, a missing link between idea and reality.

We can see that this duality mirrors that between positive religion (= understanding) and the religion of morality (= reason) in Hegel's early writings.

How does the concept of love relate to this problem?

Love, as Hegel now understands it, provides the key to a complex of events – the Last Supper, the death of Jesus, the Resurrection and Pentecost – that collectively symbolize humanity's realization that the law of externality does not define or limit their capacities: the disciples' experience of the loss of Christ is transformed by their rediscovery of his presence in Spirit in the common experiences of Eucharist and Pentecost. Hegel argues that this process of loss and recovery is very closely analogous to what we see in normal human love, when two separate, isolated individuals come together in love, are fused together in the act of sexual union and this act issues in the birth of a child, a new life that synthesizes and carries forward the meaning of the love that brought them together. So too in the pivotal moments of the Christian story: the understanding of head and heart, of God and humanity, of the teacher and his disciples, as separate, opposed entities, standing over against each other as mutually exclusive, is broken down and overcome. This goes so far that even death, the ultimate externality, the power that most limits, inhibits and thwarts human life, the most immovable power of all, comes to be seen as only a moment in the ongoing movement of Spirit. As Hegel was to put it in the *Phenomenology of Spirit*, the way of philosophical understanding was a way not merely of doubt, as for Descartes, but of despair, in which philosophy confronted the utter dismemberment and death of all received representations of the world, a speculative Good Friday.[5]

Such reflections mark the origins of what would come to be one of the paradigmatic features of Hegel's mature philosophy: the concept of *Aufhebung*, variously translated 'sublation', 'cancellation' and 'transcendence'. The movement of *Aufhebung* has the twofold connotation of marking the end and supersession of one stage of a process, but not in the sense of that simply coming to an end and being discarded. It is rather a matter of the essential content of this stage being taken up and carried forward as the basis for the next part of the process. A familiar example of this would be the movement whereby, in Christian theology, Judaism was both superseded but also fulfilled in Christianity itself. Putting it more abstractly, in

Hegel's own terminology, it is the movement whereby the mutually opposed elements of the dialectic, the thesis and antithesis, are at once overcome yet united and transformed in the synthesis. It is important, however, to see that the catalyst leading to the formulation of the logical algebra of thesis-antithesis-synthesis came from Hegel's reflections on the pattern of death-and-rebirth figured both in our general human experience of love and in the Easter cycle.

With the concept of *Aufhebung*, Hegel thus finds a means whereby he can think phenomena in terms of their actual temporal sequence. The point – if not always the achievement – of Hegelian speculation is therefore not to reduce the world on the Procrustean bed of a triadic formula, but to find a way of thinking the world in its vital, dynamic, historical actuality, a process in which all things are continually in flux, continually passing over into new forms, but, as Hegel sees it, not randomly, not arbitrarily, but according to the law of *Aufhebung*. In this way thought finds a model in and through which adequately to represent life itself in its movement through time.

Although the Passion, Death and Resurrection of Christ and the Eucharistic and Pentecostal experience of the church provided one of the stimuli for the emergence of the historical principle in Hegel's thought, he soon applied this principle more broadly to the history of religion.

This can be seen already in the *Phenomenology*. It is curious that, after his early wrestlings with the gospels and the conflict between Jesus and Judaism, Hegel now offers a completely different way of contextualizing the Christ event. Now it is no longer the crisis of first-century Judaism that provides the background for the origin of Christianity, but the crisis of Hellenistic civilization, which in turn is a further development of a story that Hegel now traces back to Persia, India and Egypt, although what he has to say about these is very brief (India gets one page).

In turning to Greece, however, Hegel is also turning back to another of his major preoccupations in his earliest writings. There is strong evidence that Hegel's ideal society had originally been envisaged along the lines of early Greek society. What particularly attracted him about that society was the way in which, he believed, the individual related spontaneously to the community, and religion offered an imaginative and non-coercive expression of this bond.

We have already seen that one of Hegel's aims in the development of the dialectic was to overcome a merely external understanding of the world, in which human beings confronted their world as something over against themselves. This applies just as much in relation to religion and to the gods as in other spheres. Thus, if we look at Egyptian religion, we see the gods depicted in half-human, half-animal form. This shows that the Egyptians still experience the highest powers of their world as somehow alien to humanity. In Greece, however, the gods are represented as perfect human beings, fully anthropomorphized. From our point of view, this may seem very inadequate, but in historical terms it is a decisive leap forward. Nevertheless, the Olympians are still represented as the inhabitants of another world. They may have human form and may from time to time descend to earth and mingle with mortals, but they are not themselves fully human. It is therefore appropriate that we first encounter them in the forms of ancient statuary: the statue, as Hegel describes it, stands over against the worshippers, confronting them blankly, as an 'Other'. It is sightless and does not see. It is silent and does not speak.

In the world of Homer, a further change occurs. Now the gods really do speak, they continually interact with human affairs, although, as Hegel says, their speech is only reported speech – *we* do not hear them, we hear only the poet telling us what they said. In tragedy, however, they no longer speak in this way in the third person, but are represented on the stage as themselves speaking. Yet it is not really the gods speaking, of course, it is only actors. In comedy, the actors themselves come out from behind their masks. Now we can see that the 'gods' are only human products, sculptures made by men, poems written by men, masks put on by men: the Athenians look at what is going on on stage and they see – themselves. At first it seems as if this humanization of the gods is what Hegel has been wanting all along, but the story has another side to it. For this humanization is at the same time a desacralization, a depopulation of heaven. This humanized world is empty of ultimate values. There are in it only human beings – and the utterly impersonal, inexorable law of fate. Far from bringing about a synthesis, the course of Greek religion ends in utter duality – and it is to this situation that the no less extreme situation of the death of God on the cross provides a solution – insofar as this same God is experienced in the risen, spiritual life of the community. And this is also a God who, at last, truly speaks in his own person, who is 'the Word incarnate'.

The story does not, of course, stop there, and – in opposition to at least some (especially Protestant) forms of Christianity–Hegel sees the after-life of the Christ event as no less important than its prehistory, as this event is taken up into and woven into the onward course of history. For the possibility of an intra-historical transcendence,

revealed in the Easter/Pentecost event, was not immediately understood by the whole of humanity but had to accommodate itself to the
forms of understanding prevalent in the world at that time. As it
encountered new historical situations, the message was further
developed, albeit often through what seemed like a falling-away
from the original truth and power of Christianity. Thus the Middle
Ages appear to Hegel as a new 'unhappy consciousness' in which
people experience the supernatural order as alien and irrational, and
it is only in the Lutheran reformation that it is rediscovered that the
truth of religion is essentially a truth of the heart or will – something
which, for Hegel, is not a limitation, since it is precisely the heart or
will that he sees as the motor force of history.

In the *Philosophy of History*, too, Hegel pays more attention than in
the *Phenomenology* or the early writings to the history of Rome and the
state of the Roman Empire as factors conditioning the rise and shape
of early Christianity. The arbitrary, domineering rule of the first-
century Emperors reflected and reinforced a dualism analogous to
that experienced at the end of Greek civilization between an utterly
alien and unpredictable fate and the actual lives of individuals. The
highest wisdom of the Roman world was the Stoicism that cultivated
indifference to fate and that turned away from society. In this context,
Hegel now offers a positive and not merely negative description of
Jewish religion. If we look at the psalms and histories of the Jewish
scriptures, he says, they give free expression to suffering, and suggest
that suffering too may be integral to the process of spiritual development. Whereas Stoicism denies pain, Judaism affirms it. The pattern
consummated in the death and resurrection of Christ is a pattern
already present in Jewish faith, a pattern whereby 'infinite loss . . .
becomes infinite gain'.[6]

On the other hand, a singular role is given to the Germanic peoples
who, Hegel argues, had no history or culture of their own prior to
their world-historical encounter with Rome. As a result of their
conquest of the Western Empire and their adoption of its religion
these peoples made Christianity the foundation of their culture in a
way that could not occur within the ancient world itself, where all
cultural forms had already reached a high level of maturity at the
time of the Christ event. They thus become the bearer of the further
development of Spirit.

In his lectures on the *Philosophy of Religion* Hegel is not, as in the
Phenomenology or *The Philosophy of History* so obviously or so immedi-
ately concerned with history. As he defines his topic in the
Introduction its object is simply religion: 'This is the highest object

that can occupy human beings; it is the absolute object. It is the region of eternal truths and eternal virtue, the region where all the riddles of thought, all contradictions, and all the sorrows of the heart should show themselves to be resolved, and the region of the eternal peace through which the human being is truly human.'[7] Its object is, still more closely defined, 'God and ... the feeling of God ... The object of religion is simply through itself and on its own account; it is the absolutely final end in and for itself, the absolutely free being. Here our concern about the final end can have no other final end than this object itself.'[8]

These words would seem to mark a turning away from history, towards the realm of timeless truths and absolute ends, the realm of what is 'in-and-for-itself', what is self-sufficient and does not depend on anything outside itself, is not a part of any chain of events.

Indeed, Hegel methodically begins with the concept of God. This 'concept', however, has no existence outside consciousness. To say 'concept' of God, implies 'consciousness of God', and this immediately points to two interrelated but distinct aspects: consciousness, the conscious mind that knows God, and God, the object of that knowing. Both of these sides have to be grasped in their utter reciprocity if justice is really to be done to the concept of God: but this state of reciprocity is precisely 'Spirit', the dynamic interrelationship of knowing subject and known object. This means that knowledge of God is inseparable from the history in which consciousness comes, as it were, to know its own mind. Consciousness is not simply the final result of a process of thinking: consciousness is the whole process, i.e. the whole process is the form consciousness takes in order to be what it is.

Later in the *Lectures* Hegel will argue analogously that 'God' can never be considered in bare, atomic individuality as an isolated single being, apart from the world. Even if, in the manner of non-trinitarian monotheism, we say that 'God' is the creator of the world, this, according to Hegel, already implies that 'being creator' is not something God happened to become, accidentally as it were, but that it belongs to God's very essence, to his very being, to be the creator. God is God only and precisely as Creator. But this is already to imply that bare unity is not adequate for grasping the true nature of God.

More appropriate, according to Hegel, is the trinitarian concept that enables us to see God as 'process, movement, life'. This alone is a truly spiritual conception of God and this ever-moving life of God that still remains at one with itself, in the unity of love, is what it means to say 'Spirit'. From the standpoint of the understanding, of a kind of reasoning that relies on distinctions and on the laws of contradiction and the excluded middle, to think of God spiritually will be to think of him as mystery. 'Father', 'Son' and 'Spirit' are not isolated predicates, and the Trinity is not a mathematical problem. It is a dynamic expression of the personal being of God.

Even in God himself, then, we never reach a still, motionless point. Versus Aristotle, Hegel's God is not an unmoved mover, but an ever-moving mover.[9]

And note: that this very dynamic movement that is God's inner-trinitarian life requires him to be the Creator, for it is characteristic of this life to continually generate differentiation in order to resolve that differentiation in ever-deepening unity. Yet whilst this is accomplished at one level within the inner-trinitarian life of God, in the relationship of Father and Son, there is a moment of 'difference' signalled by the fact that the Son is understood as a separate person and this difference is not resolved immediately in the countermovement of identity. This moment of difference finds further expression in the creation of a finite world, something which Hegel describes as seemingly inevitable once we concede the distinctive presence of a second person or element within the divine life itself. If this sits uncomfortably with Christianity's traditional doctrinal assertions concerning the complete freedom of God in creating, Hegel implies that it also underwrites the appropriateness of the dogmatic claim that it is 'by' the Son that the world was made.

The stage is set for the emergence of humanity, which, as spiritual consciousness, is to become the vehicle for the return of the world to God and its reincorporation into the divine life of the Trinity. However, precisely because separation from God – the differentiation that lies at the root of the creation of the world – is a precondition of the first human life, that life is not in its first form as it ought to be. The discovery of this situation by consciousness is the meaning of the Fall story. Thus, for Hegel – as for others in the German idealist tradition – creation itself in some way necessitates the Fall, creation is a falling-away from God. The realization by human beings of this separation is not itself a moment of actual fall, it is rather the first step on the way back to unification. It is, as for Lessing, the beginning of the education of the human race. As one commentator put it, the Fall, for Hegel, is really a successful climb.

Let us just remind ourselves of the distance we have travelled from Augustine. Certainly, when compared with Platonic thinkers such as Plotinus, Augustine gives considerable weight to history. Neverthe-less, the Augustinian view still sees the story, the narration-through-time of the pilgrim community, as a kind of accident, a by-product, as it were, of the Fall. If there had been no Fall there would have been no history. Equally, when the City of God finds its consummation in the vision of God, time will come to an end, and there will be no more history. For Hegel, however, the Fall is virtually necessary because the world is from the very beginning part of a process, a dynamic movement of differentiation leading to ever more complex unification. The journey of consciousness through time is not towards the recovery of a lost contemplation of God, but the self-discovery of Spirit itself as Spirit: God is not God apart from the human, historical events of Good Friday and Easter Day. And to philosophize is precisely to think through the totality of this journey of consciousness, including the dereliction of Golgotha, because 'the truth is the whole'.

A further implication of all this is that not only are religious narratives and doctrines embedded in history in such a way that we have to deal with religion as a historical phenomenon, but that religious history is itself part of a larger history, and is systematically interconnected with morality, law, politics, art and, indeed, all dimensions of human culture and historical experience and practice. What happens in any one of these spheres reflects and has implications for what happens in the rest.

Now clearly there are huge questions here as to how far Hegel's philosophy is compatible with Christian orthodoxy, questions to which we shall return when we come to consider the question of reductionism. The question with which I want to end this brief summary of Hegel's historicization of the question of religion, however, is this: Can we admit the thoroughly dynamic, process nature of reality to the extent Hegel does, and still claim, as he also claims, that it is possible to get a view on the whole, that history is contained within a single, unitary line of development?

Some of Hegel's sharpest critics – Feuerbach and Marx, for example – did continue to hold to the idea that history is a single process, with a single discernible end. Others took a very different view. Kierkegaard, for example, inspired largely by religious considerations concerning the 'infinite qualitative difference' between God and humanity, was to argue that it was impossible to establish a systematic overview of the whole from the standpoint of human knowledge. Later in the nineteenth century Nietzsche was to develop a still more extreme account of the world as utter flux, in which all semblance of order, purpose or unity was just that: 'semblance', a fiction we use in order to maximize our life-possibilities. Pessimistic historicists, reacting against the general atmosphere of historical optimism exuded by Hegel and the broad liberal tradition he inspired, saw the patterns of historical change less as teleologically directed towards the fulfilment of some grand, final good, than as analogues of the life and death of biological organisms. Rather than a theatre displaying the achievement and celebration of rational freedom, history became a sequence of cyclical changes in which every culture or civilization would, having exhausted its special historical essence, sink back into a decline and fall – a view of history epitomized in Oswald Spengler's massively influential *The Decline of the West*. Its influence was, of course, given added authority by the fact that it appeared in the aftermath of the First World War, and the psychological and cultural blow which that event struck against the more optimistic versions of nineteenth-century historicism.

Rejecting Spengler's reading of history as a quasi-biological phenomenon, Heidegger was, in his earlier thought, to restore the prospect of achieving authentic freedom to the idea of history, but this freedom was something very different from Hegel's freedom-as-reason. For Heidegger recast the whole concept of historicity in the context of the individual *Dasein*'s ('existing being's') confrontation with death. For Heidegger, time is the all-encompassing horizon of human existence. We *are* as temporal beings, so that it would simply not make sense to imagine human beings without or outside of the dimension of time – whereas, for Augustine, time is always a privation of the proper being of the soul. In the context of understanding and interpreting history, however, the concept of historicity advocated by *Being and Time* was won at the cost of accepting the absence of any overarching 'meaning' to the historical process. History 'means' what we make it mean through our heroic resolve – a view that could easily be assimilated to fascistic concepts of the strong leader who gives meaning and direction to national life through the sole instrumentality of his will. Heidegger himself claimed to see a connection between just this concept of historicity and his own, brief, Nazism.

In his later thought, Heidegger gave a less anthropocentric view, and spoke of a history of Being, in which Being disclosed itself according to a succession of paradigms, of which the most important, for us, is the paradigm of metaphysics, that began with Plato and ended with Nietzsche and, according to Heidegger, found its fulfilment in modern science and technology. However, unlike Hegel, Heidegger did not see these paradigms as connected by any logical sequence, or as part of any single, teleological narrative. History was more a matter of 'erring', of wandering through time like a river winding its way across the landscape, rather than a progressive movement towards a final goal.[10]

This sense of humanity as both utterly historical yet also ultimately directionless has since then (and perhaps especially since the collapse of Marxism) become an almost unquestioned assumption of much recent reflection on the human condition. For Michel Foucault history no longer turns around a single decisive rupture (e.g. the French Revolution) but is a succession of distinct 'epistemes', i.e. different configurations of construals and presuppositions about how things hang together that underlie and frame the consciousness of an age, like the sixteenth century's deep belief in a system of resemblances linking all possible phenomena across every domain of being. Thus far, we could still be in Hegelian territory, but Foucault no longer sees it as the job of the historian to 'read' or 'interpret' the documentary records of the historical past in the context of a 'total history' but, in his terms, as a 'general history' which speaks of 'series, divisions, limits, differences of level, shifts, chronological specificities, particular forms of rehandling, possible types of relation.'[11] Total history 'draws all phenomena around a single centre – a principle, a meaning, a spirit, a world-view, an overall shape; a general history, on the contrary, would deploy the space of a dispersion'.[12] Instead of turning monuments into documents to be read, this new type of history turns documents themselves into monuments: instead of archaeology aspiring to the condition of historiography he says, we now have historiography aspiring to the condition of archaeology.[13] The 'order of things' is not one that can finally be brought within the net of a meaning-oriented view of subjectivity, rational or existential. History is not only no longer the unfolding of a divine plan, it is no longer even, primarily, the 'story of man'. And if this post-humanist view of history itself now seems to have become almost popular wisdom, we can gauge its radicality by contrasting it with the kind of liberal, humanist existential view of, e.g. Karl Jaspers, for whom, even if history is no longer encased within the cone of a unitary teleological (i.e. goal-oriented) purposive, it does indeed disclose its 'meaning' through a certain great period of 'rupture' – Jaspers calls it the 'axial period' – when humanity discovered its historical, universal, spiritual ideals. These are the meaning-bestowing aspirations, Jaspers argues, that, once discovered, define humanity for all time to come. These are the things for which, as long as we continue in history, we must live, struggle and die.[14]

Another, darker view (reflecting, perhaps, its origin in the era of world wars and totalitarianism), is that condensed into Walter Benjamin's tantalizingly brief meditation on Paul Klee's painting 'Angelus Novus'. The angel depicted in this painting is interpreted by Benjamin as 'the angel of history', of which he writes

> His face is turned towards the past. Where we perceive a chain of events, he sees one single catastrophe which keeps piling wreckage upon wreckage and hurls it in front of his feet. The angel would like to stay, awaken the dead, and make whole what has been smashed. But a storm is blowing from Paradise; it has got caught in his wings with such violence that the angel can no longer close them. This storm irresistibly propels him into the future to which his back is turned, while the pile of debris before him grows skyward. This storm is what we call progress.[15]

Part of the power of this image is to do with the way in which it still holds open the possibility of a unitary vision of history whilst undermining all possibility of conceiving this unity within the constraints of any explanatory system. What the angel sees, though it is not a single chain of events linked by some kind of causality, is nevertheless the after-shock of a single historical – or, more precisely, pre- or supra-historical – catastrophe. It is, indeed, the fact that this event that both sets history in motion and gives it its specific kind of unity is catastrophic that makes it impossible for us ever to make of it a 'first cause' of the historical process. As catastrophe, it exceeds causal reckoning. The messianic longing to awaken the dead, to comprehend the whole remains alive but is conceptually weakened. Yet not eliminated: the angel may not be able to close his wings, but he keeps his eyes fixed upon the accumulation of debris we call history. In another of the theses on history Benjamin suggests that whilst the historian cannot ever adequately establish a causal explanation for historical events, he can and characteristically does leap across the supposed continuum of historical time and 'grasps the constellation which his own era has formed with a definite earlier one', i.e. creates a fruitful juxtaposition of our 'now' with the 'now' of a previous age – the fall of the Roman Empire becomes a paradigm of the decline of the West, the Exodus of Israel from Egypt a model for the black slaves' struggle for emancipation. Out of this 'constellation' or juxtaposition of historical times, our present is enlarged: it becomes, in Benjamin's terms, a 'time of the now' that, he says, 'is shot through with chips of Messianic time'.[16] In some respects Benjamin's view seems to hint at a return to the typological approach to history found in biblical and subsequent Christian literature, weaving together a unified view of history out of apparently disparate historical events. Yet, unlike the Christian version, Benjamin's typology, though 'messianic' in an adjectival sense, is missing its Messiah. His types have no final, defining antitype, no eschaton, no end. The view of the whole remains, must remain, forever elusive in face of the actual catastrophe of what happens in history. Whether happiness is possible under the reign of time is a question to which we do not have any conclusive answer.[17]

Seen from the twentieth century, then, even the radicality of Hegel's innovative fusion of philosophy and history seemed like a halfway house, and Hegel himself a bit too Platonic. Nevertheless, at least for those who stand in the line of continental philosophy, Hegel has demonstrated that our understanding of ourselves and of our world cannot be separated from history and that, if we are to question our presuppositions, the hidden assumptions behind our everyday understanding, we have to uncover the history out of which that understanding grew. History is no longer simply the stage on which the dramatic conflict between good and evil gets acted out. History is the very process of this drama.[18]

All this, of course, affects the way in which we think about religion as much as any other sphere of life. Religion is for us embedded in history, and we cannot understand what is meant by religious language, religious institutions or religious actions unless or until we see the historical horizon within which they belong. It is therefore no accident that history has been at the centre of modern Christian theology, not least in the form of the historical questioning of the founding documents of Christianity. Over against the classical, metaphysically formulated claims of Christianity and some other religions, history may well seem to be a sceptical and corrosive power, especially if, with Foucault and others, we conclude that historical study shows that history isn't actually going anywhere in particular. In this sense, history may appear in theological literature as, first and foremost, the 'problem' of history. As Rudolf Bultmann put it in the eloquent conclusion to the first of his 1955 Gifford lectures:

What is the result of all this? It seems to be a consistent *relativism*. The belief in an eternal order, ruling the life of men, broke down, and with it the ideas of absolute goodness and absolute truth. All this is handed over to the historical process which for its part is understood as a natural process ruled not by spiritual but by economic laws. History begins to become sociology, and therefore man is no longer understood as an autonomous being, but as at the mercy of historical conditions. His historicity does not consist in the fact that he is an individual who passes through history, who meets with history. No, man is nothing but history, for he is, so to speak, not an active being but someone to whom things happen. Man is only a process without 'true existence'. The end, it seems, is *nihilism*.[19]

Is this, then, the outcome of Hegel's historicization of philosophy and, with it, of the philosophy of religion? If so, then we seem to be faced with the paradox that the very same intellectual move that made possible the conceptualization of religion as a distinctive form of human activity and thought leads also to its relativization. Or does this historicization bring to light one of the necessary presuppositions that condition our understanding of religion in the modern period and, moreover, does so in such a way as to allow us to re-envisage religion as a continuing possibility for human living and no mere survival from another historical age?

This question will continue to accompany us throughout this short course, and we shall seek to develop it further when we look at the tension between, on the one hand, a reductionist, and, on the other, a hermeneutical approach to the truth and meaning of religion. Now, however, we turn to two further factors that condition the general sweep of the modern approach to religion: the turn to the subject and the preoccupation of modern philosophy with language.

Modern Trends (ii):
The Turn to the Subject

If the rise of the historical consciousness is one of the defining trends of modern thought, what has come to be called the 'turn to the subject' is another. It is easy to see that these two are closely connected, in that history is precisely understood as human history, and therefore as centring on the experiences and actions of the human subject. It is no coincidence in this respect that we find Hegel saying 'substance is subject'. By this he meant that, whereas Aristotle had conceived of the primary substance as outside of or external to the human subject, we could now see that it was the human subject itself that was the motor force, the active, causal power at work in history, the power that made things happen.

The key figure in the 'turn to the subject' is usually taken to be Descartes, but, of course, it would be foolish to say that Descartes somehow invented or discovered human subjectivity. By the time Descartes began to doubt, Shakespeare had written the sequence of plays that even today throw the sharpest light on the passions and struggles of the human person. Two centuries before that, Petrarch had scaled Mount Ventoux and realized that this outer journey was but an inverse image of a human being's ascent to self-understanding.[1] And we can go much further back still for evidence of a sense of the special place of the human subject within the cosmos. The oracle at Delphi issued the instruction '*Gnothi seauton*' ('Know thyself') and it was a Presocratic thinker, Protagoras, who declared that 'Man is the measure of all things'. I mentioned Shakespeare, and, of course, many of the poems, dramas and works of art of the ancient world speak powerfully of the subjective feeling and insight of their creators. For all that the philosophy of modernity following Hegel judged the thought-world of the Greeks to be essentially mythical and therefore finally incapable of grasping the human subject in its authentic autonomy, it has been easy for such a resolutely modern approach to the question of the self as that of Sigmund Freud to utilize Greek

drama and myth in order to exemplify the most fundamental dynamics of the mind – as in Freud's most widely quoted (if not always
clearly understood) contribution to our self-knowledge, the Oedipus
complex. The psalms, St Paul, Augustine and Luther are no less
important in the emergence of the modern sense of subjectivity. The
religious crises of Paul and Luther especially emphasize how the
decisive moment of the religious life falls upon the individual. For
them it proved to be not enough simply to follow the religious way of
their ancestors or of the surrounding society. The way to faith was a
way in which they had to repudiate everything they had been taught
and decide their fate on the basis of conscience alone. In this respect
they have often been hailed, not implausibly, as precursors of modern
existentialism.[2] For each of them, faith cannot be abstracted from the
life of the believer, from the process of conversion and sanctification.
Faith is not exhausted by the exposition of doctrine, what is believed,
but depends, crucially, on the one who believes and how he believes.

Augustine's *Confessions* also tell the story of a crisis-ridden journey
towards faith. Moreover, in the extraordinary tenth book of the
Confessions, Augustine embarks upon an extensive analysis of
memory, in order to find the traces of God impressed upon his mind,
since, for Augustine, it is in relation to the inner self, not the outer
world, that we come to know God. Augustine laments that it was
precisely the fault of his youth to seek God outside himself, in the
things of the world, when all the time God was already present
within him. In the course of this investigation memory is revealed to
be nothing other than mind itself in its synthesizing activity, and it
is through our minds being deeply structured in terms of a fundamental orientation towards truth and the impress in them of the
dynamics of the divine mind itself that we are able to attain some
knowledge of God – even if, at the last, the human mind cannot go all
the way without a special illumination from above. This vision of the
spiritual life, also developed in his exegetical writings, was to be
profoundly influential for the course of the Western understanding of
the religious life and its high valuation of interiority and recollection
as the mode and the means of arriving at the vision of God. No less
importantly, and in contrast to Paul (probably) and Luther (certainly),
Augustine's way of emphasizing the subject was not simply to
oppose the self-understanding of faith to that of philosophy or
worldly wisdom. Augustine's journey towards faith is also a philosopher's journey towards truth and the relationship remains two-sided.
As we saw in Chapter One, Augustine could speak of his relation to
the philosophy of Platonism in terms of the Israelites taking with

them the treasures of the Egyptians on their journey out of slavery. What should be emphasized here is that this philosophy was understood in a way congruent with what we would now regard as subjectivity. However, we should resist too easy a reading back of 'existentialist' concerns into Augustine, for whom the subject's exploration of the laws of its inner being was a way of following the traces ordained by God himself for its ascent towards spiritual truth. The subject was not the exception, the absurd, wilfully paradoxical entity of twentieth-century existentialism, but the appointed point of access to the spiritual realm whose laws were both rational and universal. At the same time, Augustine's later meditations on the self-contradiction of the human will, and his increasingly dark view of the incapacitating effects of sin, do resonate with much in existentialism, and it is perhaps no coincidence that Augustine was a significant – though by no means unique – source and focus for Heidegger in the period preparatory to *Being and Time*.[3]

Yet if it is hard for us to make the kind of clear-cut distinction between ancient and modern accounts of subjectivity that seemed self-evident to earlier intellectual generations (a difficulty closely connected with our loss of faith in the possibility of a 'scientific' periodization of history, as discussed at the end of the previous chapter), such a distinction retains considerable force, and is attested across a range of cultural domains, in art and politics no less than in philosophy and religion. Descartes may, then, not be the simple 'founder' of modern philosophy, but he remains a monumental figure on the threshold of the modern, and one in whom many of the shifts that cumulatively build up the profile of modernity come together. In his *Discourse on Method* Descartes explains how, confronted with a range of learned opinions and beliefs, he set out to find what could really be known indubitably, with absolute certainty. This led him to a programme of systematic doubt, in which he resolved to doubt everything that could possibly be doubted. As he put it in the first of his four fundamental methodical rules, he resolved 'never to accept anything as true that I did not know to be evidently so: that is to say, carefully to avoid precipitancy and prejudice, and to include in my judgements nothing more than what presented itself so clearly and so distinctly to my mind that I might have no occasion to place it in doubt.'[4] As is well-known (at least to every first-year philosophy student), the application of this led Descartes to the point where the only thing he could not doubt was the fact that he himself was continuously thinking. This in turn gave him the assurance that whether or not there were any objects out there in the external world corresponding to his thoughts, he at least existed. In his famous formulation: 'I think therefore I am', '*Cogito ergo sum*'. But his meditations do not stop there. The very process of doubting itself also suggested to him that there were different kinds of thought. There was the kind of thought that occurred in doubt itself, and the kind of thought that occurred when doubt came to an end and one arrived at clear and distinct knowledge, such as the knowledge that because one thinks, one exists. The very fact of having doubts, therefore, implies that the doubting mind is less perfect than the knowing mind. This in turn implies the idea of a being, a perfectly knowing intellect, that was superior to Descartes the doubter. But from whence could the doubter have derived such an idea? Surely an imperfect being cannot itself be the source of the idea of a perfect being? Surely such an idea can only derive from a perfect being itself, 'a being whose nature was truly more perfect than mine and which even had in itself all the perfections of which I could have any idea, that is to say, in a single word, which was God'.[5] As Descartes further develops his argument, the very perfection of God implies both that God exists and that the external world also exists, since a perfect God could not be a deceiver, who would set us in the midst of a merely illusory world.

Descartes' best-known argument for the existence of God is a reworking of what is known as the ontological argument. According to this argument, the existence of God can be deduced from the idea of God: God is conceived as the most perfect being, but the idea of perfection must include existence, since a purportedly perfect being that did not exist would be less perfect than a perfect being that did exist and therefore the most perfect being must exist. It is, Descartes says, like the three angles of a triangle that must add up to 180 degrees, or like the interdependence of a mountain and a valley. They are inseparable. As Rodgers and Hammerstein would sing of love and marriage and horse and carriage, 'you can't have one without the other'.

Now notice the structure of Descartes' argument and the way in which it contrasts with the previously dominant arguments for the existence of God. Descartes begins with himself, with his own thought processes and what he can deduce immediately from that. In this way he already differs from St Anselm, the eleventh-century Archbishop of Canterbury who had also propounded a form of the ontological argument. Anselm's argument, set in the context of prayer and not of a meditation upon knowledge, simply begins with the idea of God. Anselm does not see this idea as the product of his own mind, but as something offered to him in and by faith. By way of contrast Descartes deduces the idea of a perfect being from the idea of perfection present in his own mind. The idea of God is for Anselm a datum, something given, not something deduced. We may put the difference like this: whereas the sequence of Anselm's argument is God–self–existence–salvation from the world (for the sake of which the argument is being conducted in the first place), that of Descartes' argument is self–God–existence–world.

Both forms of the argument contrast with the 'five ways' of Thomas Aquinas, which we examined briefly in the first chapter. These arguments, from motion, from causality, from necessity and contingency, from gradation and from design, all involve observations about the world. Confronted with the world as it is, the argument goes, we are compelled to see that there are a number of universal laws or structures that apply to all possible beings. From reflecting on these laws we can see that they are not self-explanatory, but each of them points to a higher, ultimate ground, God. The pattern of this argument reflects Thomas's Aristotelian empiricism. As he put it elsewhere, there is nothing in the intellect that is not first in the senses. We have no immediate, intuitive knowledge of metaphysical principles, but have to infer them from our concrete empirical experience. Over against Descartes' sequence of self–God–existence–world, Thomas' is more like existence–world–God–self. The self is what it is because it inhabits a world created, sustained and directed by its divine ground. One argues from existence, not towards it.

However, the picture of the early modern period as marked by a 'turn to the subject' might seem rather naive. In the light of Galileo's demolition of the belief that the earth (and man as its premier inhabitant) stood at the centre of God's universe and of Newton's further extension of the system of universal mechanics, wouldn't it be more accurate to say that the world came to look like one in which human beings are mere products and not the causes of things being the way they are? As the implications of the new cosmology sank in and it became apparent that the earth was simply one planet amongst many, the special place of humanity was inevitably shaken.

The idea of a 'turn to the subject' should not, however, be simply taken as identical with humanism in the sense of the Renaissance's understanding of 'Man the Measure of All Things'. Instead it can better be understood as a new problematization of the human subject, a sharpening of the question as to what exactly human being is: how far does our remit run; and what, if anything, justifies our existence and our unique mode of consciousness?

The figure in whose writings these questions find their most dramatic expression is Blaise Pascal, a younger contemporary of Descartes. In Pascal's aphoristic *Pensées* we can see how the new cosmology could sharpen rather than deaden the sense of humanity's uniqueness. Pascal wrote of the infinite dread that fell upon him when he considered humanity's place in the universe. First, he suggests that his reader should consider the immensity of the cosmos in which even the orbit of the sun is merely 'the tiniest point compared to that described by the stars revolving in the firmament' and then turn to the microscopic world where we find worlds within worlds. 'Let a mite show [us] in its minute body incomparably more minute parts, legs with joints, veins in its legs, blood in the veins, humours in the blood, drops in the humours, vapours in the drops; let [us] divide these things still further until [we have] exhausted [our] powers of imagination . . .'[6] Thus we find ourselves caught between 'these two abysses of infinity and nothingness . . . [Humanity is] A nothing compared to the infinite, a whole compared to the nothing, a middle point between all and nothing, infinitely remote from an understanding of the extremes'.[7] In this situation, we seem to move in a fog of uncertainty, there are no fixed points: 'We burn with desire to find a firm footing, an ultimate, lasting base on which to build a tower rising up to infinity, but our whole foundation cracks and the earth opens up into the depth of the abyss'.[8] Yet for all the horror of this situation, Pascal writes, we have one advantage over the universe, even though the universe can crush us at any moment: uniquely in the universe we have thought, consciousness.

In many respects – and in closer historical proximity than either Augustine or Luther (especially on account of his having experience of the early scientific revolution) – Pascal anticipates many of the features of later existentialism. Others, however, sought to develop an understanding of the nature of things that, whilst accepting Newton, allowed for the proper dignity and freedom of human beings. The starry heavens above might exemplify one kind of law, but the moral law within was no less precise in its implications for our self-understanding.

This was one element in the hopes held for his philosophical enterprise by Immanuel Kant. Kant was unable to follow Descartes' argument that a priori rational reflection could give us assured knowledge of the existence of God. As Kant saw it, Descartes' ontological argument did not so much offer a 'proof' as stipulate a requirement. It did not show that God existed, but revealed our deepest intellectual conviction that there is a fundamental congruence between the way our minds work and the way things are in themselves. This was doubly important in that, for Kant, the ontological argument was not so much to be opposed to cosmological forms of argument as the basis of their appeal. As he put it, all philosophical arguments for the existence of God resolve down to the ontological argument. At first this seems an odd, counter-intuitive claim. How can arguments that proceed from such different starting-points and that follow such different trajectories be, ultimately, 'the same'? Yet Kant's reasoning is essentially quite simple. For, as he sees it, the claims on which the cosmological type of argument rest (e.g. that there is such a thing as causality undergirding the world of everyday experience) are not – as they seem to their proponents to be – derived from a recognition of how the world actually is but are reflections of the subjective conditions of knowledge, i.e. of the necessity for rational beings to conceive of the world as held together by a uniform system of causes. Thus the cosmological arguments also, like the ontological argument, proceed from what is a necessity for thought to claims about existence. Now Kant did not doubt that this was important, and important for science. If we are to make any progress in science, we simply have to assume that the world is a unitary, law-governed, purposive whole. Without making such an assumption we cannot explain anything. Nevertheless it is no more than an assumption. We do not actually know whether the world is a unitary whole, whether it is the creation of an all-powerful and benevolent supreme being or not. As we saw previously, Kant could only allow for a regulative use of metaphysical ideas. He could not allow them a constitutive role. That is to say, we had to proceed as if the world was a rationally organized whole, but we will never be in a position to affirm that it is. We do not have access to things-in-themselves, since we can never get outside of the formative processes of our own minds, processes that imaginatively work the data of sense-experience into meaningful representations – meaningful to us, but not necessarily true depictions of how things are out there.

In relation to both Thomas Aquinas and Descartes, then, Kant's position must appear sceptical. Nevertheless, what he took away with one hand, he seemed to give back with another. If God could no longer be proved to exist on the basis of cosmological speculations, nor even on the basis of an examination of the immediate data of our own consciousness, the idea of God remained important and necessary for us. Not only in relation to the practice of science but also, and more urgently, in relation to moral life. In our own selves we do not have immediate access to God, but we do have immediate access to the moral law, to the categorical imperative that requires us to act morally in such a way that our action might justifiably be regarded as a law for all. If we cannot imagine that our course of action could be adopted universally, then it is not moral, and we should not pursue it. In accordance with this principle, for example, we should never lie, because we could never wish for lying to be adopted as a universal rule of conduct.

But what if the universe itself is indifferent to our moral strivings? After all, Kant seemed to have shown that we cannot know theoretically whether or not there is an all-powerful and all-good supreme being governing the universe. If the universe turns out to be the product of sheer, purposeless chance, what is the point of trying to act morally? It would seem, then, that in order to take the claims of the moral law seriously, we have to believe that that law in some way corresponds to the way things are. Thus, although we should not do the good for the sake of any selfish reward, Kant believes that it is appropriate for us to believe in a future life in which virtue will be rewarded, because, he argues, the idea of the supreme good combines both virtue and happiness. A world in which the practice of virtue was not in any way connected to the happiness of the practitioner (or, conversely where evil-living coexisted with happiness) would be less good than a world in which virtue and happiness were conjoined. Clearly, we do not see any such conjunction in this life except fitfully and intermittently, therefore we are obligated to posit a future life in which virtue is rewarded and vice punished.

And there is another problem, intimately interconnected with these. The kind of scepticism Kant expressed in relation to metaphysical knowledge of God as the cause or ground of the cosmos, also applied to the self. Even our self-knowledge is mediated by those structures of consciousness that shape all our thinking in an a priori fashion. We think of ourselves as the subjects of our actions, and we cannot help doing so. But I never see my self-as-a-whole any more than I ever get to see the world-as-a-whole, and I never get to have an intuition of my self as the causal agent of my actions, any more than I get to have an intuition of God actively creating and sustaining the universe. Nevertheless, the moral law remained as the postulated goal of universal history, and even if Kant would not allow the possibility of insight into things-in-themselves, he reported a personal sense of harmony between the 'starry heavens above and the moral law within'. So, in contrast to Pascal who saw the iron laws of the cosmos as a kind of annihilating fate, crushing the individual human being, Kant sought to harmonize the laws of Newtonian mechanics (the best available scientific account of the external, objective world) with the intellectual and moral strivings of the human subject – even if it was not possible, he thought, to ground this harmony theoretically.

One way of telling the story of German idealism after Kant is to say that the next philosophical generation (Fichte, etc.) proved impatient with Kant's residual scepticism and, in their different ways, insisted that we are able to have an intuition of the absolute ground in which subject and object co-inhere. However, what is important is that for each of them it is precisely this intuition that is experienced by the subject of knowledge. There is no proof of the final co-inherence of subject and object outside or apart from the subject's own experience. For this reason their positions are often, justly or not, described as 'subjective idealism'.

For the history of religious thought, an important, indeed epochal, figure of this period is Friedrich Schleiermacher (1768–1834), sometimes referred to as the Father of Modern Theology. Schleiermacher's early thought found eloquent expression in his 1799 *Speeches on Religion to its Cultured Despisers*, perhaps one of the last works of theology to have any deep or extensive influence on the secular world. Schleiermacher's position in these speeches both reflected and helped to shape the Romantic milieu to which he belonged. He was intimately involved with many of the seminal figures of early Romanticism, especially Friedrich Schlegel, with whom he lived and with whom he collaborated on the translation of Plato. Although close to a Romantic philosopher such as Schelling, Schleiermacher was not so concerned to establish the absolute validity of knowledge. Indeed, one of the key arguments of the speeches is that religion is something in its own right, and is neither to be confused with knowledge nor with morality but is prior to both.

How can this be?

To answer this question we need to follow Schleiermacher's account of the development of consciousness. As he sees it, consciousness is rooted in two elements, intuition and feeling. Intuition gives us a picture of the world. I glance about me, and as my eye scans the visual field I notice a succession of objects. 'What do you see?' asks my friend. 'I see a tree, clouds, a river,' I reply. These are my intuitions of the world. But, at the same time, inseparable from these, I have a feeling-response to the world, and am continually being attracted or repelled by what I encounter. A beautiful face or a sublime sunset attract me, dog faeces or the sight of a dead body repel me. These processes, Schleiermacher suggests, reach down into the fundamental strata of our mental life. However, as creatures of civilization, we experience them as distinguishable. We are able to put our feelings on hold while we clinically examine the contents of our knowledge and in our science attempt to build up a unified system of such abstract representations of the world, a full and complete description of what the world is. On the other hand, we reserve our capacity for feeling for things that have no standing in the world of knowledge, for matters of the heart, for art, for enjoying the beauties of nature. In this schizophrenic existence, however, we are cut off from life itself, for in life as it is lived both of these powers are originally at one. Yet such separation is the precondition for ethics, since ethics, no less than does science, presupposes that we stand over against the world and over against one another as moral agents and we can only do so when we know ourselves to be distinct, separate individuals. It is therefore intrinsically impossible to re-establish the original unity of consciousness on the basis of science or knowledge (as Fichte claimed), since this is ultimately limited by the sphere of representation and intuition, or on the basis of aesthetic experience alone (as Schelling had claimed) or on the basis of ethics (as, it seemed, the Kantians claimed). If each of these 'solutions' presupposes a prior splitting of consciousness, Schleiermacher asks, how can they be the means for re-establishing the unity?

Such a reunification, as Schleiermacher argues the case, is the peculiar task of religion. Now Schleiermacher can be quoted to make it sound as if he is, in turn, privileging intuition and feeling. Thus at one point he proclaims 'intuition of the universe' as 'the hinge of my whole speech; it is the highest and most universal formula of religion . . .'[9] And then, reminding us (and perhaps himself) that intuition is always connected with feeling, he declares that 'religious feelings should accompany every human deed like a holy music'.[10] However, he then acknowledges that '[I] mourn the fact that I cannot speak of both [intuitions and feelings] other than separately. The finest spirit of religion is thereby lost for my speech and I can disclose its innermost secret only unsteadily and uncertainly'.[11] To 'speak' of them at all we must use language, and language presupposes reflection, and reflection presupposes the separation of intuition and feeling. What he wants to point to, however, is what he describes as

That first mysterious moment that occurs in every sensory perception, before intuition and feeling have separated, where sense and its objects have, as it were, flowed into one another and become one, before both turn back to their original position – I know how indescribable it is and how quickly it passes away. But I wish that you were able to hold on to it and also to recognize it again in the higher and divine religious activity of the mind. Would that I could and might express it, at least indicate it, without having to desecrate it! It is as fleeting and transparent as the first scent with which the dew gently caresses the waking flowers, as modest and delicate as a maiden's kiss, as holy and fruitful as a nuptial embrace; indeed not *like* these, but it is *itself* all of these. A manifestation, an event develops quickly and magically into an image of the universe. Even as the beloved and ever-sought-for form fashions itself, my soul flees toward it; I embrace it, not as a shadow, but as the holy essence itself. I lie on the bosom of the infinite world. At this moment I am its soul, for I feel all it powers and its infinite life as my own; at this moment it is my body for I penetrate its muscles and limbs as my own, and its innermost nerves move according to my sense and my presentiment as my own . . . This moment is the highest flowering of religion. If I could create it in you, I would be a god; may holy fate forgive me that I have had to disclose more than the Eleusinian mysteries.[12]

What becomes ever clearer is that our most privileged access to such moments is the experience of love: that moment in which intuition and feeling are one – 'to see her is to love her' – and in which subject and object, lover and beloved, encounter one another in complete reciprocity. It is through the beloved that we rediscover our lost unity with the world.

It is thus easy to see that although Schleiermacher tries to argue that he is going beyond both intuition and feeling, he is generally taken as laying the emphasis on feeling, on what lies outside of and is prior to the sphere of knowledge. Later, in his *Christian Doctrine*, Schleiermacher adjusts his position somewhat. Many regarded the *Speeches* as teaching a kind of Romantic pantheism rather than Christianity, and so the later work makes clearer Schleiermacher's Christian intentions. Now he speaks of the foundational element in religion as 'the feeling of absolute dependence'. But note that both the earlier and the later formulations involve seeing the human being as a dependent or interdependent being, and both offer a critique of the pursuit of absolute autonomy that some would see in, e.g. Fichte.

Schleiermacher can, however, along with Fichte and Schelling, not entirely unfairly, be described as a subjective idealist, even though he does not share their interest in constructing a system of knowledge. In opposition to all of them, Hegel is sometimes defined as an 'objective idealist' in that he did not base the unity of subject and object on a subjective feeling or intuition, but on what he regarded as the objectively binding laws of logic, laws revealed in the overall objective structures and development of nature, history, law, art and religion. Nevertheless, there is an important sense in which Hegel too belongs to the history of modern subjective thought. As we have seen, he claimed that 'substance is subject', i.e. that the 'substance', the real matter of history (what is revealed in the phenomenological view of history), is not an Aristotelian substance, existing eternally for itself in a state of detached self-sufficiency, but, rather, the dynamic, active agency of spiritual subjectivity. I shall return in a later chapter to the difficult question as to whether this 'spiritual subjectivity' is, as understood by Hegel, conceived in a genuinely theological way, or whether it is merely anthropological. But it is only fair to Hegel to remember, against many of his critics, that the dynamic role of the creative subject is an inexpungible element of his thought.

Søren Kierkegaard was, of course, one such critic, who regarded Hegel's whole enterprise as one-sidedly overemphasizing the objective element to the detriment and, indeed, to the ruination of the subjective element. As he saw it, Hegel's ambition of constructing an objective system of knowledge transgressed the proper limits of all human knowledge. Such a system might be possible – but only from the standpoint of God. Over against Hegelian objectivity, Kierkegaard insisted on the ineluctability of the subjective dimension. 'Subjectivity is truth', as he declared via the mouth of his pseudonym Johannes Climacus. He went on to define this more closely. *'The objective accent,'* he wrote, *'falls on WHAT is said, the subjective accent on HOW it is said'*.[13] What is a matter of objective truth is independent of the passion of the existing subject. The laws of mathematics and logic, the movements of the heavenly bodies – with regard to such things, objectivity, content, is indeed decisive. A mathematical truth is not more or less true because I am feeling bad about learning it or am tired or angry. Subjective truths, however, are truths that really do involve the subject. Whether or not I believe in Christ, for example, is not something that can be decided with scientific detachment, but is something infinitely important to me. I can only consider such a question appropriately if I consider it as the most important question of my life, if I pursue it with burning passion. But, for Kierkegaard at least, it is not just a matter of adding subjective concern to scientific enquiry. It is not as if, for example, we might find out by scientific enquiry whether or not Jesus Christ was God. Such a truth can only be decided subjectively. Objectively it will always remain uncertain. There is no conclusive evidence we could ever call on that would decide the issue once and for all. A subjective truth is therefore '*An objective uncertainty held fast in an appropriation-process of the most passionate inwardness . . .*' and, as such, this is 'the highest truth attainable for an *existing* individual'.[14] It is therefore intrinsically important for Kierkegaard that although the Bible bears witness to Christ, it does not prove that he was who he claimed to be. Neither history nor logic can give a firm objective basis for faith, and if they did so they would make faith itself into something objective, which, in Kierkegaard's eyes, would be ridiculous – and he spends many hundreds of pages satirizing what he sees as the outcome of such an objectivizing approach to Christianity. This, as he sees it, is one aspect of the situation of established Christianity, that Christianity has been normalized and made a part of the social and metaphysical world-order. More constructively, various of Kierkegaard's books illuminate the psychological problems and processes involved in the subject's attempt to find faith and to live by it, confronting and surmounting despair, anxiety, self-contradiction, suffering, annihilation, hope, patience and active discipleship.

As Kierkegaard sees it, most of his contemporaries live in essentially aesthetic categories. Life is seen by them simply as something to be enjoyed (if one can), and knowing how to enjoy life is regarded as the highest good; thus the virtual deification of poetry and art in bourgeois society. The best may try to rise above this, and to live by ethical standards, but even they will, for the most part, not challenge the limits laid down by the prevailing society. They will marry, raise a family, hold down a job, do their civic duty and avoid any sort of clash with the powers-that-be. What they have forgotten is that religion might call us to perform exceptional acts, like Abraham called upon to sacrifice his son, or, perhaps like Kierkegaard himself, who felt compelled to break off his engagement to the girl he loved, in order to fulfil what he regarded as God's call to him. Such an act was a clear breach of moral and social norms, but precisely such immorality was what faith required. This he called 'the teleological suspension of the ethical'. Kierkegaard's Abraham has, in this respect, a certain similarity to Nietzsche's Zarathustra – but he does not act simply in order to demonstrate the power of his own will; he acts in obedience to the will of God as he understands it and in fear and trembling, fully aware of the objective unjustifiability of his actions. Those who act in this way will be on their own, stripped of the guidelines and resources that sustain the majority. They have only their faith.

The situation is deepened however by Kierkegaard's characteristically Lutheran insistence on the seriousness of the Fall and of the state of sin in which human life is typically lived. In this state we have no immediate access to truth. To say that 'subjectivity is untruth'[15] is in fact a still higher statement of subjectivity than 'subjectivity is truth' for those who know themselves to be sinners, i.e. who know themselves to be in untruth, will realize all the more sharply, all the more urgently and all the more completely how much depends on their decisions and actions, and how easy it is in every case for them to decide and act wrongly and to deceive themselves as to their motivations.

In such ways Kierkegaard not only provided a modern redescription of Christian faith, he also laid the foundations for modern existentialism, with its account of the human subject as being continually brought to nothing, and striving, like Sisyphus in the Greek legend, to complete a task that can never be completed.

Kierkegaard was not, of course, the only source for either Heidegger or Sartre, but we can see a lot of Kierkegaard in both of them, and perhaps – if paradoxically – especially in Sartre's existentialism.[16] For Sartre there is no external moral law. The human subject is the sole arbiter of values, and we have absolute responsibility for the values we choose and the actions we take. There is no other basis for this than our own freedom, and freedom itself is not a product of our nature or environment. Freedom is, in Sartre's expression, the result of an 'upsurge of nothingness' in the heart of the world, i.e. that we are beings who are not determined by environment or heredity nor, for Sartre, by divine law. We are 'the sum of our actions'. Of course, this is frightening, and most of the time we flee our responsibility, living in what Sartre calls 'bad faith', blaming circumstances or the demands of our job or the needs of our families or our parents for the beliefs we hold and the things we do. But all such explanations are excuses, flights from freedom. For Sartre, it seems, there just isn't a God and we are therefore condemned, ultimately, to fail. The best we can achieve is a kind of stoical heroism, to be as honest as we can, and not to submit to any external law or code. Despair, he says, is the foundation of philosophy. For Kierkegaard on the other hand, whilst it is true that we are repeatedly brought to experience our failure and nothingness, we do so 'before God' and, in a formulation that is crucial for the whole understanding of Kierkegaard, not only are all things possible for God, but 'God is – that all things are possible'. Faith will never find support in knowledge, but it itself is always the occasion for hope.

Beyond Kierkegaard, of course, the turn to the subject seems to be more clearly a turn away from religious belief. Nietzsche seems to attribute to the self a virtually unqualified power of self-invention, a power he sees as closely resembling artistic creativity. Whereas Kant's view of enlightenment as a process of maximizing our personal autonomy innately recognized limits to what we might actually achieve, Nietzsche's vision of the death of God implied that there were no a priori limits as to what we could be or become. We are not bound by any pre-existent law of nature, morality or deity. As Nietzsche's Zarathustra puts it to himself

'You, however, O Zarathustra, have wanted to behold the ground of things and their background: so you must climb above yourself – up and beyond, until you have even your stars *under* you!'

Yes to look down upon myself and even upon my stars: that alone would I call my *summit*, that has remained for me my *ultimate* summit![17]

Becoming who we are, becoming a self, is thus, for Nietzsche, an endless process of self-overcoming, the path not so much of an explorer aiming at a specific and definable goal (the North Pole, say, or climbing Mount Everest) as of a wanderer, ever vigilant to resist the temptation to turn the beauty of a particular view or encounter into a possession or home. Such a self has no need of anything outside himself, but only of his own will to self-transcendence.[18]

So, we have seen various forms of modern thought that emphasize the element of subjectivity, with particular emphasis on Descartes, Pascal, Kant, Schleiermacher, Kierkegaard and, briefly, Nietzsche. All of these, except for Nietzsche, saw the human subject as the key to the knowledge of God or, in some cases, to faith in but not knowledge of God. In the case of Descartes it was the immediate content of human consciousness that laid the basis for a deduction of the necessary existence of God; in Pascal the uniqueness and isolation of the human subject in the cosmos confronts us with the religious question; for Kant it is the moral law that raises our sights to God; for Schleiermacher, the feeling of oneness with the universe awakened in us by love; for Kierkegaard it is the passion of faith that seeks to break out of the grip of intellectual, moral and social systems and to experience its own truth as subjective truth, truth of and for the living subject.[19] In these ways the thinkers of subjectivity articulated a determinate content and form for religious faith in, with and under the conditions of modernity. Yet, as both the existentialist reading of

Kierkegaard and the example of Nietzsche might be taken as having demonstrated, the self or subject would seem to be a very unstable and slender basis on which to erect the edifice of religion. What is there, really, to prevent a religion of the subject from collapsing back into subjectivism? What preserves truth from dissolving into 'truth is what seems to be true (or what works) for me'? Doesn't the testimony of Pascal at the very beginning of the modern era underline the point that left to ourselves we are nothing without God, merely a tremulous and evanescent mirage-like moment of consciousness in a hostile universe?

Such objections to a purely subjectivist account of faith have been made repeatedly by religious apologists who see religion as inseparable from claims to objective truth, or who see it as the business of religion to give an account of how things are in the cosmos as a whole, rather than to reflect back to itself the self's own self-images. However, it may be that we are giving an excessively abstract view of the turn to the subject and there are two further points that should be added to this brief and very broad-stroke account, points that suggest a larger picture of the subject than that given so far.

The first is that 'the subject' should not be identified simply with 'the individual'. It is undeniably true that for several of those we have been considering such an identification seems to be almost a matter of course – Kierkegaard, for example, spoke specifically and forcefully about 'the individual' as the decisive category of modern Christian thought, whilst for Sartre other people are, simply, 'hell'. Nevertheless there have also been examples of subjective thought that do not conceive of subjectivity as simply an individual thing, but, rather, as a dimension of existence in which the self finds itself as involved in defining relationships with others.

Perhaps the best-known example of this, within the field of the philosophy of religion, is Martin Buber, with his dialogical philosophy of I-and-Thou. Buber first set out his understanding of 'I and Thou' in the book of that name published in 1922. In his earlier works published before the First World War Buber had expressed a passionate spiritual vision framed – however inadequately – in individualistic terms, and inspired by Kierkegaard, Nietzsche and the vogue for mysticism prevalent in the first decade of the century. In *I and Thou*, however, he depicts the self as never existing outside a relation to the other, a relation which can either take the form of I-and-Thou or I-and-It. The latter is the mode in which we relate to the world as an ensemble of objectified, quantified, manipulable things or objects, the world of capitalist economics, of industrial production, of science and technology – but also of carefully cultivated aesthetic or religious experiences. The former, necessarily harder to define, is the opposite of all this. In the relation of I and Thou the world reveals itself to me as personal, as requiring my utmost and total engagement and attention, whether it is a matter of encountering a tree, a cat, another human presence or God – and the depth of the I and Thou encounter is always, for Buber, open to God, to the exclusive, demanding and promising claim of the Holy.[20]

Buber may be taken as the exception that proves the rule. However, he is not really that exceptional, except for the forcefulness, vividness and consistency with which he places being-in-relation at the centre of his mature thought. It is striking that other thinkers who have espoused 'dialogue' or 'dialogism' as a philosophical position have also been closely connected with existentialism and phenomenology, Mikhail Bakhtin and Gabriel Marcel being two prominent examples. We may also recall the massive emphasis placed by the 'subjective' thinker Schleiermacher on love, such that the beloved is the mode and moment of the revelation of the divine face of the universe.[21]

The other point is the intimate connection between the account of the self in the existentialist tradition and the historicization of the human subject. The question of time and of the self's relation to time is at the heart of Kierkegaard's religious and philosophical writing. Here, for all his opposition to Hegel, Kierkegaard remains a child of the Hegelian era and the categories in which he conceptualizes both the self's failure to be itself and its self-recovery are characteristically temporal: boredom, recollection/remembrance, patience, expectation and 'the moment'. Becoming a self is inseparable from acquiring what Kierkegaard calls an 'inner history'. If Kierkegaard here anticipates Heidegger, Bultmann gives a religious turn to the Heideggerian question about whether beings such as we are, beings whose existence is temporal through and through, can find their way to authentic life. For Bultmann, in close connection to both Kierkegaard and Heidegger, the future has a crucial role in authentic life, for authenticity is based on decision, on the free resolve to become or to choose what or who I am, and this necessarily involves a committing of myself in relation to a projected future, however vaguely conceived or imagined. But, Bultmann says, 'Christian faith believes that man does not have the freedom which is presupposed for historical decisions'.[22] Why not? Because, Bultmann says, we are what we are by virtue of our past – our biological ancestry, our family and social background, what we have done or failed to do thus far in our lives – which, although at one level simply a matter of how things are, typically leads us into curtailing, limiting or distorting our possibilities. Bultmann envisages the situation in terms of the Pauline view of '"the old man", fettered by his past'.[23] It is, in other words, the situation of one in whom – in contrast to the Sartrean view of the self – essence precedes existence: one who allows what he is or has become by virtue of his history to predetermine what he does or becomes in the future. Over against this Bultmann posits the picture of one who knows a 'radical freedom', 'freedom from himself': 'The man who understands his historicity radically, that is, the man who radically understands himself as someone future, or in other words, who understands his genuine self as an ever-future one, has to know that his genuine self can only be offered to him as a gift by the future ... Man cannot get such freedom by his own will and strength, for in such effort he would remain "the old man"; he can only receive this freedom as gift.'[24] Authenticity, freedom, and the possibility of self-commitment – for Bultmann, faith – are thus issues that have intrinsically to do with our temporal, historical way of being.

The relation to the other and the temporality of the self are not, it should be said, simply separate subheadings of the modern turn to the subject. Rather, the complex of problems they bring to expression lies at the very heart of the question as to what it is or what it means to be a subject at all. Both problematize a certain view of the self as self-sufficient reason or rational will, both suggest crucial limits to the aspiration towards autonomy and self-direction, but both also suggest something of the direction in which a resolution of the question of the self might be sought: the realization of a historical time in which the other is encountered not as a constraint on my freedom but, in love, as the one by whom I first become what I am, the one who brings me the gift of the freedom from my self which, as Bultmann puts it, is also the freedom to be myself.

These do not, of course, exhaust the manifestations of the turn to the subject in the modern era. In a very different tradition, for example, the tradition of empirical science, we find a psychologist such as William James looking to the phenomenon of religious experience as a possible, indeed, the best possible, basis from which to argue for the validity of religious claims. In his 1900 Gifford Lectures *The Varieties of Religious Experience* James did just what the title suggests and examined a vast range of accounts of religious experience, purely as an empirical psychologist. He concluded that as such experiences had a positive value for human life, they should be treasured, although it could not be decided on the evidence of such experiences alone, whether the claims of theism were really 'true'.

Following after James has been a succession of psychological and biological approaches to faith, such as those of Alister Hardy in Britain, that have seen religious experience as a manifestation of some objective force or power, more or less easily identifiable with the God of Christianity, that points beyond the limitations of the mechanistic world-view of popular science towards a truly personal universe.[25]

However, the objections to subjective approaches to religion are not easily disposed of. A particular problem is that of reductionism. For, the charge is, such approaches necessarily limit what can be said of the transcendence of God, tying God to the capacities, experiences and mental capacities of human beings. From religious experience it is but a short step to Feuerbach's slogan that 'The secret of theology is anthropology' and it is perhaps no accident that the early pages of Feuerbach's ground-breaking reductionist textbook *The Essence of Christianity* make significant allusions to Schleiermacher. For a religion that makes feeling the sole organon of religion, Feuerbach argues, feeling itself has become religion.

Before coming to a fuller exploration of the challenge of reductionism, however, we must take note of a third dimension to modern philosophical treatments of religion: the so-called 'linguistic turn'.

4

Modern Trends (iii): The Linguistic Turn

The discovery of history and the turn to the subject are two of the distinctive features that characterize the emerging profile of the philosophy of religion in the early modern and high modern period. And if we look at some of the great movements in ideas that dominated the twentieth century we can see how these features could be so important. Marxism and existentialism, so dominant in the secular thought of that time, were nothing if not historical and subjective – though each with very different conceptions of historicity and subjectivity. To the extent that such tendencies defined the intellectual situation of their age, any serious philosophical reflection on the question of religion would have to address the same core issues of historicity and subjectivity. Inevitably, the various exponents of the philosophy of religion came at these issues from a variety of directions and with varying commitments, some seeking to refute the perceived relativism of secular views of history and subjectivity, others identifying points of convergence. Nor should we regard 'Marxism' and 'existentialism' as internally monolithic entities (much as Soviet Communism might have attempted to impose such uniformity on the Marxist world). Although Marxists like George Lukacs (one of the most influential communist theoreticians) could denounce existentialism in terms of 'parasitic subjectivism', Lukács himself, if we look at his work as a whole, can be seen to be arguing for a kind of existentialist orientation – in contrast to those versions of Marxism that simply treated historical laws as being a species of laws of nature, i.e. deterministically.[1] Similarly, for all their differences, Hegel and Kierkegaard can each be seen as representing an approach that was simultaneously historical and subjective. The cross-fertilization of these two aspects (and the influence of both Hegel and Kierkegaard) can be seen, in the West at least, in the intellectual tradition of critical theory, associated with the Frankfurt School. In their early years the leading figures of this school (such as Max Horkheimer, Theodor Adorno and Herbert Marcuse) had important connections with existential theologians like Martin Buber and Paul Tillich, and Marcuse studied under Heidegger. Whether their project of having the best of Marxism and existentialism succeeded at all – indeed, whether it is intrinsically coherent – lies beyond the scope of this course. However, their example highlights the way in which the two emphases on history and subjectivity are by no means opposed, but interact and even merge in a whole range of modernist theories and approaches.[2]

Another characteristic feature of modern thought is what has been called the linguistic turn. However, according to the usual way in which the story is told, this comes into play somewhat later than the rise of the historical consciousness and the turn to the subject. These had already reached prominence by the early nineteenth century, but, it is said, it was only in the twentieth century that the linguistic turn really came into its own.

Now, just as it would be foolish to say that people who lived before Hegel had no sense of history (and we alluded to the Bible itself as an important precursor of historical thought) or that people who lived before Descartes or Kierkegaard had no sense of subjectivity (and here Paul, Augustine and Luther were adduced as examples of intense subjective self-consciousness), so too it would be ridiculous to claim that before Wittgenstein, for example, thinkers had not noticed just how deeply the processes of thinking and understanding are connected to the structures and forms of language. The extraordinary mystery of language has long moved those who have reflected on the meaning of human life. The opening lines of St John's Gospel, 'In the beginning was the Word', may be taken as symptomatic of the Bible's deep and far-ranging contribution to reflection on language, and both in Jewish and Christian traditions the ongoing attempt to interpret the biblical word provided the opportunity for many comments on the nature of image, symbol and word. The Jewish cabbalistic tradition, for example, argued for the formative role of the Hebrew alphabet itself in the creation of the world, and saw in the numerical significations of words a potential key to the hidden structures of the divine plan.[3] John Milbank has recently argued that the linguistic turn should be seen 'as a theological turn', and that although the early church fathers took over a rationalist and instrumentalist view of language, the decisive steps 'towards a modern "linguistic turn", beyond linguistic instrumentalism, foundational reason and a nominalist instrumentalism' came from 'profoundly orthodox Christian thinkers' whose thought was shaped by the christological and textual concerns of theology itself.[4]

Certainly, the importance of questions of meaning, symbol and interpretation are central to the Christian tradition. Building on the brilliant re-reading of Scripture by the Jewish Platonic commentator Philo of Alexandria, the early church saw the rise of allegorical and typological schools of interpretation, which again provided the occasion for reflections on the connections between words, meanings, symbols and events. Augustine (once more playing a crucial role) developed a sophisticated theory of language and meaning, and it is not perhaps coincidental that Wittgenstein's *Philosophical Investigations* opens with a quotation from Augustine's *Confessions*, in which Augustine describes how, as a child, he first learned the meanings of words. Wittgenstein goes on to attack Augustine's view, but the fact that he takes it as the object of critical reflection suggests that he finds it both interesting and important.

So, throughout the Christian centuries, we could find many points at which to stop and take note of striking or illuminating arguments about how language works or about the limits of language in relation to religious life and experience. It is perhaps no coincidence that in the wake of the twentieth century's discovery of the ubiquity of language, there is a wide-ranging revisiting of Aquinas' theory of analogy, of the medieval mystical tradition and the apophaticism associated with it – not (as in the earlier part of the twentieth century) with a view to reanimating the tradition of Christian mystical experience but precisely with regard to the kind of understanding of language at work in such sources.[5]

A crucial figure in the argument for the theological origins of the linguistic turn is the late-eighteenth-century figure of J. G. Hamann. A contemporary (and sometime friend) of Kant, Hamann is generally regarded as an eccentric and marginal thinker, representing a counter-Enlightenment position and associated with the cultural movement of *Sturm und Drang* and its rediscovery of the passionate and irrational side of human nature. However, the issue for Hamann was not simply that of reason versus feeling, since, for him, neither was separable from language as simultaneously the only possible organ of thought and yet necessarily embodied and, as such, the bearer of the lived historical and cultural experiences of humankind. It was in the light of this conviction that Hamann characteristically took upon himself the role of a 'philologian' rather than that of a philosopher, and, brilliantly, intriguingly yet infuriatingly, wrote in a complex polyglottal style, mixing quotations and references from and in a range of classical and modern languages and sources in the course of his exposition. (Hamann's writings – consistently enough –

tend more to expound a single point or insight rather than to constitute anything like a reasoned argument.)

Responding to Herder's claim – made in the context of an ongoing eighteenth-century debate – that language was a human invention, Hamann proclaimed the inseparability of human life and experience from language. God created the world by means of his Word ('And God said . . . '), so that, in the beginning

> Every natural phenomenon was a word – the sign, image and pledge of a new, secret, unspeakable, yet all the more inward unification, communication, and community of divine energies and ideas. Everything that Man at first heard, saw with his eyes, beheld or handled, was a living word; for God was the Word. With this word in his mouth and heart, the origin of language was so natural, so near at hand and so easy as a children's game . . . [6]

Hamann saw this fundamental determination of humanity in terms of its capacity for language as something that had, typically, been overlooked by the philosophical tradition. This neglect was, in his view, brought to a head in Kant's idea of 'pure reason', which, as Hamann saw it, was reason stripped of the essential conditions of all genuine thought, pre-eminently the reliance of thought on the actual experience of objects, on tradition and on language. Kant's attempt to establish pure forms of intuition and judgment occupying some kind of a priori conceptual space that was prior to all concrete experience and thought was, according to Hamann, the outcome of a 'gnostic hatred of matter', 'a mystical infatuation with form' or, simply, 'an old, cold prejudice in favour of the mathematical'. But whilst geometry, he countered, still made use of empirical, visible designs and illustrations, metaphysics abandons even this concession to reality, and dissolves the concreteness of the world into an empty x. If the mathematical is to be the supreme standard of reason, then human beings must 'be placed below the infallible and undeceiving instinct of insects' – a comment that reflects a long tradition of comparing a world shaped by pure rationality to the functional efficiency of the ant-hill or beehive.[7]

Against this Hamann sets the claim that 'the whole of our capacity to think rests on language'. Moreover, since language is inseparable from sounds and letters which are 'the true aesthetic elements of all human cognition and reason'[8] it constitutes the unity of sensuousness and intuition with reason and understanding, and if philosophy chooses to separate these by abstracting from the actual pith and stuff of language it will consign itself to an endless exile in vacuity.

Hamann can by no means be said to have had an effect on subsequent philosophy of anything like the same magnitude as Kant, yet, in conjunction with more formally 'scholarly' thinkers like Herder (despite Hamann's polemic against him), the Schlegel brothers and von Humboldt, Hamann did put down a marker concerning the necessity for thought of language in its concrete, historical specificity that was to resurface periodically in the later history of German idealism and its critics.

This, despite the extreme difference between Hamann's and Hegel's ultimate orientation, can be seen in Hegel's account of the development and crisis of Greek culture and the coming of Christianity as the 'answer' to that crisis. For this account is largely driven by the dynamics of symbolization and language, with history being carried by the inner thrust of symbolization towards the self-expression of the speaking subject. Remember how in Hegel's account of early Greek religion the cult statue, although addressed by them in hymns and prayers, stood silently over against the worshipping community; then came the poets, who spoke for the gods, but in the third person; then came the tragedians who gave the gods living voices, but speaking from behind the actors' masks; then the comedians, who allowed the audience to see the man behind the mask, and to see that it was they themselves who were, as it were, giving the gods a voice. Only with Christianity did the real, actual speaking subjectivity of God enter into history.

Even earlier in the *Phenomenology*, in the opening chapter on 'Sense Certainty', Hegel had drawn attention to the philosophical importance of language. Arguing against those who sought to explain meaning by simple acts of ostensive definition, he emphasized the universalizing power of language. Suppose a person is asked to explain what he means by a tree, and he points to a tree saying 'This!' – this might seem to support the argument that meaning is built on such simple acts of ostensive definition and that language is ultimately made up of an innumerable multitude of such individual acts of pointing. Not so, says Hegel, for even a word such as 'this' is not all it seems. In fact, it is already universal, since the same word is not tied to the phenomenon 'tree', but we can equally well use it of 'house', 'egg', 'woman' or 'painting' or whatever. Even such a simple word points beyond the immediacy of sense-certainty towards the universal.[9] Language is not fulfilled, then, until it finds a full and adequate form for expressing this inherent universality (something which Hegel believes occurs in logic, in which the inner universal form of language is presented in its purest form).

In a very different way, issues of language and communication lie at the heart of Kierkegaard's work. We have seen how his emphasis on subjectivity problematized any form of objective representation, and this included language. Part of the paradox of Christ is the paradoxical character of the communicative event he enacts as God Incarnate. The human form contradicts the divine meaning, such that he is a 'sign of contradiction', and this slippage between outward expression and inner meaning runs through the whole realm of Christian concepts and communication. So, in his *Works of Love*, he wrote

> There is no word in human language, not a single one, not the holiest, of which we can say: if a man uses this word, then it is thereby unconditionally proved that he has love within him. On the contrary, it is even thus: that a word spoken by one man can assure us that there is love in him, and the opposite word spoken by another man can assure us that equally there is love in him: it is so that one and the same word can assure us that love dwells in the one who spoke it, and not in another who nevertheless spoke the same word.[10]

Later Kierkegaard explains that the reason for this is to do with the fact that, although human beings are spiritual beings from the moment of birth, and we regard even the new-born baby as a full human being who has the protection of law and a claim on the offices of religion, they do not acquire the capacity for spiritual self-expression until a later age. Even when they first acquire language they do so in the first instance without understanding it, merely learning it as a physical system of material signs and sounds. There is thus a certain disjunction between language and spirit, although the purpose of language is precisely to be a vehicle for spiritual communication. This disjunction is expressed in the situation that all language is metaphorical, 'carried-over' as the Danish term Kierkegaard uses means literally. Because, as we have seen, language is at first acquired solely in its material externality, spiritual meaning is always 'carried over' into this materiality, and, simply in terms of this materiality itself, it is never possible to tell whether the language user 'really' understands the spiritual meaning, whether they are just saying the words, or truly understand them. Kierkegaard's complex use of pseudonyms and what he called 'indirect' communication is a response to this problem and an attempt to forge a distinctively modern art of Christian communication against the stream of the relentlessly trivializing 'idle talk' that, taking its starting point from the general ambiguity of language, flattens all speech into monochrome meaninglessness and the scientific objectivity that stifles the expression of deep passion.[11]

The earlier Christian tradition and the eighteenth and nineteenth century stirrings of reflection on the linguistic dimension of religious belief are by no means simply to be relegated to the past. As we shall see in Chapter Six, the past can remain or become a vital resource for contemporary understanding. However, neither Hamann nor Kierkegaard immediately frames the shape in which the question of language exists for us today. Let us then, briefly, rehearse some of the more prominent moments in the twentieth century's discussion of religious language.

One place to start is with the logical positivism of the Vienna circle, and its adoption in England under the influence of the early Wittgenstein and A. J. Ayer. Wittgenstein's *Tractatus Logico-Philosophicus* is one of those books that may not be all that it seems. Closing with the reflection that the whole sphere of the ethical lies outside its field of enquiry, and remarking 'Of what we cannot speak, thereof we must keep silent', it is sometimes judged to be a kind of 'indirect communication' *à la* Kierkegaard (whom Wittgenstein greatly admired, it seems[12]). However, it was mostly seen at first as very much a textbook for logical positivism. Wittgenstein's view seemed to be that language could be broken down into simple propositions, each of which 'pictured' a simple state of affairs in the external world. The truth of a statement, then, consisted in the correctness with which the proposition represented the relations it depicted.

But how could one tell whether or not a proposition was 'correct'? A. J. Ayer answered this question in terms of the verification principle, later amended to the falsification principle. What did this mean? A proposition was meaningful, Ayer claimed, if we could state a procedure for verifying it, i.e. for effecting that correlation between proposition and state of affairs that the *Tractatus* seemed to call for. Thus, 'tomatoes are red' is a meaningful assertion since I can tell you how I would go about verifying it, namely, by taking every proffered object that was named as a 'tomato' and checking its colour. However, it soon became clear that this was a very inelegant procedure. Much simpler was the falsification principle, since that meant simply being able to say what would need to be the case for the proposition to be proved false. Whereas the verification principle could doom me to counting tomatoes by the million, all the falsification principle would require of me would be one yellow or one green tomato and the proposition 'tomatoes are red' would be proved false. Nevertheless, even though it was false it would still be meaningful, whereas propositions that could not be falsified were, Ayer claimed, neither true nor false but meaningless. Such were the propositions of metaphysics. Precisely because of the generality of metaphysical propositions, a generality that embraced all possible states of affairs, there could never be a counter-instance. Take a metaphysical statement like 'God is Being Itself'[13]: what possible state of affairs could count against that? What would falsify that? Nothing. Therefore, Ayer concluded, it was meaningless. Metaphysical and religious claims, Ayer argued, could still be allowed, but basically they had the same function as poetry. They didn't say anything significant about the world; they just expressed conceptually empty feelings.

These claims provoked fierce debate amongst philosophers interested in questions of religion. In the 1960s a series of publications in Britain, known as the 'University Debate' reflected many of the possible responses to this kind of approach to language.

One seminal essay was by the Cambridge philosopher John Wisdom. Entitled 'Gods' it contained the following parable.

Two people return to their long neglected garden and find among the weeds a few of the old plants surprisingly vigorous. One says to the other 'It must be that a gardener has been coming and doing something about these plants'. Upon enquiry they find that no neighbour has ever seen anyone at work in their garden. The first man says to the other 'he must have worked while people slept'. The other says 'No, someone would have heard him and besides, anyone who cared about the plants would have kept down these weeds'.[14]

And so the argument continues. Both make further researches; both come across new pieces of evidence – sometimes pointing to one conclusion, sometimes to the other. Yet they still disagree. Moreover, Wisdom claims, this disagreement is not simply 'a difference in how they feel towards the garden'. Both men are confronted with the same set of facts. Both agree as to the nature and layout of what they see before them, but they interpret it quite differently. This difference, then, cannot be settled by new pieces of evidence nor even by further experiments on the evidence already available since it is not to do with facts, but with how the facts are understood. Not all disputes, then – contra Ayer – are to be resolved by appeal to facts or states of affairs. And yet, Wisdom insisted, the disputants speak – and speak justifiably – 'as if they were concerned with a matter of scientific fact, or of trans-sensual, trans-scientific and metaphysical fact', about something 'about which reasons for and against may be offered'.[15] Wisdom also pointed to legal cases where the same chain of events might either be construed as manslaughter or murder, as involving or not involving 'reasonable care'. So (not Wisdom's example) if a railway company is being prosecuted for criminal negligence in the wake of a crash, it may be that both the prosecution and the defence agree as to the sequence of events: what happened, what went wrong and why, mechanically speaking, the crash took place. But that is very different from assigning guilt – and yet there is a real issue at stake here. It is not just a matter of words. But it cannot be resolved by evidence. It is a matter of weighing and evaluating the evidence.

So maybe metaphysical and theological assertions, then, are of this kind.

Wisdom's parable of the garden was taken up by the sceptical philosopher Anthony Flew who turned it into a story about two explorers coming across a clearing in the jungle. So, said Flew, what happens next? Presumably our explorers will lie in wait until they see this gardener. But they wait night and day and no one shows up. Still one of them believes that there must be a gardener, but, he says, he's an invisible gardener. They put up fences, lay traps, but to no purpose. It seems that the gardener is not only invisible but can pass through walls and do all sorts of other amazing things that no other gardener has ever been able to do. Gradually it becomes clear, says Flew, that the believer will not allow anything to count against his belief. Nothing that could possibly occur could falsify it. And so his belief is meaningless. More forcefully still, he adduces the example of a child dying of cancer. Christians, he says, call God a loving father. However, any human father whose child was dying of cancer would do everything possible to help it. If it were within his power he would heal it. If he could not do that he would eliminate the child's pain if he could. He cannot do these things because he is merely a human father. God, however, is almighty, so it is said, and yet he does nothing to prevent innocent children dying in terrible pain. How, then, can we call him a loving father, since he fails every possible test we might apply in the case of a human father. Such a God, says Flew, has died the death of a thousand qualifications. Believers, he complained, just won't say what they really mean and stick with it.[16]

Nevertheless, responded the theists, things are not that simple. John Hick, for example, argued that, despite appearances, religious assertions are verifiable. Not in this life, to be sure, but in the future. Christian faith depends on the possibility of eschatological verification. And, Hick pointed out, if it is objected that we are unable to test that ourselves this doesn't matter, for the requirement of the principle is not that we should actually carry out the verifying or falsifying operation ourselves, but that we know what would count as verification or what would count as falsification. And that is what the principle of eschatological verification delivers. The point is not to prove religious language true or false, but to defend it as meaningful.[17]

From another direction R. M. Hare argued that there are certain basic assumptions, for some reason he perhaps unhelpfully called them 'bliks', assumptions that shape our world and that direct our view of things. One person, for example, might have the basic conviction that his colleagues are out to kill him. No matter what is said to him, no matter how friendly they seem, it is all part of the plot. It has to be said that Hare's example was extraordinarily badly chosen if it was intended to support the claims of religious language, and we could easily think of better ones. But his point is clear enough: that there are all sorts of situations in life, including situations that are very important to us, in which we do not rely on verification or falsification but on our basic, untested and untestable hunches. Even so, we might still feel our philosophical hackles rising at a too glib invocation of pre-critical assumptions – particularly if it belongs to our basic understanding of philosophy that its task is crucially to do with exposing such assumptions to the light of critical debate.[18]

For Basil Mitchell, by way of contrast, there *was* evidence that counted for or against the hypothesis of God's existence – but it was necessarily inconclusive. Mitchell's parable was of a mysterious stranger who informs a member of the resistance forces in an occupied country that he is in fact the commander of the resistance movement but, precisely for that reason, cannot be seen to be such. Sometimes, therefore, he behaves in ways that seem to contradict this role. Nevertheless, such is the trust that the partisan fighter has in him that no matter what happens publicly (even when the stranger behaves in ways that would be more suited to a collaborator or quisling) he still believes in him. Thus, as for Wisdom, religious belief does involve assertions ('The stranger is on our side') but, in the nature of the case, there can be no decisive arguments one way or another.[19]

Another much-discussed contribution to this debate was Richard Braithwaite's essay 'An Empiricist's View of the Nature of Religious Belief'.[20] For Braithwaite the really distinctive thing about religious language was the relationship between its form and its function. Its form is typically that of stories, parables or narratives: its function to express a commitment to a particular way of acting in the world. The language of Christianity, then, consists of stories, including the teaching parables of Jesus and the doctrinal narrative of the God who came down from heaven to save us from our sins, that promote an agapeistic life.[21] By believing the stories we commit ourselves to living agapeistically.

Like Hare's 'bliks', Braithwaite's stories seem to fall short of what most theologians would want to claim for religious language. What is there to distinguish his position from that of a purely human morality, dressed up in an appealing way? The story is that when Braithwaite was baptized as an adult in King's College Chapel, Wittgenstein, who was invited, refused to attend, since he claimed that someone who held the views Braithwaite held did not believe in the way the church itself required.

The 'University Debate' had no definite outcome (itself a comment, perhaps, on the nature of philosophical debates about religion!), but it did suggest that the logical positivist project, strictly understood, was much too rigid and much too narrow to do justice to the many ways in which we use language and, especially, the many ways in which we use language in the context of religion. Far from being a 'philosophy of language' this was a philosophy that utterly failed to take account of the multidimensional, multilevelled and manifestly complex reality of language 'as it is spoke'.

But by this time Wittgenstein himself had moved on from the position reached in the *Tractatus*. His second major work, the *Philosophical Investigations* published in 1953, developed a whole new way of looking at language. As noted earlier, Wittgenstein begins with a passage from Augustine's *Confessions*, in which Augustine defines how, as a child, he learned the meaning of words by a continual association of sounds, gestures and things. Essentially this is the ostensive principle criticized by Hegel at the beginning of the *Phenomenology*. But, as Wittgenstein now immediately comments, there are all sorts of uses of language that can't be explained that way. 'The philosophical concept of meaning,' he says, 'has its place in a primitive idea of the way language functions. But one can also say that it is the idea of a language more primitive than ours'.[22] Now, then, it is a matter of 'Don't ask for the meaning, ask for the use'. And once we start to do this, we will discover that language is used in all sorts of different ways.

'Think of the tools in a tool-box', writes Wittgenstein,

> . . . there is a hammer, pliers, a saw, a screw-driver, a rule, a glue-pot, glue, nails and screws – the functions of words are as diverse as the functions of these objects. (And in both cases there are similarities.)
>
> Of course, what confuses us is the uniform appearance of words when we hear them spoken or meet them in script and print. For their application is not presented to us so clearly. Especially when we are doing philosophy!
>
> It is like looking into the cabin of a locomotive. We see handles all looking more or less alike. (Naturally, since they are supposed to be handled.) But one is the handle of a crank which can be moved continuously (it regulates the opening of a valve); another is the handle of a switch, which has only two effective positions, it is either off or on; a third is the handle of a brake lever, the harder one pulls on it, the harder it brakes; a fourth, the handle of a pump: it has an effect only so long as it is used to and fro.[23]

The attempt of logical positivism to find a single, uniform and universal formula for language, then, was mistaken from the ground up. Language isn't the sort of thing you can do that to. Instead, said Wittgenstein, learning a language is like learning to play a game, and just as there is an infinite variety of games in human societies, so there is an open-ended number of possible language games, each embedded in a particular form of life that is not necessarily visible or understandable from the outside. We have to be in it, to live in it, to experience it from within before we are 'players' in the full sense. Instead of philosophers trying to legislate what games should or shouldn't be played or what counts as meaningful language, they should simply accept that 'this game is being played' and, in face of the actual language games being played, content themselves with trying to work out the relevant grammar to apply to each particular case.

The appeal of this to philosophers of religion is clear, in that it seemed to draw the sting of logical positivism once and for all. On the other hand, there did seem to be a price to pay. For the fact that language games are being played does not mean that those language games provide significant information about the universe. The religious language game, or the whole complex of religious language games we encounter in the world, is no longer to be dismissed: but whether they are being used in the way that their players imagine is another matter. And whether any religious language game is really fitted to tell us of the nature or existence of metaphysical beings is a whole other question. But, of course, the reply will come: maybe it never was the point of religious language games to impart metaphysical information. Maybe the aim was more to shape deep attitudes, to articulate the hinterground against which our personal and moral strivings best make sense.[24] Maybe religious words are just the right words to use in some contexts, even if they have no particular instantiations.

Much depends, of course, on how we understand the idea of 'forms of life' in which language games are embedded. For some theologians who have made use of Wittgenstein, the form of life means something like the whole ensemble of church practices, of liturgy, of doctrine, of social formations. This is how it seems to be for George Lindbeck, an American theologian. According to Lindbeck the modern era has been dominated by an emotive-expressive view of religious language, reflecting the turn to the subject discussed in the previous chapter. Now, however, we can see that that is a misunderstanding. Religious language does not primarily express the inner subjective states of believers. What it does is to articulate the cultural-linguistic situation within which believers situate themselves.[25] Let us take an example. The Virgin Birth and analogous miracles were for a long time discussed in the philosophy of religion in terms of whether such a thing was objectively possible. The question was: is it reasonable to suppose that God would intervene in history in this way, suspending or disrupting the normal operation of the laws of nature? Of course, some drew analogies with parthenogenesis in some animals, and argued that this was not an absolute breach in the laws of nature, but simply an extremely rare but biologically possible occurrence. Others addressed it in terms of the nature of the textual evidence. But in any case what seemed to be at issue was whether or not such a thing could have happened and did, in this particular case, happen. To those who stand this side of the turn to the subject, however, other possibilities of interpretation also come into view. In the subjective perspective it might be seen as a symbol of the radical novelty that is experienced as the basic event underlying or initiating the religious life. In this case the argument is not about whether it really happened, but about whether it is appropriately expressive of the religious life. From the cultural-linguistic point of view, however, both these approaches are misdirected. A doctrine such as this cannot be abstracted from its overall context in Scripture, in liturgy, in devotional practice. Only by being a believing reader of Scripture, a participant in liturgy, a practitioner of prayer do we get to know how, in Wittgensteinian terms, to make use of this doctrine. It is not a question for natural science or historical research, but a rule-like sign within, and only within the form of life of the church. Doctrines themselves are primarily to be understood as rules for using Christian language.

This way of using the Wittgensteinian ideas of language games and forms of life thus connects up with the more general turning against the appeal to experience that characterized a lot of Christian theology in the 1970s and 1980s (possibly in reaction against the experientialism of 'alternative' approaches to religion associated with the counter-culture of the 1960s) and, more broadly, illustrates how one way of invoking the linguistic turn may work against the turn to the subject.[26] Wittgenstein himself can certainly be used to debunk the myth of an absolutized individual subject, occupying a kind of mental space independent of any involvement in the transpersonal web of language and culture, though whether this necessarily dissolves *all* forms of subjectivity is a whole other matter.[27]

Related to this approach is what has come to be known as narrative theology. Narrative theology, as its name suggests, draws attention to the importance of narrative forms in Scripture and, indeed, in Christian credal formulations. What Christians believe is not a list of facts, nor yet a theory of history or metaphysics. Christians commit themselves to a complex of narratives, linked in the unifying master narrative of creation, Fall and redemption. These narratives define the membership and life of religious communities; 'we are the people who tell this story', and, in connection with this function of community identification, the dominant narratives of a community are ascribed a determinative role in shaping the dispositions and values that we call on in making moral judgments. It is essential to their ability to operate in this way that they are not broken up into their constituent parts and checked out against reality. That is not what they are for. They 'work' only so long as we respect and enter into their narrative coherence and take them as a whole. The story of the birth of Christ, narrated as the Incarnation of the divine Word, the second person of the Trinity, is not something we can treat as a historical claim amongst others, like the claim that Napoleon invaded Russia in 1812, as something that either did or didn't happen, and for which there is quantifiable historical evidence. What the story of the Incarnation shows us is God's way of acting and, consequently, the kind of spiritual attitude and the kind of moral behaviour that is truly godly. In order to get the message we have to take it as a whole, or not at all. On this view narratives are therefore not reducible to moral prescriptions, but rather the opposite. Such narratives are not directly ethical but provide the context, the framework, within which moral principles and judgments are formulated, communicated and enacted.[28]

Clearly such an approach does offer an approach to religious texts that recognizes the interdependence of different elements in belief-systems, and the need to see how they work as a whole. Nevertheless, it can be seen as sidestepping some of the difficult questions of truth that, for example, a historical approach to religion poses. Miracles may well make sense within certain religious language games; indeed they may be necessary for the proper playing of those language games. But that cannot entirely absolve us from asking the question as to whether miracles are at all possible and, if so, under what conditions. And there are innumerable other points at which religious narratives and doctrines seem, on any ordinary under-standing of language, to broach analogous questions. What does the archaeological record tell us of the Hebrew conquest of Canaan and does it square with the account of Joshua/Judges? What are we to make of the differences between the gospels with regard to specific words and actions of Jesus, e.g. was the Last Supper a Passover meal or not? How important are the variations in the accounts of Paul's conversion given in the book of Acts and by Paul himself? What really happened on the Damascus Road? Or, in another context, how does what is known historically of the life of Muhammad and of the social context in which he operated affect our understanding of his revelation? How do we hold together the historical life of the Buddha with, for example, the cult of the Amida Buddha of the Pure Land School, for whom the simple teacher of self-discipline has become a cosmic redeemer? And, of course, when we move into the history of religious communities similar questions crowd in on us with regard to the legends, stories and commemorated events that mould the lives of those communities. Now if it is claimed that such debates are irrelevant to the specifically religious meaning of these texts and narratives, we nevertheless then have to face the question as to what exactly the proper scope of a purely religious reading involves. The fact that many religious believers themselves seem to regard the factuality of at least some of their claims as essential to the truth of the faith suggests that the answer to such a question is not at all self-evident. In any case, it is very difficult to know when a fact is not a fact in the context of religion. Does the doctrine of the Virgin Birth rest on 'fact' in the same way as the claim that Jesus was sentenced to death by Pontius Pilate or the record of Muhammad's *hijra*? Clearly not in exactly 'the same' way – but where are the lines to be drawn? And how do we know, how do we decide, when a matter of fact is or isn't significant? And if a religious reading of narratives simply declares all facts to be irrelevant, aren't we back with the problem faced by medieval theologians as to whether there are two levels of truth, whether something can be true according to philosophy that is false according to revelation and vice versa? Certainly it is nothing new for theologians to recognize that Scripture is not merely historical narrative. The early church had already developed sophisticated typological, allegorical and other symbolic readings of Scripture: but it also insisted, as most churches still insist, on the primacy of the historical reading. And if narrative theology abandons what we might call the 'control' provided by the historical level, is there anything left at all to limit the possible range of interpretations and reinterpretations of the saving events? Narrative theology for the most part understands itself as aiming to preserve and to rescue the whole body of Scripture and doctrine, rather than succumbing to what it regards as the piecemeal approach of liberal theology. Lindbeck calls his own position 'post-liberal'. But can it entirely escape the charge it levels against the liberals in the sense that we must ultimately have some kind of reason for preferring one narrative or one cultural-linguistic formation to another and, if this is not to resolve back into a matter of purely arbitrary subjective decision then it is going to involve matters of fact, of moral evaluation, experiential or existential relevance or persuasiveness, etc. – i.e. all the criteria used by liberal theologians in their revision of the tradition?

Another problem is that, given the interdependence between narrative and community, narrative theology doesn't seem to be able to offer a basis for self-criticism on the part of the community. Don't reform movements, including those that subsequently get incorporated into the mainstream of tradition, often start with experiences and counter-narratives that work against the prevailing discourse of the community? This has been recently the case with feminist theology in the Western church, but we can see something similar in many reforming or schismatic movements in quite diverse religious contexts (even when these adopt a fundamentalist rhetoric that may seem to be looking to a return to origins rather than appealing to contemporary experiences). Narrative theology, however, seems to be too static to allow for such new formations or for a genuinely dynamic understanding of tradition.

There is a quite different approach to the question 'how large are forms of life?' that does not see them in terms of macro-structures like the whole life of the church or of Christendom, but, basing itself upon some remarks of Wittgenstein, looks instead to micro-situations and micro-practices. Examples of such micro-situations and practices that Wittgenstein himself gives include comforting a wounded or dying man, or we might think of lighting a candle for a friend or loved one.[29] If we take this seriously, then a Wittgensteinian approach to religious language would not be about justifying or legitimizing the whole system of religious language and doctrine, but simply learning to recognize those situations in which religious language becomes appropriate. Such an approach might, for example, recognize that religious language is not appropriate when two nations are negotiating the terms of a diplomatic pact, or two companies drawing up a merger document, but is appropriate when visiting someone in hospital and exhorting them to face their illness acceptingly. 'We are all in the hands of God' may be the right thing to say when the doctors have given up hope, but perhaps unhelpful when negotiators are confronting a tricky point in international law (though even in such contexts one can imagine that it might have a certain use, albeit a very different one from the use appropriate to the hospital bedside). There is much that is attractive in this proposal, and philosophers such as D. Z. Phillips have done a lot of interesting analysis of what he calls 'concept formation' showing how particular religious concepts come to take the shape they do in actual usage, and how we can learn to discern when such concepts are being used appropriately.[30] Nevertheless, here as elsewhere there is a price to pay, in that we are implicitly recognizing that religion is not determinative for the whole of life, but only for certain aspects or parts of it. In other words we are allowing religion to be ghettoized or marginalized – though Phillips and others would claim that in fact those situations in which we characteristically have recourse to religious language are amongst the most decisive, the most crucial, in our lives.

A quite different approach to language is that to be found in the later philosophy of Martin Heidegger. I shall say more about Heidegger and language when we come to the question of hermeneutics, but for now I wish only to emphasize the role of language in his later thought. Heidegger never presents a systematic philosophy of language, and many of his formulations are presented in the context of 'remarks' on one or other of the poets he is typically concerned with in this period, chiefly Hölderlin.[31] Indeed, it is from Hölderlin that Heidegger takes the expression 'the conversation that we are' that does so much to capture the tenor of his approach to language and its implications for hermeneutics. If Hölderlin is in the fore-ground of Heidegger's own linguistic turn, however, we can already see that there is a striking analogy with the kind of approach exemplified by Hamann. Language is not an instrument that we have; it is the medium in which we live and move and have our being. Language itself speaks – *'Die Sprache spricht'* [Language speaks], writes Heidegger – and the task of the philosopher is not, as for the logical positivists, to put language on the rack, but to attend to what language itself says – and, pre-eminently, what language says in the mouths of the poets. This is not because poets have some kind of higher consciousness, as in Romantic aesthetics. Rather, the poetic word itself says more than the poet himself understands by it.

One of the characteristic themes of the later Heidegger is that, in an age dominated by science and technology, the 'gods have fled', and people no longer experience an immediate, living sense of divine powers at work in the world or watching over them. This thought Heidegger finds at the centre of Hölderlin's poetry. But, Heidegger says, Hölderlin's lament over the flight of the gods is not merely sentimental. Precisely as someone standing on the soil of the modern, Western, post-Enlightenment world, Hölderlin understands very well that he cannot simply recall the world of the ancient Greek gods. As opposed to the early Nietzsche who seemed to think that we could somehow reawaken the spirit of Dionysius, Hölderlin realizes that there is no transhistorical Dionysian-in-itself. For him the vanished gods live only in poetic recollection. This, then, suggests a paradox: that it is precisely the poetic act of remembrance that at one and the same time opens a relationship to the gods and also separates us from them. The poet – and, with the poet, Heidegger suggests, language – comes on the scene only as and when the gods have already fled. Language bears the trace of their having-been, but it can never deliver them up in their present actuality.

The way of language, then, is not a way with a determinate end. Language is not an instrument designed and used for specific purposes. Language is not a window on the world. Language, like the rivers of which the poet speaks and that Heidegger takes as symbol-izing the reality of the poet's own existence, wanders across the face of the earth, creating its own channels and shaping the world as it goes. Language creates the landscape within which mortals dwell.

In this regard Heidegger is remarkably close to aspects of post-Heideggerian deconstruction. Often the relationship between de-construction and Heidegger is seen in purely negative terms. Heidegger, it is said (especially by deconstructionists) taught that language is determined by presence, and always harks back to an original presence that imbues it with a fullness of meaning. This, however, is only a partial reading of Heidegger. For Heidegger, no less than for Derrida, 'every representation is a depresentation'.

In the case of deconstruction we have an additional dimension, flowing from the linguistics of Saussure. The key point here is that Saussure, as interpreted by deconstruction, regarded language as a system of mutually defining contraries, a system, in other words, of differences. Words do not acquire meaning by being attached to objects but by their difference from each other (an idea that seems to parallel the Pythagorean idea that the universe is created from a series of contraries: black/white, masculine/feminine, being/ non-being, etc.). Words thus mean what they mean only in relation to the system of language as a whole. There is no pure reference from within language to some extralinguistic reality. 'There is no *hors de texte*', as Derrida put it.[32] This means, however, that many of the values and beliefs promoted by religion (and by Christian belief in particular) cannot be what they seem, for 'goodness', 'holiness', 'life' and 'God' do not actually mean anything apart from their opposites 'badness', 'evil', 'death', 'the world'. These are not features of the world, but elements of language. Thus, for Derrida, Plato was wrong to denigrate writing in favour of speech. Writing, Derrida claimed, because it is literally spaced out across the page, preserves and reflects the original character of language as always already differentiated. More dramatically, 'Spacing as writing is the becoming-absent and the becoming-unconscious of the subject . . . All graphemes [written signs] are of a testamentary essence. And the original absence of the subject of writing is also the absence of the thing as the referent.'[33]

A full discussion of the implications of deconstruction for theology and religious thought would go beyond the limits of this introductory course. It should be said, however, that whereas many religious conservatives have seen these implications as purely destructive, there has also been a range of positive responses from within the theological community. After all, it has been said, when did theology ever stand or fall with the kind of naive theory of language attacked by Derrida? If we look back into the theological tradition itself we will see movements like apophatic or negative theology that show a clear grasp of the impossibility of any directly referential speech in relation to God.[34] Or, especially in some Lutheran and Calvinist traditions, a powerful emphasis on the simultaneity of revelation and concealment, as in the crucifixion itself, at once the revelation of the love of God but, at the very same time, the utter eclipse – even death – of God in the world.

But if language (rather than, say, 'knowledge') has become the ground on which the debate about religion is being fought in our time, and if the task of philosophy has become to reflect upon the forms and limits of the diversity of language games in which issues of religion come to articulation, this leaves many questions un-answered. Does it, for example, necessarily mean that 'language is all', or is there still a significant question as to the relationship between linguistic representations of religion and, e.g. matters of historical fact, moral obligation, non-linguistic representation (e.g. painting or music) or cognitive processes? But even if we restrict our philosophical gaze to the field of language there is no little work for a philosophical approach that is directed towards the uncovering of the unobserved presuppositions that govern the discourse of religion. For if language itself had for a long time been just such an unnoticed presupposition, the medium but not the object of philosophical reflection, we have to say that the linguistic turn itself is executed under a range of assumptions as to what does or doesn't count as an optimal case of religious language. What, in other words, are the criteria that govern the appeal to language? Which of the following, for example, is the best paradigm of religious language in use: the language of liturgy, of moral appeal, of prophetic witness or pastoral succour? What practice and what values drive the turn to language?

We must also ask how the turn to language relates to history and to subjectivity. As was seen previously, history and subjectivity have themselves been presented in a variety of combinations, in alliance or in opposition and the same pattern holds if we expand our picture to incorporate language. Is language some kind of timeless, extra-historical structure, or is it itself historically conditioned or, perhaps, the medium and matter of history? Does language displace the subject, is it perhaps the agent of the 'death of the subject' mooted in early postmodernist sources, or can the subject still be seen as the creator and exponent of language?

Traversing all such questions, however, is what has been an under-lying question for religion since at least the closing decade of the eighteenth century. This is the question of reductionism. The issue is this: does religion have a continuing role as an independent theor-etical or practical phenomenon, or can it be dissolved without remainder into one or more physical, cultural or intellectual forms? In terms of the trends characterizing the modern discipline of the philosophy of the religion that have been the subject of the last three chapters – the rise of the historical consciousness, the turn to the subject and the linguistic turn – this means asking whether these (in whatever combination) provide the base into which religion is to be resolved. Is religion, after all, nothing but a phenomenon of history? An expression of the needs and aspirations of the human subject? A way of speaking? Perhaps all these? And if we are not inclined simply to answer 'yes!' then what is it that we wish to preserve as the distinctive and irreducible domain or function of religion and how could we go about turning the reductionist tide? And can our three themes of history, subjectivity and language play some kind of constructive role in such resistance? And, in any case, is there any appropriate role for the philosophy of religion here, or is it a matter to be left to the religionists and their opponents? These last questions will, in effect, shape the remainder of this course. First, however, we must look more closely at the way in which reductionism itself emerged as an issue in the philosophy of religion.

5

'Nothing but . . .'

In each of their different ways the various trends underlying the modern philosophy of religion we have been examining have raised the spectre of reductionism. Insofar as they offer a way of understanding religion they seem at the same time to reduce it to something less than the believer understands it to be, and, more specifically, to reduce God or belief to something else: to history, to an aspect of human subjectivity, to language. This reductive tendency has been perhaps the most persistent and the most troublesome aspect of modern thought for religious believers and it might seem to be inherent in the philosophical approach to religion. At the beginning of this short course I spoke about philosophy's characteristic commitment to examining the mostly hidden presuppositions and assumptions behind our everyday habits of speech and action, including our religious speech and action. But, of course, to say that something x is a presupposition of something else y is to suggest that y is, in an important sense, dependent on x and has no independent existence apart from that. From being a necessary condition of x (or even, simply, its phenomenal accompaniment), only a slight logical slippage is needed for y to come to be seen as x's real matter, its substratum, as it were, or, in Marxist terminology, its base. The likelihood of such a slippage is all the greater if, as is the case with religion, we are dealing with a human relation to that which, in some sense, is 'beyond' the human. In this situation it is not only very easy to confuse the human condition of the appearance of this 'beyond' with the 'beyond' itself, it is perhaps almost impossible not to – i.e. if the human phenomenon of religion (or, within a given cultural situation, the dominant form of religious life) is shown to be conditioned by or dependent on some other purely worldly complex of forces, then it is hard in practice to maintain any confidence in the idea of God as the intended object of religion. Thus, in terms of the three themes we have been examining – history, the turn to the subject and language – believers have repeatedly experienced the modern focus on these as threatening the independence of religion. The rise of the historical consciousness, for example, can easily seem to reduce the religious life and its theological expression to no more than a mere part of a larger historical process, implying that such and such a theological position can be fully explained by learning about its historical background and origins. Obviously Marxism is the pre-eminent example of such a historicizing reduction of religion, but many non-Marxist approaches seem to have similar implications. Even within theology itself, the application of critical historical methods to church history and, above all, to the biblical texts, has seemed to many to undermine the basic sources of belief, and to dissolve the saving events into the stream of history, to relativize them and to make of them just one more set of historical occurrences alongside all the rest. Similarly, the turn to the subject can seem to reduce religion to no more than the expression of human needs, hopes or fears, something which has been emphasized by such critics of religion as Freud, who claimed to see in religion no more than a kind of neurosis, expressing unresolved infantile traumas. Even when the turn to the subject has been promoted in the name of religion, as by Pascal, Schleiermacher, Kierkegaard, Shestov and other existential thinkers, many church theologians have seen this as robbing faith of what they regard as its necessary objective base, and therefore as damaging to the cause of religion as any attack from without. Indeed, one of the most famous episodes in Western European theological history in the twentieth century was the passionate attack on liberal theology made by Karl Barth in his commentary on Paul's Letter to the Romans, a commentary published just after the First World War. Barth argued that critics of religion such as Feuerbach, Marx, Nietzsche and Freud were merely exposing what the church, and especially theologians, had allowed to happen to faith: that it had been humanized, and turned into a matter of human sentiment, human feeling, human morality and social ethics, and that it had lost its decisive emphasis on divine transcendence, on what Barth, quoting Kierkegaard, called 'the infinite qualitative difference' between God and humanity. And we can see the same pattern in relation to the linguistic turn. Again this can seem to contribute to a view of religion that makes of it nothing more than the expression or the articulation of cultural-linguistic systems, a language game or a narrative rather than a truth claim. Of course, although I have treated each of these movements separately, they are often deeply interconnected, and, although the emphasis on subjectivity, for example, may be in tension with some forms of the linguistic turn, they can also combine, and, in this combined form threaten religion with a thoroughgoing reductionism.

This is not only a matter of academic discussion, but has come to pervade the public perception and discussion of religion in Western culture as a whole. For many people, even for many who regard it as good and important, religion is a historically-conditioned system of verbal and ritual symbolism that expresses deep individual and collective needs, but that is essentially unprovable and makes no significant truth claims that can be tested and proved true or false. It is a part of our culture or an expression of personal longings: its truth or falsity doesn't come into it.

Less so today, perhaps, but in the 1950s and 1960s there were a number of theological movements in the West that embraced this situation positively, that called for Christian belief to strip itself of its claims to speak for or about a transcendent reality, and to limit itself to a this-worldly spirituality. Paul van Buren spoke of the secular meaning of the gospel, and called for the gospel challenge to be translated without remainder into secular terms.[1] Echoing Nietzsche, Thomas Altizer and William Hamilton spoke of a 'theology of the death of God', by which they meant that Christian faith had to dissociate itself from the kind of objective, metaphysical theological claims that had, to most people, seemed to be an intrinsic part of the Christian world-view.[2] Strikingly, however, many of the sources behind such movements were theological or, at least, Christian. Such sources included, for example, William Blake, the English Romantic poet who had drawn a strong distinction between, on the one hand, God the demiurge who, as the creator of the world according to the laws of Newtonian mechanics was a God of power and number, over against Christ, the God of pure, powerless, suffering love. Similar themes were drawn from Kierkegaard and Dostoevsky, and, in the twentieth century, from the later writings of Dietrich Bonhoeffer, who wrote that Christianity must learn to shed all vestiges of its worldly power and influence, and that Christians should live in the world as if God did not exist, *'etsi Deus non daretur'*.[3] John Robinson's enormously controversial *Honest to God* was, in this respect, only the most public of a whole current of such revisionist 'theologies' that had, to a greater or lesser extent, internalized the thrust of the reductionist argument.[4]

I shall return to the issues raised by such figures and movements, i.e. to the question as to how far Christianity can go along with or learn from reductionism. But I now turn to those forms of reductionism that have most influenced the theological agenda of the twentieth century.

Here as elsewhere, Hegel is a seminal figure in the modern philosophy of religion, and it is no accident that the definitive formulation of reductionism in the philosophy of Ludwig Feuerbach arose on the basis of and as a development of Hegelian philosophy. However, whether Hegel himself was (as was claimed by Feuerbach and, from an opposite direction, Kierkegaard) essentially reductionistic is a difficult interpretative issue.

At the most general level, Hegel's own life story might seem to encourage the charge of reductionism: the student of theology who became a professor of philosophy. More specifically, the overall structure of the Hegelian system, a system which culminates in the philosopher's claim to absolute knowledge, might seem to point necessarily to the subordination of religion to philosophy.

I have already suggested that Hegel's meditations on Good Friday, Easter, Pentecost and the Eucharistic anamnesis of the presence of Christ in the midst of his community played a crucial role in helping him to formulate his fundamental principle of historical movement, the principle of the *Aufhebung*, the passage of becoming by which even the moment of negation is incorporated into the larger story of Being. In the *Phenomenology*, religion, along with art and philosophy, appears as one of the three great forms of Spirit, and here, as in later works, Hegel seems to rank these in the following progression: art-religion-philosophy, such that each is the *Aufhebung*, the simultaneous negation and sublimation of the former. But what exactly does this mean and, in particular, what does it mean to speak of philosophy as the *Aufhebung*, the transcending, of religion?

To answer this question, let us look at the overall shape of 'Spirit' and the kind of relationship that Hegel envisages between its first two forms, religion and art. The first thing to notice is, of course, that the realm of Spirit as a whole is a realm of understanding, of reason and not, primarily, of action. Life rises to the level of Spirit when it becomes able to reflect upon itself and to understand itself and each of the three great forms of Spirit are, essentially, forms of Spirit's self-understanding.

We have already seen how, in the *Phenomenology*, the history of religion in the ancient Mediterranean world marked the gradual humanization and spiritualization of the divine, as Spirit progressed from the half-human, half-animal gods of Egypt, through the Greek Olympians, to the utterly human, utterly incarnate God of early Christian experience and faith. We can also see this as a movement from a more outward, externalizing view of divinity, to a more inward, interior view. A pivotal moment in this process is therefore the change from a form of religion in which art plays a dominant role, to one in which art is strictly subordinate, and this moment coincides with the cross over from Greek religion, that Hegel calls 'the religion of art', to Christianity. Why is this?

Art, according to Hegel, occupies a very specific 'sphere and stage of truth'. This sphere is defined by two factors. On the one hand, insofar as art is a form of Spirit it expresses the general character of Spirit as reflective self-understanding. Its inner meaning is rational. It is guided by the idea. On the other hand, art represents only that form of Spirit that is capable of being expressed in sensuous form. In art, therefore, a twofold movement occurs. In the first, Spirit projects itself expressively into its object, imbuing the object – wood, stone, paint, sound – with spiritual meaning. In the second, it beholds the object thus created as spiritually significant. The interaction of these two movements defines the realm of art or the aesthetic. Now, it might be said that this same general pattern applies for all forms of Spirit. However, in the case of art, the relation to the specific sensuous object (even when, as in the case of poetry, this is transferred onto the plane of pure imagination) remains determinative in a way that is not so for religion or philosophy. It is in the light of this definition that Hegel says, famously, that

> there is a deeper comprehension of truth which is no longer so akin and friendly to sense as to be capable of appropriate adoption and expression in this medium. The Christian view of truth is of this kind, and, above all, the spirit of our world today, or, more particularly, of our religion and the development of our reason, appears as beyond the stage at which art is the supreme mode of our knowledge of the Absolute. The peculiar nature of artistic production and of works of art no longer fills our highest need . . . Thought and reflection have spread their wings above fine art.[5]

And note, in this passage that Hegel, writing from within a Lutheran culture, links Christianity with philosophy as 'higher' forms of consciousness, that do not require sensuous externalization as a necessary condition of expressing and understanding truth.

What, then, is the Christian way of expressing truth?

In his simplest – though perhaps potentially misleading – formulation Hegel says that, in comparison with art, Christian thought is 'picture-thinking'. That is to say that although Christianity does not require external sensuous images to provide it with material for thought (and thus, for Hegel the Lutheran, the Catholic use of images and ritual is, in the last resort, a falling-away from Christianity's most characteristic form of self-understanding and self-expression), the Christian understanding of God is still governed by representations of God as, e.g. Father, or as acting in history to redeem his people, sending his Son into the world, comforting the troubled spirit, or listening to prayer. Now, in order to understand and to experience the truth of such representations the Christian consciousness does not intrinsically need to have recourse to artistic representations. Hegel is, of course, well aware that there has been a great deal of Christian art and he writes very extensively about the positive impact which Christianity had on the history of art, since, he argues, it broadened and deepened the potential subject-matter of art almost limitlessly. He has many extremely insightful and helpful things to say about the relationship between Christianity and, especially (in my view), painting and poetry. Nevertheless, at its centre, the Christian consciousness was already 'beyond' art in its earliest beginnings, something which Hegel sees as having been rediscovered and decisively reaffirmed in the Protestant Reformation. The truth of religion is understood by Christianity as being a matter of the heart, of the mind, of consciousness itself.

It is for this reason that in his lectures on the *Philosophy of Religion*, Hegel is positive about Schleiermacher, whose appeal to experience and feeling he generally dismisses as a reversion to immediacy, a falling-back from the standards of rationality to which philosophy should aspire. With regard to Schleiermacher's claim that the essence of Christianity was the feeling of absolute dependence, Hegel famously remarked that, if that were true, then a dog would be the best Christian. Nevertheless, compared with previous philosophical attempts to explain religion, Schleiermacher represented an advance, because, Hegel now says, he focused exclusively on human consciousness as the seat of religious truth (rather than, as had Aquinas or the natural theologians, on physical or cosmological structures conceived as independent of consciousness).[6]

The business of philosophy, as distinct from the sensuous representation of Spirit in art and the imaginative picture-thinking of religion, is, Hegel maintains, the pure concept, the structures of consciousness regarded for themselves, independently of any specific empirical or concrete form. Thus, although Hegel is committed to the discipline of phenomenology, of seeking to trace the manifestations of Spirit in the historical process, the purest form of philosophy is logic, in which pure reason, pure thought is itself the exclusive object of enquiry. At one point, Hegel claims that logic shows us the mind of God prior to the creation of the world.

But does this mean that Hegel is trying to create a philosophical theology independent of the actuality of religion? Or trying to deduce 'God' from the structures of human consciousness, or to limit God to what can be grasped by human logic?

Certainly this is what some of Hegel's critics have claimed. Ludwig Feuerbach, in his *Principles of the Philosophy of the Future* argued that although Hegel continued to use a theological vocabulary, speaking of God, the divine, etc., he used it in an essentially non-theistic way. 'Modern philosophy,' he wrote (meaning philosophy from Descartes to Hegel whom he described as 'the culmination of modern philosophy'), 'has realized and negated the divine being who is separated and distinguished from sensation, the world, and man. But it realized and negated this divine being only in thought, in reason . . . modern philosophy has proved only the divinity of mind; it recognized only mind, and indeed the abstract mind, as the divine and absolute being.'[7] In other words, Hegel had effectively equated God with the rational structures of human consciousness, which, for him, were also identical with the true essence of humanity (i.e. humanity was essentially identified with its rationality).

We shall come back to why Feuerbach found this unsatisfactory, and how he wanted to go beyond Hegel, but a similar criticism was also made (and has been made many times since) from the Christian side by Kierkegaard. For Kierkegaard, it was impossible to construct the kind of universal system of knowledge to which Hegel aspired from a merely human standpoint. Perhaps, he suggested, such a system would be possible from the standpoint of God, but this was not a standpoint any human being could possibly occupy. There was an 'infinite qualitative difference' between God and humanity, such that human consciousness is always and necessarily incomplete, occupying the unstable middle ground between ideality and reality. For this reason he was especially outraged when he saw theologians adopting Hegelian principles, and attempting to use these principles in the context of doctrinal theology. As he saw it, this was replacing the proper content of theology with a purely human idea, thus belittling God. A crime of *lèse-majesté*, as he put it.

Hegel's critics have, at least in this case, generally won the day in the subsequent history of ideas. However, the question as to how far Hegel himself could be understood as a reductionist is not necessarily closed. Hegel himself insisted at several points that although philosophy is 'higher' than religion in the sense that it abstracts from religion the pure conceptual structures that are implicit but not explicit in the religious life or in theology, it does not add any new content to religion. It only clarifies what it finds there, it does not alter or replace it. Its content is the same as the content decisively revealed in the Christ event, in the spiritual resurrection experience of the early church. Generally this may be understood as an example of the pattern that Hegel sums up towards the close of the Preface to the *Philosophy of Right*.

> One more word about giving instruction as to what the world ought to be. Philosophy in any case always comes on the scene too late to give it. As the thought of the world, it appears only when actuality is already there cut and dried after its process of formation has been completed. The teaching of the concept, which is also history's inescapable lesson, is that it is only when actuality is mature that the ideal first appears over against the real and that the ideal apprehends this same real world in its substance and builds it up for itself into the shape of an intellectual realm. When philosophy paints its grey in grey, then has a stage of life grown old. By philosophy's grey in grey it cannot be rejuvenated but only understood. The owl of Minerva spreads its wings only with the falling of the dusk.[8]

Applying this to religion, and to philosophizing about religion, would seem to suggest that such philosophizing does not determine or dictate to religion what it should think or do or be: it takes religion as it finds it, as an actual, legitimate phenomenon in its own right, and seeks only to understand it. It is, it might be argued, in the light of such comments that we should hear these words from the Introduction to the lectures on the *Philosophy of Religion*:

> Religion . . . is the loftiest object that can occupy human beings. It is the region of eternal truth and eternal virtue, the region where all riddles of thought, all contradictions, and all the sorrows of the heart should show themselves to be resolved, and the region of endless peace through which the human being is truly human . . . God is the beginning and end of all things. God is the sacred center, which animates and inspires all things. Religion possesses its object within itself – and that object is God, for religion is the relation of human consciousness to God.[9]

Hegel's own claim is that, far from being reductionistic, his philosophy is shaped specifically by meditation upon the mystery of God, God in his mystery, revealed as trinitarian.[10]

Feuerbach, as we have seen, regarded this as essentially fraudulent. Hegel, he said, had reduced God to the rational structures of human consciousness. Hegel's 'Trinity' was only a conventional expression for what Hegel himself conceived as an essentially logical, rational dynamic. At the most, Hegelianism issued in a kind of pantheism, and, as we have also seen, Christian critics like Kierkegaard agreed.

All that was wrong with this, from Feuerbach's point of view, was that Hegel had misconstrued the nature of human existence. Human life, as Feuerbach understood it, was not primarily rational but material. It is in the materiality of our animal being that our true life is to be found. Hegel had taken the first step, but what was needed now was to translate Hegel's idealism into materialism.

Feuerbach's most famous attempt to realize this aim was in his 1841 book *The Essence of Christianity*, a book which caused a Europe-wide controversy and which through such novels like those of George Eliot (Feuerbach's translator) and N. Chernyshevsky's *What is to be Done?*[11] permeated the cultural perception of religion in the nineteenth century.

Feuerbach's main point is basically quite simple. The human being exists primarily as a material being and is what it is by virtue of its participation in the human race, understood as a biological and historical totality. The same could, of course, also be said of caterpillars, dogs or any other natural species. What, then, distinguishes human beings? Consciousness. But what is consciousness? Not, according to Feuerbach, a reflection of the divine mind, or an intimation of a spiritual destiny. Instead, consciousness is consciousness of our species-being, i.e. consciousness of our interdependence as individuals with the human race as a whole. Moreover, this consciousness can itself become an object of thought and action. This sounds somewhat abstract, but the point is not as difficult to grasp as Feuerbach makes it sound. An animal, for example, will flee at the appearance of danger. Instinctively, a human being will also be moved to flee, from a fire or a sinking ship for example. However, our consciousness of humanity may lead us, and often does, to rise above such a merely instinctive reaction. We may go back into the burning house to rescue a trapped child, or stay on board the sinking ship, if we are the captain, until all the passengers and crew have left. In such situations we show – even though we don't always articulate or express it this way – our consciousness of our species-being. We speak of acting with human dignity or for the sake of humanity, of our duties to others, which may, as in such examples, involve the sacrifice of our own individual lives for the good of the species, the whole. However, such a clear understanding of the true meaning of humanism did not appear suddenly in history, and, Feuerbach claims, has only gradually and relatively recently emerged. In previous ages this consciousness was mystified, and alienated, by being projected upon purely imaginary objects. Peoples of the past did not think of their duties to humanity, but their duty to God. Religion was the screen onto which humanity's relation to its species-being was projected. The secret of theology, as Feuerbach put it, was anthropology, and the task of philosophy was now to translate theological into anthropological statements.[12]

Now it is important to note that for Feuerbach religion was ambiguous. As opposed to some earlier Enlightenment rationalists who regarded all religion as simply the product of priestcraft and superstition, Feuerbach believed that the essential content of religion was true – only its form, its theological form, was false. The values expressed in religion, especially in the higher religions such as Christianity, were true: truth, goodness and beauty were still worth pursuing, but not because they manifested the divinity of God, or because God commanded us to pursue them, but because it was in the common interest of humanity to do so.

Feuerbach's comments on baptism and the Eucharist are typical. Each of these rites, he says, has a natural and true human meaning. Baptism symbolically represents the fundamental value and importance of water. Water is physically cleansing, but, he says, has 'moral and intellectual effects upon man.' After a bath we think more clearly, 'water extinguishes the fires of appetite . . . Water is the readiest means of making friends with nature . . .' etc.[13] Similarly, the Eucharist reflects the fundamental value and importance of eating and drinking. But this must now be understood anthropologically, materially, and not theologically:

> Think, therefore, with every morsel of bread which relieves thee from the pains of hunger, with every draught of wine which cheers thy heart, of the God who confers these beneficent gifts upon thee – think of man! But in thy gratitude towards man forget not gratitude towards holy Nature! Forget not that wine is the blood of plants, and flour the flesh of plants, which are sacrificed for thy well-being! Forget not that the plant typifies to thee the essence of Nature, which lovingly surrenders itself for thy enjoyment![14]

Such commentaries on religious concepts and practices are typical of Feuerbach's method. The truth of religion is, in every case, 'nothing but' its human and natural truth – but it is a kind of truth, all the same.

We can see how Feuerbach became a flag-bearer for nineteenth-century humanism, and for the cause that pitted humanistic values against the authority and the theology of church and state. But we can also see how, for Marx, Feuerbachian materialism was still inadequately historicized. For Feuerbach the true meaning of, e.g. washing, eating and drinking is not significantly altered by historical or social forces, but is always the same, waiting only for us to discover it. The essence of humanity is everywhere and always the same. The consciousness to which we should aspire is not class-consciousness, but universal human consciousness.

From the standpoint of theology, Feuerbach was, of course, unacceptable. Nevertheless, he remains in one key respect closer to the theological tradition than the so-called 'masters of suspicion' – Marx, Nietzsche and Freud – who followed him and who developed his critique of religion in new and more specific contexts. For Feuerbach, as we have seen, the content of religion was essentially true and the task was simply to free this true content from its false theological form.[15]

In the case of Marx, Nietzsche and Freud, however, the content of religion was itself twisted, warped, unhealthy. For Marx, of course, religion represented, in a suitably alienated and mystified form, the dominant class interests which were in turn determined by historical and economic conditions. For Freud, religion was a neurotic repetition of infantile feelings of helplessness (*The Future of an Illusion*) or of the assuaging of blood-guilt incurred by the sons of the primal horde who had collectively murdered their father in order to have access to his women (*Totem and Taboo*).

I shall not focus on these, however, but on Nietzsche, whom I regard (and who certainly regarded himself) as the cleverest, most complex, most dangerous of these masters of suspicion.

Nietzsche's thought is very rich, 'a feast', Heidegger called it, and is not necessarily the same in each of his works, although there are significant continuities. Many of his books were written in an aphoristic, quasi-poetic form, with brilliant imagery and a glittering use of language, and it is therefore always risky to tie them down to specific philosophical doctrines. On the other hand, to say that Nietzsche was 'merely' a poet, and that we therefore don't need to take him seriously as a thinker, would be to underestimate him. With the proviso that I am leaving out many of the nuances and rich details of his argument, then, I should like to focus on two aspects of Nietzsche's critique of religion. The first concerns the overall, one might say metaphysical, picture of the human condition that Nietzsche offers, a picture that, as he claims, is without God. The second concerns the specific genealogy of Christianity, and how Christianity came to adopt the specific form it did.

The 'metaphysical' contours of Nietzsche's thought are perhaps most easily accessed by reference to the section on nihilism in *The Will to Power*. Here, in the section entitled 'Decline of Cosmological Values', Nietzsche argues that 'nihilism as a psychological state' will come about as the result of three interconnected discoveries. The first is that there is no 'meaning' in the world, apart from the meanings we ourselves ascribe to things and events. 'Meanings' that have been believed to be true in the past include the idea of the fulfilment of the moral world-order or even the negative idea that the whole world is in a state of decay towards some final annihilation. As Nietzsche puts it, 'any goal at least constitutes some meaning'. Now, however, 'we' are beginning to realize that nothing gets achieved in history, there is no aim, neither in some supposed divine purpose nor as the *telos* of some naturalistically conceived evolutionary process. The second discovery is that whereas philosophers of the most widely varied schools have in the past envisaged the world as some kind of coherent unity, bound together in a single system, organized according to universal laws that hold for all beings without exception, there is really no such unity. Thus far, Nietzsche guesses, many religiously minded readers might have been able to go along with him. After all Christianity teaches that the world we inhabit is a fallen world and that this fall not only affects the moral capacities of human beings but has corrupted nature itself, opening a passage along which the annihilating power of non-being can force its way into the world. But, and this is Nietzsche's third discovery, there is no true world to which we can appeal in the face of the meaninglessness and chaos of this world, there is nothing behind or beyond this world that could justify or put right its shortcomings. Nietzsche sums up: 'briefly: the categories "aim," "unity," "being" which we used to project some value into the world – we *pull out* again; so the world looks *valueless*.'[16]

The world we live in is in fact a pure chaos, with no intrinsic aim, meaning, goal, unity or purpose, and we are just the chance products of this chaos. As such, our first priority is always to maximize our own life possibilities: to live as much and as fully as we can, to make the most of our short time under the sun. Now in the past it had always been assumed that acknowledging the truth of our situation would lead to discouragement and pessimism. We had to believe in a better world, a higher order of things, an ideal truth or a kingdom of God in order to motivate ourselves to go on living, to bear or to struggle against the suffering that was so deeply a part of our experience. Indeed, says Nietzsche, the first wave of modern European nihilism made just this mistake, assuming that if the world is indeed a meaningless chaos, then there is no way out of suffering except extinction and the surrender of the will to live. This was, of course, the position of Schopenhauer, for whom the world was a vast torture chamber and the only significant difference amongst its inhabitants was that some were tortured and others were torturers, a horrific struggle for survival, from which art provided a limited and ascetic religion a definitive escape – but only at the price of total detachment from life.

Such nihilism is a natural reflex in face of the discovery of cosmic meaninglessness. But, Nietzsche says, we don't need to react like this. In fact, we could just as well react in the opposite way. Precisely because there is no intrinsic meaning in things, we are all the more free to create our own meanings, to decide for ourselves what should count as values, what aims we wish to pursue, how we want to envisage the world. We should, in other words, live like artists, justifying our lives by our self-created fictions, and not being ashamed of the fact that they are fictions.

Famously, it was axiomatic for Nietzsche that 'God is dead', and even if Nietzsche himself was not the first to think or say something like this, his statement of it has become definitive for twentieth-century debates. Its supreme expression is in the parable of the Madman in *The Joyful Wisdom*. In this parable Nietzsche recounts how a madman ran into a market-place one morning, carrying a lamp, and calling out that he was seeking God. The people, many of whom do not believe in God, laugh at him. He, however, rounds on them:

> 'Where is God gone?' he called out. 'I mean to tell you! *We have killed him*, – you and I! We are all his murderers! But how have we done it? How were we able to drink up the sea? Who gave us the sponge to wipe away the whole horizon? What did we do when we loosened this earth from its sun? . . . God is dead! . . . And we have killed him! . . . Shall we not ourselves have to become Gods, merely to seem worthy of it? . . ..'[17]

What is truly radical about Nietzsche's announcement of the death of God is that it is not merely directed at ecclesiastical Christianity.

After all, philosophers had been publicly attacking Christianity for several hundred years. Many of the people in the crowd are 'atheists'. But what Nietzsche suggests is that they do not realize the logic of their own position. If there is no God, then not only does Christianity fall, but all systems of morality, all belief in social progress or laws of history. It is simply inconsistent not to believe in God but to go on believing – like Feuerbach – in goodness, truth and beauty, or in objective values of any kind. But the fact is that most people are simply afraid to face up to the abyssal responsibility that the discovery of the death of God imposes on them, and so they shelter behind quasi-theological moralities or behind the claims of nation or family. They don't claim the enjoyment of the freedom that is theirs – an analysis that will be developed further by Sartre in his account of 'bad faith' and our characteristic flight from the freedom that we are.

God, then, is dead. But where did he come from in the first place? Nietzsche tells us this in his *Genealogy of Morals*. Like Hegel in this respect, Nietzsche sees the early development and subsequent crisis of ancient Mediterranean civilization as decisive for the modern world. In the earliest period, the period portrayed by Homer, men were not yet ashamed of their natural animal instinct for self-assertion. The strong lorded it over the weak and this was regarded as right and proper. Instead of the polarities of good and evil, men then thought in terms of noble versus base. The noble warrior thought no more of killing his enemy than an eagle would think of killing a sheep. The strong inherited the earth. So what happened?

What happened, according to Nietzsche, was what he called the 'slave revolt in morals'. The two main symptoms of this were Socratic philosophy, and the rise, from within its original Jewish matrix, of early Christianity. Socrates (whose famous ugliness, Nietzsche thought, was not accidental, since it betrayed his biological inferiority) subverted the natural self-confidence of Athenian society, and laid the ground for the Platonic projection of a 'true' world, defined in opposition to the world of everyday experience.[18] Perhaps of more immediate concern to Nietzsche (at least in The *Genealogy*) is the impact of Judaeo-Christian beliefs. The cauldron in which these beliefs were formed was that of political subjugation and slavery. Now, obviously, the position of oppressed peoples and slaves is not a happy one. They do not enjoy the free exercise of their powers in the manner of their owners or masters. However, the circumstances of their lives compel them to be more quick-witted and, gradually, to become more intelligent than these masters. They develop cunning, duplicity, and an ability to wait. Unable to overcome their rulers physically or militarily, over the centuries they create a mythology that ultimately proves devastating. They sow the seeds of the idea that power is not good, that it is the weak and not the mighty who are the special objects of God's favour, that eternal punishments await those who sin against their God. They invent conscience and a sense of sin. And it is this which proves the downfall of, pre-eminently, the Roman *imperium*, as the ruling class loses faith in its own right to rule. The seeds of the Christian era, Nietzsche says, are in the *ressentiment* of the slave.[19] Perhaps Nietzsche's account sounds crude in its bare outlines, but his narration of it is executed with brilliant virtuosity. Take what he writes about conscience:

> Hostility, cruelty, the delight in persecution, raids, excitement, destruction all turned against their begetter. Lacking external enemies and resistances, and confined within an oppressive narrowness and regularity, man began rending, persecuting, terrifying himself, like a wild beast, hurling itself against the bars of its cage. This languisher, devoured by nostalgia for the desert, who had to turn *himself* into an adventure, a torture chamber, an insecure and dangerous wilderness – this fool, this pining and desperate prisoner, became the inventor of 'bad conscience'.[20]

Having thus exposed the origins of Christian ideals of goodness and virtue, and of the popularized version of Platonic metaphysics with which the church, historically, backed them up, Nietzsche calls upon his readers to cast those ideals aside, to reclaim their animal innocence, to throw themselves into the maelstrom of becoming, into the Heraclitean flux, and to live as they would if they were condemned to live the same life over and over again, with no otherworldly fantasies to sustain them.

It is a strange, harsh, but often eerily beautiful vision. Once we are touched by it, it is hard to shake it off. As Nietzsche wrote, towards the end of his sane life, to the literary critic George Brandes, whose lectures and book about Nietzsche had first established his international reputation, 'Having been discovered by you no trick was necessary for the others to find me. The difficulty is now to get rid of me.'[21] Nietzsche has inspired, rightly or wrongly, generations of modernist artists, Nazis and, now, postmodernists. Whether or not his arguments have been convincing, his brilliant poetic diction has helped persuade many that living without God is, after all, a real possibility. For Nietzsche's philosophical project was not simply to offer an alternative 'scientific' explanation for what had in previous ages been ascribed to God or the gods. It was rather to show how what had been assumed to be the necessary consequences of abandoning a transcendent framework for human beliefs and values (such as a loss of faith in life itself) just didn't follow; that belief and disbelief were not so much a matter of knowledge as of taste; that religion was, in the last resort, no more than an *aesthetic* option – but one which, Nietzsche declared, we have become too sophisticated to entertain.

There have been other advocates of reductionism. Freud has been mentioned. Durkheim is another seminal figure, whose study *The Elementary Forms of the Religious Life* laid the foundation for subsequent non-Marxist sociological and socio-anthropological approaches to religion. In this work, Durkheim argued that religion was, in effect, the voice of the social body, transmitting through belief and ritual the binding power that held society together.[22] In contrast to Marx's stance of active hostility towards religion and his judgment that religion, like the state, will wither away in the classless society, Durkheim sees religion or religion-like forms as a permanent feature of social life. Nevertheless, the fact that Durkheim says, as it were, 'nice things' about religion does not make his position any less reductionistic in principle. A similar point can be illustrated by the case of Carl Jung. Jung seems at first glance to be more sympathetic to religion than his mentor, Freud, and is indeed almost venerated by many as one of the twentieth century's great spiritual masters. However, a close examination of his work shows that although Jung accepted the creative value of religious experiences in life and the importance of religious symbolism in dream interpretation (and its irreducibility to a more fundamental sexual origin), there is nothing in his account of it to suggest that these experiences and symbols are of a more-than-human origin. As far as he is concerned, they are a purely psychological phenomenon. Jung writes that

> Religion appears to me to be a peculiar attitude of mind which could be formulated in accordance with the original use of the word *religio*, which means a careful consideration and observation of certain dynamic factors that are conceived as 'powers': spirits, daemons, gods, laws, ideas, ideals, or whatever name man has given to such factors in his world as he has found powerful, dangerous, or helpful enough to be taken into careful consideration, or grand, beautiful, and meaningful enough to be devoutly worshipped and loved.[23]

Religion, according to Jung, has a valuable part to play in the individual's quest for wholeness, but he is entirely agnostic as to whether it has any extra-psychological reality, and his teaching and psychological practice do not require it to have any such reality. Note, however, that for Jung – in almost diametrical opposition to Durkheim – the locus of religion is not society but the individual: 'Religion means dependence on and submission to the irrational facts of experience. These do not refer directly to social and physical conditions; they concern far more the individual's psychic attitude'.[24]

In the contemporary world, the most potent forms of reductionism are probably those that stem from the Darwinian-oriented biological anthropologists and psychologists, for whom the universe reveals design without a designer and consciousness is a system of net-worked computers.[25] Religion, for them, is simply an epiphenomenon of more fundamental psycho-biological processes. As the title of one of his most influential books suggests, Daniel C. Dennett argues in this mode that consciousness can be exhaustively explained and that although the lived experience of consciousness will continue to strike those who experience it as mysterious, thorough-going demystification is possible. 'Mind' is not the appearance in us 'spiritual beings' of another dimension of existence, but simply the outworking of physical processes.[26]

It is not immediately obvious that such Neo-Darwinist accounts are adding anything significantly new to the philosophical question of reductionism as that was posed by Hegel (perhaps) and Feuerbach, Marx, Nietzsche and Freud (certainly). Moreover, the religious apologist might point out that the greater the number of reductionist theories, the more likely they are to cancel each other out: if Durkheim is right, Jung must be wrong and vice versa. However, this is more of a debating point than a substantial blow to the reductionist principle. For the fact is that the reductionist case has a cumulative effect. If different reductionist theories can on occasion neutralize one or other element in their various theoretical presentations, what is more significant is the way in which they progressively colonize more and more of the territory once occupied by religion. Early reductionist accounts typically attempted to explain religion in terms of one particular cause or base (a manifestation of class-struggle, for example, or the Oedipus complex), leaving religionists room to point to various kinds of religious activity or belief that just didn't seem to be explicable in those terms. Over the last two centuries, however, a reductionist alternative to the religious case seems to be lying in wait wherever the religious apologist turns. In the case of the contemporary Neo-Darwinians (as opposed to, e.g. Feuerbach or Nietzsche) the reductionist case is able to mobilize the detailed and sophisticated findings of natural science in its support. Is there anything now of which we can confidently say: this is not and never will be shown to be reducible to any natural or human occurrence, drive or purpose? The reductionists are now no longer lone voices, but reductionism has come to pervade both academic and popular assumptions about the status of religion.

It is therefore no longer enough simply to try to turn the tables on those who have been called 'the dissuaders' and to bring a religious suspicion to bear upon the practitioners of secular suspicion. It has long been a tactic of religious apologists to draw attention to the possibility that critics of religion are themselves driven by malice, are morally self-deceived or in the grip of psychological or social forces they do not understand.[27] However, although this may frequently succeed as an *ad hominem* argument, it can no longer convince us in the face of the ever-wider and ever-deeper extent of the secular world-view. Of course, the case brought against religion is itself freighted with unexamined presuppositions and those who make the case are, sometimes, doubtless driven by ignoble motives, but this does not of itself weaken the cumulative force of the case that the reductionist tendency as a whole has built up.[28]

Of course, it is possible for Christians and other religionists to go some way with the reductionists. Clearly there is much in religion that is conditioned and shaped by history, culture and human interests (and, for that matter, biology). And perhaps there are some aspects or forms of religion that deserve everything the reductionists say. Clearly (I think) there are or have been forms of religion in which doctrine was used as a tool of oppression by particular ruling classes, or that betray psychologically morbid conditions. Think of Father Ferrapont in *The Brothers Karamazov* (a crazy monk, who sees devils everywhere) – isn't it in the interests of religion itself to expose such neurotic forms of religion for what they are? For Karl Barth, basing himself on the Calvinist conviction as to the utter fallenness of human beings, it was even possible to say that Nietzsche and the others were right as far as the external phenomenon of religion in the modern world was concerned and that Schleiermacherian theology itself gives the game away by effectively reducing religion to human feelings and mental states. Such a religion, Barth claimed, obscures any possible grasp of the truly transcendent God, or of faith in all its unworldly otherness, and Christians should join with the critics in dispelling this unwholesome mishmash of humanity and divinity.

But even for Barth not everything was to be sacrificed on the altar of Nietzschean reductionism. The Word of Scripture itself stood above the storm, and we could appeal to Scripture for a judgment on the world. The central affirmations of Christian faith, Jesus Christ as true God and true man, were, for Barth, unaffected by the storm of criticism.

But how can such claims be justified? What grounds can be given for excepting specific Christian doctrines or texts from reductionist critique? Why these texts and not those of Islam, for example? Surely it is not enough simply to assert that certain beliefs are not merely human but are of divine origin?

But if they go beyond mere assertion, then, it seems, believers have to enter into the to and fro of argument and debate, into the relativity of psychology, sociology, history, philology and philosophy. That is daunting: but is there any way for religion to confront the challenge of reductionism other than by attempting to understand religious claims themselves, to show how and why they make sense and should command attention, to confront our own presuppositions and assumptions with as honest a gaze as we can, and to be more, not less, willing to face up to our own endless capacities for self-deception than any Nietzschean? Perhaps, instead of trying to show that they are above the storm, that their faith is an immovable rock that cannot be shaken, they might – to invert an image of Feuerbach's – do better to show themselves willing to plunge into the heart of the storm and learn how to swim in it: to show that their faith is not a weight that drags them down, but a liberating power that buoys them up; that it does not bring about a decrease of vitality, as Nietzsche claimed, but the opposite; that it does not lead to intellectual cowardice but the opposite. But the proof of this cannot be in any grand claims. Rather, it demands a willingness to engage with the detail of what religion – its practices, traditions, texts and models of sanctity – means to those who still treasure it, and to seek, in that detail, for something that can make sense to those (ourselves!) whose world is permeated by the spirit of the secular. It is such a requirement that irresistibly moves the contemporary philosophy of religion towards a hermeneutic approach, an approach to which this short course itself now turns.

A Matter of Interpretation

If the historical, subjective and linguistic tendencies of the modern philosophy of religion do not necessarily amount to an endorsement of the reductionist approach to religion, they do seem to leave the door wide open to such an approach. However, there are possibilities of creative response to the reductionist challenge that incorporate just these tendencies. Foremost amongst these is the path of hermeneutics. A hermeneutic approach to philosophy is one in which the emphasis is no longer on explanation or logical analysis but on interpretation as a means of bringing out into the open the often-hidden presuppositions or assumptions behind any particular discourse. Interpretation, however, does not do this in a vacuum, or pretend to have some absolute criterion of truth by which these assumptions can be judged. An interpreter is not a judge (although she must use all her available skills of judgment) since she does not stand outside the historical flow of language but within it. She is herself situated and participant. There is something about interpretation, and about understanding the philosophical task in terms of interpretation, that implicitly acknowledges the relativity, or, better, the provisionality of the interpreter's own position and, therefore, the outcome of the interpretative process. Understood hermeneutically, the philosophical task is open-ended but not on that account sceptical or detached.

But what does the interpreter ask about?

The interpreter, I have suggested, does not ask about how things happen or why it is the case that such and such a state of affairs has come to pass. The interpreter asks what would it mean for such and such a state of affairs to hold, or for such and such a proposition to be affirmed, or such and such a ritual to be enacted or moral law invoked. The interpreter asks about the meaning of the phenomenon under consideration. In this regard the reductionist accounts of religion offered by Feuerbach, Nietzsche and others may themselves be looked at as hermeneutic exercises. Although these accounts seem to have the form of explanations, and claim to lay bare the causal nexus underlying the phenomenon of religion, we have learned, in philosophizing, that appearances may be misleading. What looks like an explanation may turn out to be something else. And perhaps that is the case here. Perhaps especially in the case of Feuerbach and Nietzsche – whose accounts are less 'scientific' in form than those of Marx, Freud or Durkheim – what we are being offered is not an aetiology (or causal explanation), in the sense that medical science might trace the aetiology of a disease, but a 'big picture', a way of looking at or representing religion, a framework within which the diverse elements of the phenomenon of religion can be understood in their interconnection and in terms of their relevance to us. As Nietzsche himself virtually says, what he is giving is an evaluation of religion, telling us what makes it important for us and why. Looked at in this way, the more specifically scientific strategies pursued by Marx, Freud and others can be seen as themselves dependent on the prior acceptance of the interpretative framework, and the initial setting up of such a framework is something more like an artistic envisioning of the matter than an analysis or explanation of it. In other words, the reductive strategies themselves only make sense within the larger framework given by the fundamental evaluative act – in Nietzsche's case the commitment to suspicion. But what is going to make us accept one framework rather than another? And can interpretation be altogether separated from explanation and analysis? Might one not turn around what has just been said, and argue that Freud, for example, was moved to adopt a hermeneutic of suspicion on the basis of his clinical experience of cases in which the religious element played a distinctly neurotic role? Equally, it might be said that we will only overturn a Nietzschean hermeneutic of suspicion if we are able to adduce plausible cases of individuals and communities for whom religious belief does not lead to pessimism and world-weariness, but inspires world- and life-affirmation? Doesn't there remain an unavoidable debate as to what is actually the case, and doesn't this suggest a limit to what we can expect of any purely hermeneutic approach to religion?

We shall return to this question later, but first we shall examine three forms of modern hermeneutics, in Schleiermacher, in Hegel and in Heidegger.

The modern hermeneutic tradition is generally traced back to Schleiermacher, whose hermeneutics reflected both his activity as a translator and also his understanding of experience as the root of religion. At the same time that Schleiermacher was writing his early speeches *On Religion*, he was also starting on a project of translating

Plato (indeed his translation was to prove immensely successful and to be the standard German translation for many generations). Also important was his experience as a theologian, seeking to make biblical texts relevant to a contemporary audience. These activities provided a fruitful ground for reflections on hermeneutics; since they necessarily involved questions of interpretation, and, generally, one might say that the phenomenon of translation is one that is particularly fruitful for raising the kinds of questions that come under the heading of hermeneutics. Let us imagine that we have come towards the end of a seminar on Plato's *Republic*, a seminar conducted in English and with an English version of the text. We think we're beginning to grasp what Plato means by 'justice' – but are we even justified in using this particular English word for Plato's Greek term? How much might our discussion have been led off course because of our importing the connotations of the English 'justice' into it? Essentially, however, the same situation is latent in every conversation or communicative exchange, as soon becomes apparent if we once stop and ask ourselves not only how we are able to understand what is being said to us and how to make an appropriate response, but how it is that we are so sure of ourselves in this regard. Look at it like this. If I am speaking to an audience who do not have English as their mother tongue, I will always have a certain anxiety that they are not correctly understanding what I am trying to say, and I will simplify or expand or repeat my words in order to maximize the opportunities for them to get a handle on what I am saying. I have no doubt that *I* know what I am saying. The question is whether they understand it. But now imagine that I am speaking to them in their own language, in which I am by no means at home. My anxiety then will not be so much about them as about myself, whether I am expressing myself clearly and correctly, or whether in fact I am making a complete fool of myself. If I see the corners of their mouths twitching in amusement, or looks of puzzlement appearing on their faces, I will wonder whether I have said something quite different from what I meant to say, or conveyed completely the wrong emphasis or tone. But, in either case, is the situation really so different when I am speaking in my 'own' language to another native speaker? Derrida has pointed out that we have only language and it is not our own.[1] For English was not invented in order to suit my communicative needs. As an English-speaker I inherit a grammar and a vocabulary that, capacious as it is, also imposes certain limitations on what can and what can't be said, and none of this is of my contriving. I have had to learn it from a starting point outside it. From where, then, do I derive my confidence that I know what I'm saying and that what I'm saying is what I mean to say? How do I understand myself in what I say? But yet (as Heidegger emphasized) our mother tongue, as the language we learn in infancy from our mothers, is precisely what gives us the possibility of inhabiting a meaningful world at all.

Previous to Schleiermacher, however, the question of hermeneutics had not been thematized in a sustained way or opened up as a fundamental philosophical question. For it was only in the light of the development of a genuinely historical consciousness that the radical hermeneutic problem of the difference in consciousness between text and reader could really be grasped. Before the rise of the historical consciousness, the hermeneutic problem seemed to be simply how to spell out the timeless meaning of the text under consideration, a problem that the church had classically solved by means of the inter-related strategies of typology and allegory, together with the require-ment of mystical and moral application. Such developments, though they reflect the hermeneutic problem, actually overlooked it, as it was simply assumed that each of these levels of meaning was what the text had always actually meant. Now, however, it became increasingly apparent that the thought-world in which ancient texts took shape was far removed from that of modern, post-Enlightenment Europeans. And, of course, this was a problem for the texts of Greek philosophy just as much as for those of the Bible.

Schleiermacher called hermeneutics 'the art of understanding' and pointed out that, as against previous theories, this was not only necessary in the case of particularly difficult texts but also applied to the whole field of linguistic discourse. 'Difficult' texts often only appear difficult because we haven't in fact understood what we assumed to be 'easier' parts. The whole field of a language hangs together, and therefore the first requirement laid on any would-be interpreter of ancient texts is familiarity with the language as a whole, as that would have been available to the author. The first part of interpretation, then, is what Schleiermacher calls 'grammatical exposition', of which the first rule (or, as he calls it, 'canon') is 'Everything that requires a more precise determination in any given discourse, may only be determined on the basis of the field of language common to the author and his original public.'[2] In other words, if we want to understand the New Testament as well as pos-sible we have to immerse ourselves in the language, including the grammar, the usage and the cultural context that conditions usage, before we can begin to make sense of such terms as '*Kyrios*' or 'Son of Man' or 'justification'. These cannot be abstracted from their linguistic-cultural context. Least of all can we assume in advance that the meanings we attach to them are the meanings current in the time of their then usage. And the same point, of course, applies to the interpretation of other texts. If, to take an example of particular interest to me, we are to understand Kierkegaard, then we must familiarize ourselves with the Danish language of his day, with the philosophical German he knew and made use of, with the literature he read, with the popular culture of the 1840s, etc. Of course, this is an almost indefinitely expandable task, and one never reaches an actual end. Nevertheless, what is aimed at is not a total contextualization, but a philological, grammatical contextualization to the highest possible attainable level. Schleiermacher's second rule of grammatical exposition is that 'The meaning of every particular word in a given place must be determined in the light of its interconnection with those that surround it.'[3] With this rule – simple to the point of obviousness – Schleiermacher puts the axe to the root of the tree of a deeply-engrained Christian habit of reading Scripture, namely, pulling proof texts out from the body of the text and building dogmatic constructions on them in detachment from the text – a practice we can in fact see at work already in the scriptural text itself.

Now, if Schleiermacher had stopped there, we might think that we were once more being confronted with a variety of reductionism, 'philological reductionism' we might call it, in which the meaning of the text was reduced to its grammatical determinants. But there is a whole other, no less necessary side to hermeneutics, as Schleiermacher goes on to explain. It is what he calls 'psychological exposition'. Now this is not something added on to the grammatical exposition. Indeed, in actual practice these are inseparable. From whichever side we begin we have to presuppose the essential unity of the work or discourse under consideration: that the grammatical form belongs to the psychological meaning, and that the psychological meaning has no existence in isolation from being given expression in, with and under its grammatical form. There is no free-floating meaning detached from the text, but, on the other hand, grammatical exposition alone will not deliver the text's meaning to us. Every writer works within the constraints of the system of language and concepts within which he was formed, and yet 'every connection of subject and predicate that has not been previously effected is something new'.[4] It is in this novelty, in this unique, personal action of the author in writing that psychological exposition finds its matter and it is most tellingly disclosed in the author's style, in his or her distinctive manner of using the language. But how can we go about discerning this inner psychological meaning? How can we interpret the style of a work?

Schleiermacher offers two methods. The first is what he calls the comparative method. This 'posits that which is to be understood as [a] universal [idea] and then proceeds to find the singular expression thereof, by comparing several expressions of the same universal [idea].'[5] So, for example, if we want to find out what Schleiermacher has to say about hermeneutics, we might bring to his work a general conception of hermeneutics and then see how what he says varies from or compares with Hegel, Dilthey, Heidegger or others. Schleiermacher calls his comparative method the 'masculine' element of interpretation. The corresponding feminine element is what he calls 'divination', in which the interpreter 'transforms herself into the other, and seeks to grasp the individual [expression] in its immediacy.'[6] This moment of divination, then, is the apex, the furthest reach of the hermeneutic art: this is the closest we get to the mind of the other, the author we seek to understand. Despite everything Schleiermacher has said about the necessity of preparing the grammatical, philological and historical foundations, and despite all that can be gained from a comparative approach, the whole process is incomplete unless or until we experience this moment of immediate rapport with the text, this moment in which we 'divine' its inner meaning, the intention, the original creative act of the author that makes his product a unique and meaningful work.

In this regard, a Schleiermacherian hermeneutics is going to look very different from, for example, a Hegelian hermeneutics. As we have seen, one way of reading the Hegelian approach to religion is to see it as essentially reductionistic. This was the line taken, with different motives, by Feuerbach and Kierkegaard. Yet it is also possible to take a more positive view and to see the Hegelian *Aufhebung*, the retrospective philosophical grey-in-grey, not as an attempt to supplant, to overcome or to reduce religion in favour of a science of pure concepts, but as an attempt to draw out and hold up to view the conceptual structure that is implicit within religion itself. In this aspect the *Aufhebung* is not the suppression or cancellation of religion, but its preservation, its elevation to the dignity of philosophical thought. It is discerning the philosophical content that is already present within religion.

I do not want to enter into a specialist debate about the interpretation of Hegel and how we are to understand his deepest philosophical intentions, but, for now, simply to highlight the possibility of a kind of hermeneutic approach developed according to the Hegelian pattern. In opposition to the Schleiermacherian approach, this would not culminate in the act of divination, in the immediate intuition of the meaning in the text, but would rather – in a manner closer to Schleiermacher's comparative method – see the meaning in terms of the text's power to illuminate a general, universal current in history. So, for example, the 'meaning' of Greek art, for Hegel, is not somehow indwelling the particular works of art, timelessly waiting for an appropriately attuned eye to behold it. Rather, this meaning is constituted in and by the historical process of which it is a part, a process that, as we have seen, can be characterized as the humanization and spiritualization of religion, a transition from the world of eastern religions to the new world of early Christianity. Nor is that history something simply 'behind' the text, since, insofar as we too are historical subjects, concerned with the text on the basis of our historical need and experience, the 'meaning' is also a question of our contemporary possibilities.

In his study *Truth and Method*, one of the defining works of twentieth-century hermeneutics, Hans-Georg Gadamer drew attention to an image used by Hegel to explain what the surviving works of art of classical antiquity might mean to his contemporaries. It is, Hegel said, like a girl who hands us beautiful fruits torn from a tree. They are no longer connected to or nourished by the life-processes that made them what they are, but what they have lost in this respect is more than compensated for by the human exchange figured for Hegel in the charm and grace of the girl who hands them to us. This real human relationship, he suggests, gives us more than the 'merely' organic process of their origin and growth. For Gadamer this image thus encapsulated the profit and the loss of the hermeneutical enterprise, but also showed the limitation inherent in Schleiermacher's apparent ideal of re-experiencing the original experience of the author.[7]

Yet, for all their differences, Schleiermacher and Hegel are not necessarily so far apart. Schleiermacher too, as we have seen, did not believe that divination could be fruitfully exercised apart from the labour of philological and comparative study. Likewise, it is clear from the way he writes about them, if not from his overall argument, that Hegel sees the spiritual content of Greek art as being still in some sense accessible to contemporary spectators. Even if, as Hegel put it, 'thought and reflection have spread their wings above fine art', art – including the art of other times and places – still has the power to seize, move and instruct us.

Later in the nineteenth century Wilhelm Dilthey attempted to promote something like a Schleiermacherian hermeneutics as the basis for a general humanistic method. As the natural sciences made ever more remarkable strides, and seemed ever more secure in their own methods, the human sciences suffered a corresponding crisis of doubt. There were, of course, those who thought that ethics, aesthetics and history could be treated in the same way as the phenomena studied by natural science, and that all fields of possible knowledge could be brought within the domain of positivistic thinking – the Russian nihilists were, perhaps, extreme in this regard, but not without parallels in the West. Dilthey, however, argued that the human *sciences*, the *Geisteswissenschaften*, had a different orientation, namely, towards the *meaning* of historical and cultural phenomena. Human life is not a purely natural phenomenon, like chemical or geological processes, but is shaped and impressed by subjective purposes and intentions. On the plane of history, these take shape as the world-views characterizing the successive ages or epochs of history.

In some ways, Dilthey can be seen as a kind of fusion of Schleiermacher and Hegel. With Schleiermacher, he sets himself the goal of 'seeking the soul' as the meaning of history. With Hegel, on the other hand, he is concerned with the large historical picture, rather than the individual expression of meaning. Unlike Hegel, however, his view of history is not teleological. He does not claim to be able to anticipate the end of history and, from that end, look back over the whole process and pass judgment on its meaning. History is still in progress, still underway. Nevertheless, because, for all the differences between different ages and different cultures, we share in a common human nature, it is possible for us to interpret the meaning of world-views alien to our own. The life and culture of every age is a variation on a common theme. There is change in history and, arguably, within certain limits, development, but there is no finality.[8]

It is not Dilthey's intention, but his view remains close to a kind of relativism that, in turn, seems defenceless against the aggressive relativism of Nietzsche. For Nietzsche the differing world-views of different epochs were not connected by any common human nature, but were all of them more or less fictional constructions imposed upon an indifferent universe. The only question is: which is the stronger, which is the more attractive, which is the more persuasive? But, since he has renounced the possibility of an overview of history *à la* Hegel, what justifies Dilthey in holding on to the presupposition of a single, common, human nature? Is Dilthey perhaps one of those onlookers in the marketplace, who have participated in the killing of

God, but who do not realize the enormity of what they have done? Is he attempting to occupy an inherently unstable and untenable middle ground between a unitary, teleological view of history and Nietzschean relativism? Or, more positively, is he perhaps pointing to the possibility that there really is a third way? That abandoning a metaphysically overdetermined view of history is not the same as giving in to nihilism? That even if we cannot get our heads round the whole, there are still possibilities of understanding, there is still meaning in history?

A decisive figure in twentieth-century Western philosophy – in the continental tradition, at least – was Martin Heidegger. Despite the damage done to Heidegger's reputation by his complicity in Nazism, his thought has been perhaps as influential as that of Hegel in the nineteenth century, and has provoked similarly antagonistic responses.

It is customary to divide Heidegger's career into two parts, early and late: the early centring on *Being and Time*; the later on a series of essays and lectures in which the themes of poetry, the critique of science and technology and the return to the pre-Socratics are dominant motifs. Both these parts of Heidegger's career are fruitful for the question of hermeneutics.

'Understanding', one of the key terms in hermeneutic theory, is likewise central to *Being and Time*. As opposed to positivism, Heidegger did not believe that anyone had ever actually inhabited the objective world as revealed by positivistic science. We do not encounter the objects in the world as fixed, determinate entities, standing over against us, subject to laws of nature. Rather, we encounter them in the course of our own lived projects. Take a hammer. We do not first learn what a hammer is by consulting a dictionary definition. We just pick up a hammer (or rock or piece of heavy wood) in order to bang a nail into a wall. It is in this way, in the course of living out our practical involvement in the world, that we discover the world and ourselves in it. And such practical involvement is always governed by implicit aims and intentions. I want to bang a nail into the wall in order to hang a picture. I want to hang a picture in order to make my house attractive, because I am newly married and setting up home, because we are planning a family and I want to get it all into good shape before the baby comes. And all these plans and projects are themselves dependent on further background assumptions about who I am and what I want to do with my life: that I want to be a father, a husband, to play my part in society, to fulfil my parents' expectations of me, etc. (or, it may be, my hammering is connected with a life-project that involves the thoroughgoing contestation of all my parents' values and of their ambitions for me).

In such ways, argues Heidegger, we bring a pre-understanding to our encounter with the world, and it is this that guides us in the first instance. 'Understanding' is not something added on to existence, after the event, as it were. But we exist understandingly, as understanding, in the world. We have to do with objects, with the world, with others, long before we stop to think about them objectively.

When, therefore, Heidegger as a philosopher wants to ask the question of Being, he does not resort to logical analysis or historical reconstruction. Instead, he asks about the kind of pre-understanding of Being that already guides us in our being-in-the-world. However, this does not mean that he takes the self-understanding we generally have of ourselves at its face value. It may be true that much of my behaviour on a day-to-day basis is governed, unconsciously, implicitly, by the kind of motivations I mentioned above in connection with hammering nails into walls – wanting to be a good father, husband, son, etc. (or, as the case may be, a rebel). But what do these sorts of wants and wishes reveal? In *Being and Time* Heidegger sees most of us most of the time as living a very degraded kind of life: we have fallen into the habits of speech and action that belong to our everyday environment without ever having subjected them to critical examination. We are what our environment expects us to be and no more. This is the situation Heidegger describes as inauthentic. Fundamentally, such inauthentic existence is a flight from what most of all concerns, or should concern, us: our death. Only the heroic, resolute confrontation with death, Heidegger claims, will deliver us from such immersion in the common life of the crowd and fit us for authentic existence.

In drawing this picture of the human condition, Heidegger was, of course, drawing on a rich heritage of philosophical and religious critiques of ordinary life. It was certainly no accident that the theologian Rudolf Bultmann, at one time a colleague and friend of Heidegger, transferred these categories of inauthentic/authentic to the Christian duality sin/faith. Indeed, Bultmann claimed (with some justification) that the Heideggerian categories themselves reflected the basic existential (though not cosmological) dualism of the New Testament. For Bultmann, as for Heidegger, human beings always live 'understandingly' in the world. The concern to think about things 'objectively' is always a late arrival and not how we engage with the world in the first instance. For this reason it is a mistake to approach the scriptural texts with such questions as: were the miracles historic facts, or, was Jesus the Messiah? The question is rather how these events and claims were understood by those by and for whom the text was formed. Moreover, we should be aware that when we ourselves are reading the Scriptures, we bring our own understanding, our own concerns into that reading. The Scriptures only ever speak to us if they do so in terms of our own horizon of understanding.

Now, for Bultmann it was axiomatic that the world-view of the New Testament, and our own world-view are radically different. Theirs was one in which the world stood at the centre of the universe. Heaven was literally a place above the earth and hell a place beneath. The atmosphere was peopled with spirits and demons, and the laws of nature were subject to frequent interruptions. Ours is shaped by science and technology. Therefore it is a mistake to require us to accept the New Testament world-view as a precondition of 'believing' its message. For this message does not depend on the world-view in which it is framed. This message itself addresses the concern for authentic existence in the face of death that Heidegger had shown was the fundamental concern of the existing human subject. The task, Bultmann claimed, was to translate, or to demythologize, this message, so that it could be heard with twentieth-century ears.[9]

This put him on a clear collision course with theologians like Karl Barth. Already the liberal, Schleiermacherian hermeneutic was too humanistic for Barth. As we have seen, Schleiermacher required us to take seriously the whole context, the whole linguistic world in which a text was produced. Of course, the final aim in, say, reading Paul's Letter to the Romans, was to divine the mind of Paul, but we could only do this alongside the grammatical and comparative strands of interpretative work. For Barth, however, faithful interpreters encounter no historical barrier between themselves and the text. As he said of Calvin's commentaries on Paul: 'Paul speaks, and the man of the sixteenth century hears.'[10] The hermeneutical way, according to Barth, meant hearing 'other spirits' in the text than the one guiding spiritual concern of Paul himself, i.e. the objective content of Paul's thought that is none other than 'the' Spirit and, in the Spirit, Jesus Christ, God himself. To hear this, however, we have to attend to the text in its own terms. Demythologizing is ruled out, not merely because it calls into question God's power to perform miracles, for example, but because it places *our* question, *our* concern about our own existence at the centre of the interpretative task. For Bultmann, this is the only way in which we can get the text to speak to us at all:

for Barth it is to reduce the text in advance of any possible reading to the limits of our understanding. It is, as he somewhat grimly put it, allowing the humanistic tail to wag the theological dog.

The debate about demythologizing was one of the great debates of twentieth-century German theology, although it has now receded into the past. Nevertheless, many of the issues it threw up are still with us. Above all, this is true of the role that hermeneutics should play in theology.[11]

I have said that the work of the later Heidegger was, amongst other things, fruitful for questions of hermeneutics. We have already seen how language became a dominant concern for Heidegger, and that the kind of importance he gave to questions of language is brought into focus by his citation of Hölderlin's reference to 'the conversation that we are'. In the light of the comments at the beginning of this chapter concerning the relationship between the basic structures of any conversation and the necessity of the hermeneutical question we can at once see how hermeneutical questions might resurface in Heidegger's work. But the theme of 'conversation', fruitful as that is for hermeneutics,[12] is by no means the only issue here.

In order to get at some of the key questions, and accepting the distortion involved in any simplistic summary of Heidegger's position, it could be said that whereas *Being and Time* took its starting point from the situation of the existing human subject, anxiously fleeing the prospect of its own death, the later philosophy turns away from man towards Being, towards what it is that lets Being, and beings, be at all. As part of this enquiry, Heidegger offers a vast and monumental re-reading of the Western philosophical tradition. A key element in this is his claim that a decisive turning point occurred in the thought of Plato when truth was, for the first time, defined as the correspondence of idea and reality, the adequation of thing and object, as medieval philosophy was to put it. This view of truth as 'correctness' was, Heidegger argued, an imposition onto the world of human beings' desire to have the world conform to their capacities and their wishes, to make the world subject to their epistemological, sociological and technological dominion. The 'secret' of Plato's philosophy was modern technology. We no longer see the river coursing its way from the mountains to the sea, said Heidegger: instead, we see a potential source of electricity, a means of transport or a political border.

Much of Heidegger's later thought is made up of readings of key philosophical texts, and showing how this hidden will to domination lay at the centre of the mainstream of Western philosophy. In this respect, although Nietzsche saw himself as an anti-metaphysical thinker, and as overturning all the values of Platonism, he is in fact the ultimate heir of Platonism, and the Nietzschean will-to-power simply spells out what has been the guiding thought of Western philosophy all along. Remember, once more, how we saw philosophy as characteristically involving the exposing and calling into question of the hidden presuppositions, preconceptions and assumptions in the discourse under consideration. In this regard Heidegger seems to be saying that philosophers themselves have not been sufficiently aware of their own presuppositions – a point we might want particularly to remember in connection with the discussion of reductionism. Because of this, because of our compulsive desire to impose a human-ly-determined value on the world, we have forgotten how to let beings be as they are and show themselves as they are. We have forgotten, simply, what it is for us to be.

How could a wrong view of truth get installed so firmly and so centrally in the philosophical mind?

To answer this question, let us note some of the fundamental principles guiding Heidegger's late hermeneutic. When we approach the works of any great thinker, says Heidegger, we have to remember that any great thinker is great precisely by virtue of the fact that they think only one thought. This is so with Plato, with Aristotle, with Descartes, with Nietzsche. An average researcher will discover many facts, experiment with many arguments, but never arrive at the over-arching simplicity of a single guiding thought. This is the preserve of true thinkers alone. This does not mean that it is obvious what that thought is or that we can restate it in words of one syllable. Particularly when we are dealing with ancient texts, we need to be sure that we are not being misled by customary translations, or by assumptions along the lines of 'what we all know about Plato'. Finding and holding onto the decisive thought of a great thinker is an arduous and testing business. But that is not the end of it. Even more far-reaching is Heidegger's claim that the thought of a great thinker is shaped and determined by what is unthought in it, and our task as interpreters is to think beyond the great thinkers to what they didn't think.

This sounds paradoxical, even absurd, but like much in Heidegger it is perhaps closer to common sense than it seems. He was, after all, not the first to say that philosophy begins with aporia, with puzzle-ment. An unlikely occurrence or a strange quirk of language gets us thinking: 'What's going on here? What's this about?' we ask ourselves. Often such questions are quickly and easily solved. But isn't a measure of the importance of a philosophical question precisely its resistance to easy and simple solutions? (As an illustration of which one might add that all there is to say about the philosophy of A. J. Ayer has probably nearly all been already said – but do we yet really know what Plato *meant*?)

Heidegger speaks of 'what calls for thinking' as that which withdraws from our gaze, what hides itself in the world we encounter and, by doing so, creating a vacuum – and thinking is the current or draught generated by this vacuum, pulling us ever toward it. He writes of this situation:

> Once we are so related and drawn to what withdraws, we are drawing into what withdraws, into the enigmatic and therefore mutable nearness of its appeal. Whenever man is properly drawing that way, he is thinking – even though he may still be far away from what withdraws, even though the withdrawal may remain as veiled as ever. All through his life and right into his death, Socrates did nothing else than place himself into this draft, this current, and maintains himself in it. This is why he is the purest thinker of the West. This is why he wrote nothing. For anyone who begins to write out of thoughtfulness must inevitably be like those people who run to seek refuge from any draft too strong for them.[13]

The interpretation of texts, therefore, is always aiming beyond the written word, beyond the external, public record of thought, not, as with Schleiermacher, to the creative mind of the writer, but to the hidden aporia, the wonderment, that *thaumazein* that first provoked the thinker into thinking. The ultimate presupposition of thought is not in thought itself, but in what precedes and provokes thought. This, Heidegger's line of thinking suggests, is what most concerns the philosopher.

Does it sound as if what is being talked about here as the ultimate presupposition behind which we can never go is some fugitive ineffable object, an unthinkable *x*? But what would such a thing be? The sheer givenness of there being something there at all to think about, perhaps? A kind of intellectual encounter with raw Being (but which, of course, it would be a mistake to interpret as a *concept* of Being – therefore something beyond both Being and non-being)? Like wanderers in a haunted forest we seem to be back once more at the site of apophatic theology, struck dumb by the presence of the wordless.

Nevertheless, it is not a matter of a simple return to an insoluble conundrum, as if nothing had changed from the last time we were here. For our reflection on the theory of interpretation points up possibilities of how we may, after all, find it worthwhile to go on talking, even in the face of the unthinkable.

The question of meaning is inseparable from the process of the historical experience of language. Meaning and truth are not the intellectual property of the originators of texts, but, by virtue of being expressed textually, they become part of history. As such they then become the object of repeated interpretation (or, it may be, of neglect) that comes to shape what they might mean to subsequent readers. The truth of *Hamlet* is not its correspondence to certain timeless truths of human nature but its power to generate ever-new literary and performed interpretations which are themselves worked out against their predecessors as well as in relation to 'the original'. As the demythologizing debate highlighted, we cannot, finally, separate the interpretation even of sacred texts from the history of their interpretation. Both sides – even the Barthian – showed by their participation in the debate that the debate itself needed to be had if Scripture was to be made accessible (or, conversely, protected) for the contemporary community of readers. Even in aiming beyond writing, even in trying to get at the truth (of Plato or of Scripture), we are led through an open-ended history of text, commentary and interpretation. If, from one angle, this threatens to engulf us in relativity, from another it provides a context in which we can learn to address 'what calls for thinking' in what we read.

Putting it like this also calls attention to the public and common nature of such learning. It is not a matter of trying to effect some kind of private inner intuition, but, as Heidegger himself often put it, to conduct a dialogue with the tradition of great thinkers of the past. (Though whether Heidegger himself is a genuinely dialogical thinker is a whole other question – his interpretations of the defining figures of the philosophical tradition, original and brilliant as they are, are often profoundly monological in tone!) The dialogue in question, however, is not just a matter of our sitting down with the works of Plato (or of Heidegger) and trying to work out for ourselves what they mean. Rather, it is a matter of participating in a conversation about what such works mean and what is really being said, what is really being offered to thought, in them. The dialogue is not just diachronic in the sense of reaching back through the tradition but synchronic in the sense that it involves active engagement with what we, now, allow to count as understanding. To the discipline of historical retrieval we add the discipline of criticism and controversy, within and between disciplines. Trying to think what precedes thought cannot therefore be conceived – as it seems to have been for Schleiermacher – as a kind of mental reconstruction of the original linguistic- and thought-world of the writer. There is always also the present issue as to what this might or could mean for us.

The fact that this contemporary horizon of meaning exists for us in the form of dialogue, however, means that we must significantly modify the so-called 'two-horizon' model of hermeneutic enquiry, according to which the task of interpretation is to say within the horizon of contemporary thought what was said within the horizon of its own time in the text under consideration. For whether there ever were historical times when the representation of the world as a whole was shared by all the participants in cultural discourse, it is characteristic of modernity that our horizon exists for us precisely as a question, as a conflict or debate between rival representations. It is, perhaps, first in the juxtaposition of two historical moments that our own time becomes, in Benjamin's sense, the 'time of the now',[14] and it is only when our own time is thus brought into focus by an historical interpretative act and therewith seen in its fundamental question-ableness that hermeneutics moves from being a simple (though never easy) matter of historical remembrance to a kind of philosophical enquiry. The question then is just what our own horizon really is, rather than assuming it to be something with which we are already familiar.

And the philosopher of religion?

If the guiding question of the philosophy of religion is: what provokes us into *thinking about God* (and not simply worshipping or believing in an unreflective way), we may say two things by analogy with the preceding comments about hermeneutics in general. The first is that the word 'God', even in this, its simplest, most stripped-down form, is (like all words) historically transmitted and, therefore, historically conditioned. In seeking to work our way into the question we are, by analogy with what has been said above, also seeking to think our way through it and to arrive at the truth of the word, what it 'really' means. But this will always be positioned for us, as histori-cally existing beings, by our history and the history of our language. As we have seen this means engaging in what is simultaneously a diachronic and a synchronic argument as to what the historical tradi-tion of religion gives us to think and what it can mean for us now.

The twentieth-century discussion of hermeneutics was dominated by the assumption that language occupied a justifiably privileged place in the communication of truth and meaning. In the case of some exponents this has seemed to involve subordinating the autonomy of the personal subject to a hypostatized 'language' as not merely the medium but the functional determinant of all meaning. Heidegger himself, no less than some of his postmodern critics and interpreters, seems to come close to such a view. However, as the emphasis of these thoughts on hermeneutics might suggest, we can understand the hermeneutic process itself – as a process of actual and continual argument and dispute – as the way in which language is humanized and set to work for humanly significant commitments. At the same time we should not allow the understandable privilege given to language to obliterate the ways in which other form-bearing media (painting, ritual, sculpture, music, architecture, dance, or the bodily dimension of acted drama, for example) contribute dimensions of meaning that give thinking in language something to think about. Nor can we simply exclude the kinds of questions that concern a more factually-oriented historian. It may in the end be the case that meaning breaks loose from the factual constraints of its origin (so that, for example, 'resurrection' can become a powerful symbol even for those who do not believe in the actual physical resurrection of Jesus of Nazareth), but if that is so, then the interpreter still owes the historian the courtesy of acknowledging that such a transformation has indeed occurred.

But is the correspondence between philosophy in general and the philosophy of religion in terms of the general shape of the hermeneutic task merely formal, in the sense of sharing an overall orientation towards what is prior to every conscious assumption within a specified field of discourse? In this case 'God' would be the necessary presupposition of religion in the same sense that farming is the necessary presupposition of there being such a thing as agricultural science. Or does God coincide with what fundamental philosophy seeks to uncover as the ever-intended but ever-unthought presupposition of thought? In this case, God would not only be the 'special' meaning of religion, but of all conscious life as such. In other words: is philosophy's intellectual *eros* merely *analogous* to the aspiration of religion, or is what philosophy and religion long for finally and actually the same? In the light of everything that has been said here that is not a question to which we can expect any simple or direct answer. Rather it is a question to be pursued through the prism of historical and textual enquiry (taking 'text' in the largest sense), and always accompanied by the critical debate as to what kind of sense and what kind of implications that historical enquiry might have for all who participate in the contemporary debate concerning philosophy and religion. That is, in a sense, *the* question – and one which the hermeneutical principle suggests will never be brought to a final conclusion. Only the argument itself will decide what the question could possibly mean for us. This is why, although the hermeneutic process is inseparable from history and the interpretation of history, it can never be simply a historical science, a bare retrieval of a past truth. It also, necessarily, points to a decision concerning the present and, as such, might be described not so much as the continual retrieval of the past as its recreation or reinvention, or as a way of understanding and of self-commitment to the never-before-experienced actuality of the present moment.

It is worth adding to these remarks the following two further comments. Firstly, that hermeneutical approaches to philosophy characteristically oscillate between aesthetics and ethics. On the one hand, philosophical interpretation (in this case the philosophical interpretation of religion) will be seeking an aesthetic image of its object (the religious life) capable of giving direction and shape to the interpretative process. On the other hand, such interpretation will also evaluate a religious text in the light of its possible function as a guide to life, i.e. with a view to such questions as 'How would someone who believed this behave?' The meaning of a religious text is not a purely noetic or intellectual matter, nor yet an intellectual matter with an aesthetic dimension. It is also, and may be always, a matter of what is the supreme good for human beings, and how we should be living in order to best give effect to our understanding of that supreme good. In this connection we may recall that, in addition to translation and exegesis, an important context for the early development of hermeneutic theory was law, where, of course, the interpretation of the meaning of a legal text (a statute, a principle or a case-law judgment) has immediate implications for action. Moreover (and this is, in effect, the second concluding comment), insofar as our contemporary horizon is itself brought into question by the hermeneutic process, the resolution of the interpretative process in its ethical aspect will open up towards the whole business of political and cultural life. In this way it becomes the process whereby we collectively enact the multidimensional dialogue that itself determines, for our time, what that horizon is to be, yet does so in continuous and conscious relation to the presence of the past in our present decision-making.

Beyond Criticism

One of the guiding threads of this short course has been the idea that philosophizing characteristically involves the critical questioning of assumptions and, by such questioning, seeks to bring to light the hidden presuppositions that inform but also very frequently distort and undermine the various realms of human discourse. In connection with this it was noted that the initial encounter with philosophy is likely to be disturbing, vertiginous even, as what had been assumed to be self-evident forms of argument and understanding are undermined or problematized, and we ourselves are revealed as not really knowing what we are saying. The irritation and anger with which many of his interlocutors responded to Socrates' critical questioning powerfully attest to the negative impact of philosophy on the everyday understanding of things, as does the exclamation by the first-year philosophy student that it does his head in. But an analogous story is repeated even in the more rarefied realms of science and the philosophy of science, where the philosopher's view as to what science is aiming at and what it can achieve may go against the grain of working scientists' own understanding of what they are doing. And, of course, the same is true in religion, where religious believers, including those whose faith has been disciplined by scholarly research, may experience the philosopher of religion's niggling questions as gratuitously subversive and altogether unwelcome. 'Why can't we just get on with believing!' the believer exclaims. 'What's the point of all these endless questions that don't get us anywhere?'

Philosophy, as we have been thinking about it here, indeed doesn't 'get us anywhere'. Philosophy is not a positive science; it does not have a field of enquiry of its own like chemistry, biology, history or English literature. There is not something out there 'about' which philosophers and philosophers alone know, it seems. In probing the assumptions of any particular discourse, philosophy itself does not lead on to new findings, but simply, via the initial disorientation it brings about, leads us to understand what we already know (or think we know) differently. Philosophy does not make discoveries, if, as

Hegel put it, the owl of wisdom spreads its wings only at nightfall, when the business of the day has been brought to a conclusion. In this respect philosophy would seem to be parasitic, dependent on the pre-existence of the discourse it seeks to clarify, tidying up the jungle-like profusion of language-games that have overrun their limits, but never itself planting or harvesting.

In the face of which, inevitably, the question will be asked, 'So what?' Such a modest mode of questioning may have a certain curiosity value and even a quiet dignity, but does it really matter? What, if anything, gives philosophical questioning its urgency? If I were to claim that the philosophy of religion is the most important and decisive line of approach to the understanding of religion today, wouldn't this seem like a massive overstatement in the light of everything that has been said thus far?

In this chapter, then, I shall try to sketch a constructive understanding of the philosophy of religion, and to show that philosophy of religion is not only the core discipline of the academic study of religion, but that it can be a vital resource for the living of the religious life itself. In setting out to do this, however, it should be emphasized from the very beginning that such a 'positive' outcome, if achieved, does not simply cancel the 'labour of the negative' that precedes it. Speculation does not and cannot break loose from questioning, and philosophy cannot free itself from philosophizing, as if it might put its own assumptions and foundations beyond the reach of any possible critique. On the contrary – philosophy is most itself when it is most attentive to the questionableness of its own aims and methods. It is the enemy of inflated claims and hyperbolic discourse – at least when such claims and such discourse pretend to truth, importance or compulsion. Philosophy, by way of contrast, will bear the imprint of irony, self-effacement and the hypothetical.[1] If philosophy's way of questioning will, as it must, nevertheless have a certain decisiveness, that does not mean that the philosophy of religion can be elevated to a positive science or made into religious doctrine. What can be said positively cannot be said otherwise than questioningly – and if that seems paradoxical, then perhaps that is indicative of one more assumption that needs questioning.

I shall begin by looking at the constructive role that philosophy of religion might play in the contemporary academic study of religion, where, I shall argue, it – and it alone – is able to maintain the coherence of the subject as a whole. Even if it usually is (and, in a sense, *must* be) a minority subject within the field, the kind of reflection undertaken in philosophizing about religion pre-eminently secures, justifies and maintains any claim by theology and religious studies, separately or in unison, to be a bona fide field of enquiry, teaching and research – but it does so only when understood as a process of questioning and not as the securing of certain results.

However, the academic study of religion is only a small part of humanity's overall religious activity, and there are many other ways in which religion appears as public discourse or personal commitment. Consequently, the question arises as to whether the philosophy of religion is 'merely' an academic exercise (though this 'merely' need not necessarily be heard as dismissive) or whether it has a possible role within the religious life itself. In pursuing this question, I shall return to and carry further the discussion of the preceding two chapters concerning the relationship between reductionism and hermeneutics, exploring further how this relates to two understandings of philosophy: philosophy as world-view and philosophy as critique. What I shall then suggest is that the hermeneutical requirement of a world-view, in the sense of a general horizon of representation within which meaning can be established and explicated, will, if left to itself, revert to a pre-philosophical world-view, in the sense of an unexamined adherence to tradition, ideology or even mythology. Nevertheless the interplay of constructive hermeneutics and philosophical critique allows for the positing of possible horizons of interpretation and understanding that, whilst critically prevented from petrifying into dogmatic world-views, are sufficiently stable and extensive to give individuals and communities the possibility of constructing and transmitting identity and meaning.

Finally, I shall go back to the characterization of religion (given in the first chapter) as being essentially concerned with human salvation and ask whether the philosophy of religion can contribute to that concern, whether, in other words, philosophy can give us direction in our search for what it is best for us to be, what it is best for us to do, and how we may best name God.

Philosophy and the study of religion

The academic study of religion today is, in many respects, thriving. New departments are springing up, new topics are proposed and pursued for teaching and research, and conferences and publishers' lists convey a sense of things on the move. In schools and universities new generations of students are bringing new interests and perspectives to bear. All is as it should be in what, globally, is a situation of ever-expanding religious pluralism, in which (contrary to earlier

Marxian and Freudian predictions) religion is not only not withering away but is continuously generating new forms and interacting with other dimensions of human life and understanding in new and often unexpected ways. Many of the phenomena of contemporary religion may be deeply unappealing to Western liberals (including religious liberals), but the sheer dynamism, scope and importance of these phenomena is scarcely deniable. All to the good, then, that the study of religion is itself an increasingly pluralistic enterprise. Nevertheless, as in many other areas, the rapidity of change is outstripping the responsive ability of institutions, and it often seems as if, having abandoned one model for understanding itself (traditional theology), the academic study of religion is gyrating around somewhat aimlessly, unable to resolve upon a new paradigm for deciding what its subject matter and procedures should be.

In order to clarify just what is at issue here, let us step back a generation. In the early 1960s, it was generally (obviously not universally, but generally) assumed that if one wanted to study religion at a university or equivalent level one did so under the aegis of theology – and, for the most part, that meant (in Europe and North America) Christian theology. In some contexts, such as Germany and Scandinavia, the links between the confessional theology of particular churches and the academy were (and still are) strongly institutionalized and embedded in law. Elsewhere, as in Britain, the identification of academic theology with, e.g. the theology of the Church of England, occurred more by default. In the United States the most exciting and radical religious thinkers – Paul Tillich, and the 'secular' and 'death of God' theologians such as Paul van Buren, Harvey Cox, Thomas Altizer and William Hamilton – still wrote as 'theologians'. Since then, however, the picture has gradually changed. Alongside the traditional institutions of 'theology' there have developed new departments or sub-departments of 'Religion' or 'Religious Studies', in which the exclusive claim of confessional theology to determine the academic agenda has been both explicitly and implicitly challenged. In some cases this has resulted in a more or less acquiescent acceptance of cohabitation, in others in an outright 'conflict of faculties' – or, rather, of conflict *within* the faculty: conflict as to just what it is that should be the proper object of the academic study of religion, and how it should be studied.

One extreme view is that 'theology' is essentially an improper presence within the academy, and that if religion is indeed a bona fide subject for academic study, then it can only be on the basis of prescinding from any particular religious perspective or commitment. This view has been powerfully stated by Sam Gill, writing in the *Journal of the American Academy of Religion*: 'The academic study of religion must not depend upon or require of its researchers, teachers or students any specific religious belief or affiliation, race, culture or gender . . . the term "religion" must be understood as designating an academically constructed discourse inclusive of all religions as historically and culturally manifest . . . [in the light of this] dual motivations arise for the study of religion. On the one hand is the desire to appreciate, understand, and comprehend specific religions in their historical and cultural particularity. On the other hand is the opportunity . . . to learn more about ourselves as human beings'.[2] Here is a bold affirmation of 'religion' as an academic construct, independent of the actual life of religious communities. The study of religion is, in this sense, a part of a larger programme of humanistic science, the never-ending expansion of human beings' self-understanding. Nothing, it would seem, either should or can be said about the truth of any particular religious claim, or of any truth concerning transcendent beings or states (God, immortality, salvation) in the context of such study. The concern for God as God cannot be a part of this academic construct, still less the researcher's own quest for salvation or blessedness.

On the other hand there remains a vigorous reaction against such a secular, academic approach, represented in recent years by the so-called 'radical orthodoxy', associated with John Milbank. According to Milbank 'only theology can overcome metaphysics', i.e. only theology (and theology in the strongest of senses) can provide a basis for resolving the crisis of knowledge adumbrated by Heidegger and expanded upon in what has been called the condition of postmodernity. For such radically orthodox thinkers the Christian Eucharist (indeed, the Christian Eucharist understood in terms of transubstantiation) gives us, in the fullest sense of the term 'gives', the paradigm for understanding Being as the analogical bond between God and humans, and a pattern for the optimum manner of living the life of the postmodern city. Over against the solvents of pluralism, the call is to the reintegration of knowledge under the rule of theology as Queen of the Sciences (although theology, it is claimed, is here understood in thoroughly linguistic terms and not as a simple 'realist' 'science of God'). Philosophy, for Milbank, has nothing of spiritual value to say unless it is taken over and 'consummated' by Christian theology: left to itself it is inevitably 'a secularizing immanentism' and, finally, 'malicious'.[3]

Such arguments between 'religious studies' and 'theology' will not easily go away, least of all when the participants share a common institutional space – a university department or a larger body such as the American Academy of Religion. At the same time, there are, perhaps, deeper and still more intractable problems lurking below the surface of such polemics. For, even when theology was itself unchallenged by religious studies, there was room for considerable internal debate as to the proper prioritization of the various sub-disciplines. Classical Christian theology, after all, necessarily involved a range of interacting disciplines: the systematic exposition of doctrine (including apologetics, dogmatics and philosophical theology), church history, the study of Scripture (incorporating both the philological discipline required for the study of ancient texts and the hermeneutical discipline of exegesis and exposition), as well as homiletics, canon law, Christian ethics, etc., etc. What, within this kaleidoscope of disciplines, subjects and methods, gave unity to the field as a whole? Ought dogmatics to be dependent on the study of Scripture – or should the study of Scripture take its lead from dogmatics? Were the preaching, pastoral and ethical requirements of church ministry to be understood as merely the practical application of theological science, or did theological science itself exist to serve the lived practice of Christian church life?

Looking at, but also through (or, as it were, to one side of) the present dispute between theology and religious studies, we can see that analogous questions press upon the subject today, whatever it is called and in whatever context, academic or ecclesiastical, it is practised. Given the diverse, polychrome and multifaceted nature of the phenomenon of religion, is it at all possible to identify any one method or family of methods as best able to facilitate the maximal opening-up and understanding of the field?

Put like this, it immediately becomes apparent that any one of the many disciplines that are potentially relevant to the study of religion – social science, comparative literature, philology, history, philosophy, etc. – is going to be hard-pressed to establish exclusive global rights. It may also seem likely that, *pace* Sam Gill, it is not self-evident in advance of the actual process of enquiry that being a religious believer or practitioner is irrelevant or discreditable to the pursuit of the subject itself, any more than the practice of law or medicine is irrelevant or discreditable to the study and teaching of these subjects in the context of the university. By the same token, however, it has to be no less emphatically asserted that no particular form of religious belief has any self-evident right to determine in advance the outcome of research or the planning of curricula for the subject as a whole.

Now it may well be said that other subjects are experiencing similar turmoil – that historians have for many years engaged in ongoing disputes as to whether history is about the establishing of facts or the construction of interpretative frameworks, and social scientists have likewise argued about whether or not their subject is indeed a 'science'. But if the identity crisis of the study of religion is in this way a local instance of the more general identity crisis of contemporary academic life, that does not make our present enquiry as to what, if anything, can give coherence to this particular field any the less urgent. On the contrary, it may well be that a model developed here might also serve elsewhere, especially if, as may well be the case, the crisis of knowledge began – and runs most deeply – in just this sphere. But to discuss that would be the business of another day (and perhaps not, in any case, a matter for theologians or philosophers of religion themselves to decide).

How, then, are we to balance the centrifugal forces that threaten to pull the subject to pieces, to reduce it to incoherence, making of it whatever anyone wants it to be?

This, I suggest, is one important task for the philosophy of religion.

But how can philosophy of religion help, if, as has been emphasized at many points, the leading characteristic of philosophical activity is critical, calling into question the principles and presuppositions of any particular discourse?

Strangely, perhaps, it is just this that makes philosophical reflection vital to the study of religion. For, as I have indicated, the study of religion today is a territory fought over by a veritable multitude of conflicting disciplines and methodologies, not to mention the dispute between those who require a faith commitment or existential involvement in the subject at issue and those who wish, in principle, to exclude any such commitment or involvement from the academy. Despite the vociferousness of some of the claims being made, it is not at all obvious as to which, if any, of the current competitors has the best title to determine the scope and nature of the field as such. Consequently, the first step towards stabilizing and clarifying the situation is simply for each participant in the debate to clarify to the others their various self-understandings as to what they are about. But, if there is no master-discipline or scientific 'Queen' to adjudicate on the outcome, this will mean a continuing process of mutual interrogation, in the course of which the respective aims, methods and limits of the different disciplines and commitments will be reciprocally clarified – albeit absolute clarity and final agreement may be an imaginary focus to which we may hope to approximate but never attain.

Whether or not there is an individual present called a 'philosopher of religion' is, in the first instance, not so important, for this process of mutual interrogation and clarification is already itself a kind of philosophizing, and it is the activity itself, not personal or institutional status, that is the primary factor here.

Let us not be too grandiose about this. The first step will often be no more than that the members of a faculty talk to each other in a sustained and purposeful manner about their work, or experiment with new ways of working together. The Orthodox liturgist must sit down with the social anthropologist, and the commentator on Shankara must sit down with the Anglo-Saxon philosopher, not to mention the biblical scholar and the psychologist. Such things do, of course, happen constantly, and perhaps not every such encounter, two-way or polyphonous, is genuinely 'philosophical'. There may be many marriages of mere convenience, bursts of fellow-travelling for the purposes of livening up courses and boosting student admissions. Nevertheless, every such moment of dialogue does have within it the possibility of genuine philosophical activity, if what is at stake in the encounter is pursued for its own sake with a resolute concern for the matter itself, over and beyond the simple adjustment of established positions.

It should be clear from all I have been saying, that I do not envisage any short- or even long-term final resolution of the discussion. The need for active, committed, self-critical reflection will never abate, but must accompany the continuing work of substantive enquiry at every step, and, in the context of modern, pluralistic academic life, this reflection will necessarily take the form of inter- and intra-disciplinary dialogue.

The philosophy of religion, then (and, indeed, the philosopher of religion), is not being appealed to as to a judicial authority. Clearly there have been those in the history of philosophy who saw this, or something like it, as the special task of philosophy: to prescribe to each of the sciences the proper boundaries of its field and, as with Hegel's ambition of constructing an encyclopedia of all the sciences, ordering the mutual relations of all the sciences in a unitary and hierarchical system. But philosophy does not need to raise the stakes as high as that in order to justify its claim to a central place in intellectual life. It is already something if it can set in motion and sustain a process of mutual definition that is itself the necessary precondition for common work within a unified field. It is in this sense that I have elsewhere spoken of philosophy of religion as offering 'a kind of translation service to the academy' or, more strongly, as potentially 'the conscience of the academy'. But, once more, this is not to be understood in the sense of claiming superior status. Language itself is constantly changing, and the good translator must be alert to the ever-changing nuances of the living languages between which translation is to occur, and conscience is not conscience if it sleeps. Both metaphors point to the obligation of incessant, painstaking and, even, painful vigilance. This is not an overview kind of thing: philosophy does not have special access to the kinds of things there are in the universe or control the borrowing rights on the kinds of methods needed to unlock the mysteries of life. It works (metaphorically speaking) in the market-place as much as, if not more than, in the courts or parliaments where laws are made effectual and defined.

But although any 'authority' the philosopher of religion might claim is of a horizontal rather than a vertical kind and is, in any case, an authority in some sense derived from the other participants in the continuing debate about the matter itself, this does not make philosophy of religion a mere shadow of other, more substantive disputes. Although neither an aptitude for translation nor conscientiousness are goods that can be possessed without being continually relearned and re-applied, it may be the case that, through the practice of intellectual translation and the practice of intellectual conscience, a certain practical wisdom is built up, a certain direction and orientation of mind of a distinctive kind. Correspondingly, the philosopher of religion who has engaged over a long period of time with the kinds of questions we have been considering, who has listened long and hard and continues to listen long and hard to the many varieties of theorizing about religion will never be able to supplant or bypass the knowledge of specialist scholars, but will for all that be in a unique position to suggest how such specialist knowledge hangs together – or fails to hang together – with the shape and direction of the subject as a whole. If, then, the philosopher of religion can only become such by virtue of a willingness to attend to the contributions and claims of specialist scholars, the philosopher of religion who has become and who truly practises what the name implies will also be a voice to which specialist scholars will want to attend, and one that will have a unique relation to the meaning of the overall study of religion.

Perhaps we might look at it like this. From Clement of Alexandria, through Thomas Aquinas and down to the present, Western theology has spoken of philosophy as the handmaid of theology (apart, of course, from those like Luther who simply wanted to expel 'the whore reason' from the domains of religion altogether). This is somehow a very passive image. We imagine theology, Queen of the

Sciences, seated upon her throne, being waited on by philosophy. Let me suggest an alternative. Philosophy is the guide of theology, in the sense of a guide who leads a traveller through wild and unfamiliar territory. Such a guide need not himself be familiar with the land, but will have the kind of skills that enable him to find his way, to spot and to pre-empt dangers. In one sense the guide is the leader of the expedition. He goes on ahead and prepares the way. Yet it is for the sake of the one being guided that the journey is undertaken. However, we also need to remember that the one being guided is also at risk in this potentially dangerous land. There is no sitting on thrones here, for we are out in the open, not in palaces of gold and ivory. Moreover, in such conditions it may from time to time be the case that the guide himself gets into trouble, and then guide and guided must work together for the sake of their common journey.

The 'leadership' exercised by philosophy, then, is not a matter of promulgating decrees or imposing definitions, but is more characteristically expressed by a repeated call to intellectual modesty, and the urging of an ever more careful, ever more open qualification of substantive claims and an ever-heightened sense of the necessary interdependence of all scholarly enquiry, in the light of the limitations and constraints of any particular form that such enquiry may take.

But can philosophy do more than this? Can it expect to achieve more than contribute to the development of a culture of vigilant self-critique and respectful cooperation amongst scholars? Can philosophy itself, if it is dependent on the substantive research of others, justify any positive claims in relation to religious life and to the God or to the search for salvation spoken of in that life?

Philosophy and world-view

Even if it is accepted that what has been said thus far goes some way towards justifying the claim that the philosophy of religion is or should be a central element in the academic study of religion, it may nevertheless seem as if the position reached is somewhat negative and even bleak. If the significance and truth of the whole rich variegated phenomena of historical and contemporary religious life comes to depend on the ongoing and reciprocal critique of the diverse motives and methods of academic enquiry, won't this necessarily end in a situation of continual irresolution, with each cancelling the other out or, at best, drawing attention to the limits of each other's approach and findings in such a way as to spread a cloud of uncertainty across the whole field? Won't it only succeed in telling us what we don't know rather than what we do know about religion, about our own final destiny and about God? Is it really necessary to impose such antiseptic but devitalizing constraints upon the study of religion, upon philosophizing and upon ourselves? Don't the issues at stake in religion call for more than this, one way or the other?

Certainly the human mind seems reluctant to stop with the negative, the critical, the purely hypothetical. The radical irony of Socratic questioning was rapidly succeeded by the visionary doctrines of Plato, and maybe even Socrates himself had motives and beliefs that went beyond what critical dialogue could establish. Beyond Plato, Aristotle transformed philosophy yet further into a programme for the setting-forth and explaining of the truth of things across the whole domain of theory and practice.

In the modern period, the story has been the same. Descartes' programme of systematic doubt led him to establish, as he thought, the existence of mind, of the objective world and of God as the ground and guarantor of both, putting in place firm principles for the further pursuance of science. Hegel declared in the Preface to the *Phenomenology* that he would proceed more radically than Descartes, pushing beyond doubt (*Zweifel*) to despair (*Verzweifelung*) as the ultimate intensification of doubt, looking at the utter disintegration, dismemberment and negation of meaning in, e.g. the death of God on the cross – but then, somehow, the way of negation itself becomes the foundation for a new, totalizing systematic view of the whole, and, as such, the revelation of truth. However, since Marx and Kierkegaard, from quite diverse standpoints, ridiculed both the ambition and the achievement of the Hegelian system, it seems that each philosophical generation has sought to outbid its predecessor in the thoroughness of its negativity, in its acknowledgement of difference, in its advocacy of otherness, and in its recognition of the impossibility of closure. Each one-time radical must ritually submit to the critical scrutiny that, like any well-conducted interrogation, will sooner or later unearth some residue of guilty dogmatism.

But is it really an intellectual crime to seek out sure and certain foundations for knowledge? Surely science, law and even art require us to believe in some kind of basis or some kind of standard in the light of which we can say 'This is truer than that' or 'That is preferable to this'? An anarchic free-for-all may seem desirable from the experiential standpoint of a summer of love or an explosion of angry insurgency, but don't the long-term achievements of science, the long-term needs of society and the permanence of great, canonical art point in another direction? The critical voice may be necessary as (in Kierkegaard's phrase) 'a corrective', to stop us all from getting too boring, or as a Socratic means to push or pull us towards more exact definition, but doesn't it become empty and trivial if we absolutize the negative itself? The Hegelian system may, as a particular instance of philosophical construction, have been over-ambitious, but does it follow that all construction, all foundationalism is equally to be condemned?

Perhaps we have already taken a step towards a more positive and more constructive view in what was said in the previous chapter about hermeneutics. For if the critical task is itself dependent on an understanding of the meaning of that which is to be subjected to criticism, doesn't that of itself suggest that there is a positive supplement to any possible labour of the negative? Isn't the horizon of criticism itself predetermined by a field of meaningful discourse?[4] Nor do we have to imagine this as congealing into an impermeable and indivisible dogmatism, since, if we allow for a continuing and creative interplay between meaning and criticism, then meaning itself will allow for and welcome the critical voice. Seen in this light, even the Hegelian system itself can be understood as a hermeneutic construct, as a synthesizing of all possible fields within which or in relation to which both meaning and criticism can freely operate. Far from imposing closure, such system-building is permissive, freeing up manifold possibilities of discourse – as, one might say, the Hegelian system itself can be shown, historically, to have done (even if many of the discourses facilitated by Hegel have been overtly anti-Hegelian: such is filial gratitude in the world of ideas!).

Let us put it like this. Philosophical questioning cannot of itself endorse or establish the foundations of any particular world-view. Yet the business of living in the world pragmatically requires the support of some more or less clearly delineated, more or less explicit world-view. For if we understand world-view here to mean the coherent synthesis of a maximum number of theoretical and practical commitments across the whole range of human experience and activity, then the demand for a world-view simply reflects the everyday assumption that we exist and act in a consistent and self-consistent manner.[5] It is the philosophical articulation of the principle enunciated in E. M. Forster's injunction: 'Only connect!' The assumption that this is a requirement we need to take seriously is, like all assumptions, questionable. It cannot of itself guarantee that the world *is* a unitary whole or that we ourselves have a continuous identity through time. Nevertheless, it would seem that if we do not make some such assumption, however provisionally, then the very possibility of meaningful discourse is discarded since it would become possible to say anything about anything at any time and in any sequence or connection. Minimally, it would seem that a life (which would not, of course, be 'a' life at all) exemplifying such intellectual Dadaism would be incapable of recognizing or responding to any significant claim made upon it by others, or even of recognizing any obligation of consistency in the language it used.[6]

If, then, we reject epistemological anarchism as a life-option, we owe it to ourselves and to those with whom we participate in a common discourse to show, or to be able to show if called upon to do so, the assumptions that guide us. The attempt to be clear about this will, probably, expose contradictions between our guiding assumptions, or demonstrate that they do not relate to our judgments about life in the way we had supposed. I may, for example, operate in my daily life with a maxim such as 'Everyone should stand on their own two feet' but also from time to time avail myself of the conflicting maxim 'We ought to help each other out when called upon to do so'. These seem, at first, to be contradictory, and if I am to harmonize my life-view I may have to change one or other of them, taking into account which most closely reflects my ethical practice. Or they may turn out to be reconcilable in the sense that the one holds good for a certain range of activities whilst the other is brought on line only in certain cases. I may thus turn out to have a more coherent moral outlook than my random comments on life suggest. Nevertheless, even prior to such self-examination, there may well be many areas of our lives where we are not consciously guided by a consistent set of social, personal or intellectual values or principles, but where, once we think about it, we can see that some kind of all-round view of life is in play. I may not immediately connect the way in which I behave in the milieu of my family with the kind of decisions I make in the context of my career or with the judgments I arrive at on literary texts, but unless I am a multiple personality, all such areas of my life are likely to bear a common imprint, and to be guided by a common set of values, principles and aims. This, as I have said, is likely to be pre-reflective. It is also likely to be flawed. Literature, public life and private experience are rich in examples of those who contradict in one part of their lives what they proclaim or practise in another: the politician who proclaims family values whilst practising serial adultery, the comedian driven by suicidal demons, the artist who portrays a beauty he cannot attain, etc. Some such cases we regard as hypocritical, others as pitiable, and, in many, we see something of ourselves, or would if we only cared to look. Reflection on our own assumptions, then, is not only a matter of bringing to the surface the actual view of life that guides us in the manifold dimensions of living. It is also an aid to self-assessment and, beyond that, self-correction, as we seek to bring our inconsistencies, our hypocrisy or our self-contradiction, into a larger unity.[7]

Philosophy, in its constructive aspect, has long been associated with the task of promoting some such personal view of life or world-view. But it may be objected that whereas this is indeed a legitimate and a pragmatically beneficial exercise for the individual, it falls far short of deciding whether such a world-view can hold for society as a whole. Since the break up of the unitary society of the pre-modern period at least, we have been plunged in a situation of inescapable epistemological, speculative, social and moral pluralism. In this situation it may still be possible and even obligatory for each of us to attain maximum self-awareness and to be as consistent and as truthful as may be in our dealings with one another, but none of us can raise our personal view of life to be a standard for the whole. I owe it to you to tell you what guides my life, to bear witness to what I hold to be most true, most important to me, and you owe me a reciprocal obligation. At the same time it is precisely a condition of such exchange that each of us accept the rubric 'This is how it seems to me'. 'Here I stand, I can do no other' in this context, represents the only remaining justification for intellectual, moral or religious decisiveness and testimony, and though we can do our best to explain to each other why it should be so, we all know that the very finality of such declarations can never be made entirely transparent, and that that is partly why they carry such force.

We seem, then, to be back not only to the view that, in relation to public discourse, the best that philosophical reflection can achieve is to level the playing field for the diversity of human discourses and to enable these discourses to engage, dialogically, in a process of mutual critique and limitation. Within these discourses we may find the stories that individuals tell about themselves, their beliefs, their aspirations, their hopes and fears, in short, their views of life, their 'philosophies', but these will never be able to claim decisiveness for others' construction of their own, differing views of life.

But are we accepting too easily a kind of distinction between private and public discourse? Isn't the picture actually more compli-cated than that? And isn't that especially apparent in the case of religion? Indeed, might we not say that one of the pre-eminent sites of religious discourse in the modern world is on the boundary between private and public discourse, where the individual seeks orientation in relation to the larger social body, or where the inner discourse of family or tribe encounters the universalizing discourse of a globalized humanity? For in setting out their view of life in religious terms, human beings are necessarily saying that that view of life is more than individual, or that, precisely as an individual understanding of life, it is embedded in a larger, social and transhistorical tradition: that I am certain as to what it is good for me to be, to do or to hope for, because this is how I have been instructed by the community of faith. And it may be that no individual view of life is ever entirely invented, but depends in some manner and some measure on a broader, common story. The task of the philosophy of religion, then, is not merely to bring about a dialogue between individuals, swapping stories and views of life, but to operate on the level of views that claim a certain publicity and a certain historical durability, views that claim to express or to project a 'world'. If these views cannot necessarily compel universal assent, they must at the very least make some kind of sense in relation to the public discourse of the society in which they are put forward.

It would go against the grain of everything I have been urging with regard to the nature of philosophical enquiry to suggest that the philosophy of religion might finally be able to declare one or other religion to be the true philosophical faith, a world-view to which all right-thinking people should subscribe. And yet it does not follow from this that philosophy is dogmatically hostile to the formation of such world-views, any more than it is hostile to individuals developing their private philosophies of life. If philosophy will necessarily maintain a certain reserve in relation to any particular world-view it will at the same time require that religion be understood and evaluated precisely in its fullest dimensions, intellectually as worldview and practically as the embodiment of that world-view in the whole life of the religious community and of each individual within that community. In other words, part of the process of drawing out the assumptions of religious discourse will be to show the discourse of a particular religion in the full extent of its interconnectedness. When we look to understand a particular doctrine (say, the doctrine of divine omniscience) or practice (say, the phenomenon of sacrifice), we do not do so by reducing the object of our investigation to an ever more precise formulation, as if we might that way discover the atomic building blocks of religious discourse. Or, not only that. We also look to see the place, the function and the meaning of the doctrine or practice in relation to the whole, as far as we are able to do so.

If the philosopher of religion wants in this way to see the fullest possible picture of religion before, or as a condition of, or as one outcome of the critical questioning of the phenomenon of religion, this still (to say it again) falls short of endorsing any particular religion. Nevertheless, it may still be a result, or provisional result, of the process of philosophical enquiry that some religious world-views come to appear more deserving than others of serious intellectual and moral attention; that out of the sifting and discrimination of question and counter-question a number of specific religious world-views emerge as possible vehicles for the articulation and nurturing of individual life-views in the contemporary world. The philosopher is unlikely to end up saying 'This religion is true', but may well say of several religions that 'These religions provide for the possibility of living a religious life that is not in contradiction to the best attainable understanding of life open to contemporary humanity'. Or, to use a Kantian formulation, the philosopher might judge that, articulated in the form of a concrete religious world-view, such-and-such a religion proves itself to be a 'religion of reason'. Part of the evidence for such a (provisional) conclusion would, clearly, be whether the religious world-view itself was willing to accept the invitation to enter the space of philosophical interrogation. However, recalling everything said in earlier chapters about the dialogical nature of philosophy and about the hermeneutical situation in which our own contemporary horizon is itself one aspect of what interpretative enquiry exposes to questioning, it should be emphasized that philosophy and reason are not being understood (as another Kantian formulation hints) as some kind of intellectual magistrate empowered to adjudicate on what is or isn't reasonable in any particular case. Rather, what counts as reasonable is itself only decidable in and through the questioning process.

Historically, something like this has repeatedly been the case, with philosophy acting as a kind of culture or medium within which religious doctrines and theologies can acquire their specific shape. Thus, the philosophies of the ancient world – and pre-eminently Platonism – provided a milieu within which pagan, Jewish and Christian beliefs were able to take a shape and form that commended them to seekers and practitioners. Similarly the rediscovery of Aristotle in the Middle Ages provided an intellectual space in which Jewish, Muslim and Christian theologians could raise their confessional debates to the level at which some of the decisive issues between them could first come into view. Since the Enlightenment various views of history or of natural science have provided analogous media in which the religions – or different movements within the religions – have been able to show the kind of meaning or the kind of truth they believe themselves to offer. Most recently of all, the advent of postmodernism has likewise provided a common site for the continuing debate between liberals and conservatives within Christian theology, and the quasi-Nietzscheanism of a Don Cupitt and the quasi-Neothomism of radical orthodoxy have staked out a quarrel precisely on the basis of the possibilities projected by radical phenomenology and poststructuralism. And doubtless the passing of postmodernity will see analogous developments.[8]

Philosophy and salvation

Despite the initial anxiety and disorientation it is likely to occasion, philosophy, then, can be understood as having a positive role, both as giving overall shape and direction to the field in question (in this case the study of religion) and as the permissive setting out of a critically tempered horizon within which world-views can be developed and articulated as part of the context that enables individuals to form their own life-views within the process of forming and sustaining their personal sense of identity and value.

Nevertheless, even these 'positive' developments of the philosophy of religion may still sound somewhat over-intellectualistic, somewhat 'academic'. I have heard a leading teacher of philosophical theology assert that most theology is done in the context of academic teaching. If this were true, I would find it highly depressing. Theology, at least, should have deep roots in human beings' actual attempts at living the religious life, their searching for salvation, their efforts of praise. It would, of course, take a whole new book to argue through this understanding of theology, and it would be necessary to take account of the many alternative views of the subject in play. Nevertheless, somewhat rashly – unphilosophically, even – assuming that there is or should be such an existential dimension to theology, can we say something similar of philosophy, especially, in this case, of philosophy of religion? Even if it is only at one remove, may there not be something of the soteriological motivation of theology operative in the philosophy of religion also? If so, then the 'positivity' of such philosophizing would not simply consist in what might almost appear as quasi-accidental outcomes of critical practice and, in any case, as 'merely' academic, but would relate to the most powerfully personal strivings of the living philosopher.

Let us put it another way: if it is of the essence of the critical task of philosophy to bring to light the hidden presuppositions of any given discourse, and if seeking salvation is the lifeblood of the religious life such that that life itself presupposes at every turn that the desire for salvation is integral to our being human, then the philosophy of religion too must concern itself with that desire. But what if that desire is itself something that resists objectifying clarification, if it is something that must be experienced and lived if it is even to be recognized for what it is? What if the core element of religion requires that those who would understand it must, in some sense, participate in it?

These questions could be taken as pointing towards the kind of defensive strategy that religionists have often adopted in the face of philosophical criticisms, appealing to a purported cognitive privilege on the part of believers, and refusing to concede to 'outsiders' the kind of access to religious truth that would enable them to pass judgment on it. This has been the strategy both of those who have looked to religious experience as grounding belief, and of those who have taken a more linguistic approach, arguing that only participants in the religious language-game (of which the religious form of life is the necessary context) can understand what it's all about. Only the regenerate mind, it has been said, can understand theology. But this present essay began by calling into question the kind of insider/outside duality that is often taken for granted in discussions of the relationship between faith and philosophy. My present point, then, is not to put a fence about religious truth, but to raise a question about the philosopher's own assumptions. For maybe the search for salvation is not, after all, alien to philosophy itself.

Although I have repeatedly emphasized the critical, subversive function of philosophy, there are many historical precedents for understanding philosophy itself as the love of or quest for wisdom, and, as such (as exemplified in texts such as Plato's *Phaedo* or *Banquet* and Plotinus' *Enneads*), as engaged in a search for salvation. In the nineteenth century the German historian of ideas, F. C. Baur, argued that the 'main idea and final goal that inspired Platonic philosophy' was itself 'salvation' (*Heil*) and that Socrates himself was not merely portrayed by Plato as a midwife, drawing others' thoughts to birth, but as 'a divine nature in human form, an image of the divine, whose outer form, like a noble container, enclosed a divine content.'[9] This is, of course, contestable, but Baur is well supported by the kind of praise attributed to Socrates by Alcibiades at the end of the *Symposium*:

> . . . if anyone will listen to the talk of Socrates, it will appear to him at first extremely ridiculous; the phrases and expressions which he

employs, fold around his exterior the skin, as it were, of a rude and wanton Satyr. He is always talking about great market-asses, and brass-founders, and leather-cutters, and skin-dressers; and this is his perpetual custom, so that any dull and unobservant person might easily laugh at his discourse. But if anyone should see it opened, as it were, and get within the sense of his words, he would then find that they alone of all that enters into the mind of man to utter, had a profound and persuasive meaning, and that they were most divine; and that they presented to the mind innumerable images of every excellence, and that they tended towards objects of the highest moment, or rather towards all that he who seeks the possession of what is supremely beautiful and good need regard as essential to the accomplishment of his ambition.[10]

The practice of critical irony is not for nothing, but for a more perfect fulfilment by human beings of their divine potential – an understanding of the Socratic task that Plato most dramatically sets out in the *Phaedo*, where even if the hope of eternal blessedness is never decisively justified at the level of argument it is nevertheless held out as 'fitting to be believed, and worthy the hazard for one who trusts in its reality; for the hazard is noble, and it is right to allure ourselves with such things as with enchantments . . .'[11]

The many philosophies of the ancient world were not simply forms of primitive science but were also forms of therapy, quests for a better way of living in the world or even for redemption from it. When the early apologists, beginning perhaps with Paul on the Areopagus, sought to expound Christian thought in terms readily comprehensible by their pagan interlocutors, they were responding to a recognition by many that Christianity too was, in these terms, a kind of philosophy. Later, Augustine could agree with his pagan opponents, that all were alike in seeking 'a blessed life', the *beata vita* aimed at by pagan philosophers and Christian believers alike.

More recently, philosophies such as existentialism have also sought to root philosophy in the context of humanity's lived needs and anxieties. Although many of the existentialist philosophers themselves judged that humanity's longing for deliverance from its onto-logical self-contradiction was incurable, others, such as Gabriel Marcel, did see the desire for a greater fullness of being as itself a response to a profound, pre-reflective revelation of Being. Against Sartre, Marcel argued that hope and not despair was the best founda-tion for philosophy. Even after his existentialist period, Heidegger too was prepared to speak about the 'need' and 'destitution' of human beings in an epoch in which technology had overrun the planet, reducing to the flatness of one dimension the possibilities for encountering and attending to the call of Being. That this situation was at one and the same time the impulse to the renewal of philosophy (provoked by the recognition that, as the wasteland grows around us, 'we are not yet thinking') and a search for salvation was indicated by his famous comment in an interview with the journal *Der Spiegel* that 'Only a god can save us'.

For pagans and Christians alike the quest for salvation early on became linked to the quest for an all-inclusive explanatory view of the world. Although philosophers and believers have since then argued as to the respective roles of reason and revelation in establishing this view of the world, their arguments have often been about means, not ends. Both have agreed that what is desirable is a total explanation. However, it is just this that Heidegger's critique of metaphysics calls into question. For Heidegger the demand for such an explanation is of itself indicative of the hegemony of technological thinking. The path of thinking opened up by his later thought takes a very different form. It is not so much an attempt at an explanation, but an attempt to reorientate thought towards another kind of thinking, closer to poetry, but no less precise for that. As such it is offered as a countermovement to what Heidegger called 'planetary homelessness', the ever-increasing rootlessness, fragmentation and estrangement of human consciousness, cut off from what Heidegger allusively called the fourfold of earth, sky, death and the gods.

Whether, finally, Heidegger's later work can be related to the religious quest for salvation and, if so, how, are difficult and, in the present context, distracting questions. Nevertheless his decisiveness in moving philosophy away from the search for explanations and the justification of all-inclusive world-views opens other, interesting possibilities for future conversations between philosophy and religion. Not accidental in this respect is his concern to revisit the Pre-Socratic thinkers in order to uncover ways of thinking that were suppressed when philosophy was taken over by logic and science. Although Heidegger himself does not comment on this, it interestingly moves the philosophical task into a certain proximity to elements of biblical teaching about wisdom. Biblical wisdom is precisely not about knowing everything but about knowing the limits of our knowledge, and this is offered by the wisdom writers as the necessary condition of a right relation to God. Not knowledge of God but fear of God is the beginning of wisdom. In this perspective, then, the critical concern of the philosophy of religion harmonizes with the philosophical and religious quest for saving wisdom. The question is not 'what is the nature of things?' but 'what is best for human beings to believe?'[12] Or (with an eye on both the turn to the subject and the linguistic turn) 'how should we best speak in order to help bring about the best life?'

Salvation, these words imply, is not, or need not (perhaps must not), be understood exclusively in terms of deliverance from the world. It may also concern how it is best for us to live in the world and, consequently, cannot be understood other than in connection with the ethical – a further frontier for the philosophy of religion, where we must engage with the paradox that whilst all philosophy is fundamentally ethical insofar as it is guided by a concern for the best possible way for us to live, the practice of ethics must itself lie outside philosophy.

In its struggle to decide and to say how it is best for us to be, philosophy too, out of its own concerns, will be moved to reflect on what might make possible the transition from the life we now lead to that better life. To assume, as theologians usually do, that philosophy must always issue in a programme of self-help, whether on the basis of optimistic rationalism or of existential resolution, is, maybe, already to assume too much. Perhaps philosophy too can arrive in its own way at the thought that 'Only a god can save us', and that some analogue of what believers call grace must complement or contextualize philosophical questioning concerning the view of life that best opens to us the prospect of good living; that, consequently, we owe an impulse of gratitude, of reverence, or minimally, of respect to that which gives us the possibility of living the best life and, indeed, the possibility of being able to direct our thoughts to such questions in the first place.[13] Whether that from which help comes is what religion has named as 'God', remains, of course, a question, *the* question. But, in posing it, can we even assume that we already understand what 'God' means? And if, in the midst of all the talk about and against God, the divine remains unknown, it also remains a question as to whether that unknowability is, in the end, an epistemological issue at all or a problem of a different kind. In the closing verse of his poem 'Homecoming', Hölderlin – writing with a poet's sense of the limitations of language – asked 'How shall I offer thanks? Should I name the Exalted One then? A God does not like what's unseemly; to grasp him, our joy is almost too small. Often we must be silent; there is a lack of holy names . . .'[14] If the question as to rightly naming what gives us the possibility of being all we could be is a question to which such factors as 'too small joy' are crucially relevant, then the issue between religion and philosophy is going to look very different from when it is conceived purely as a relation of belief and knowledge.

Beyond the question of knowledge are poetry, madness, love – but if these are not and cannot be knowledge, they may yet be best of all. The question of meaning presupposes at every step the revelation of that to which such words allude (we might call it 'the aesthetic dimension'), as, at the same time, it turns towards the ethical task of living in the light of what matters most and doing so self-critically and understandingly.

Theodicy

Up until this point the emphasis of this short course has largely been on general questions concerning the nature and scope of the philosophy of religion. Now, however, we change direction, and attempt to see how the kind of approach developed in the preceding chapters might look in the detailed working out of a particular substantive issue. The issue I have chosen is what has been called 'the problem of evil'. It is, of course, not a matter of simply applying a formal method to a designated subject matter since the dialogical and hermeneutical conception of the subject that has been advanced here sees every process of questioning as inseparable from the unique configuration of the subject matter being addressed. In other words, how we understand the question will itself interact with the kind of approach we bring to bear on it, as well as on the kind of impact we allow it to have upon us.

The choice of this question is by no means random, for, situating ourselves within the modern experience of religion and the modern conceptualization of the philosophy of religion, it could well be said that in the modern period perhaps no other question has been so existentially urgent in the experience of the believer or so prominent in the argument about the meaning of religion. This has been a point at which the spirits divide, not only with regard to the decision for or against belief, but also concerning what is to be looked for from religious doctrine and philosophical argument in relation to religion. Unsurprisingly, there have been many hints already as to how the topics discussed in previous chapters (the rise of the historical consciousness, the turn to the subject, the linguistic turn and the tussle between reductionism and hermeneutics) are all, in complex ways, interwoven with the characteristically modern reworking of this fundamental question. I shall, shortly, return to this point, but it will prove useful firstly to recap on the basic terms and forms of the question, because although it is a question that has been so central to the modern philosophy of religion it is by no means an exclusively modern question. The complaint of suffering human beings against the bitterness of their fate, however articulated, is attested in the earliest strata of the written record, and it is a likely speculation that preliterate societies too had and have their ways of formulating it and of seeking, somehow, to explain it.

As far as the theistic tradition is concerned, the question was given its most succinct and definitive expression in Hume's reworking of Epicurus' questions: 'Is he [God] willing to prevent evil, but not able? Then is he impotent. Is he able but not willing? Then he is malevolent. Is he both able and willing? Whence then is evil?'[1] This, in essence, is the 'problem' of evil, which, whether in its ancient or its modern guise, can seemingly only be resolved by eliminating one of the three terms (God's almightiness, God's benevolence or the fact of evil itself), or by redefining one of them in such a way as to allow for an accommodation of some sort with the other two.

Within Platonic thought, for example, the apparent 'fact' of evil is disarmed by defining evil itself in terms of non-being, an argument taken up into Christianity by, amongst others, Augustine. On this view evil is not a reality in itself but a restriction, a diminishment, a privation of some good. Perverted or violent sex is not a positive phenomenon in itself, but a misdirected attempt to find love. Because of that residual orientation towards love, however, it is also, in some measure, a 'good', no matter how limited or reduced. Integral to this argument is that whatever is, whatever has a share in Being, is, to the degree that it *is* or *exists* in the strong sense, good. Thus, according to Plato's account of creation in the *Timaeus*, the best world is one in which the greatest possible number of beings exist in such a way as to fill up every possible permutation and degree of being. This is how Plato puts it:

Let us then state for what reason becoming and the universe were framed by their constructor. He was good; and in the good no jealousy in respect of anything ever arises. Being devoid of jealousy, therefore, he desired that all things should approach as near as possible to being like himself.[2]

However, the Platonic creator does not act with the total freedom of the Creator in Christian doctrine, but works with pre-existent chaotic matter, giving it form, order and measure and in this sense bringing it into being. The state of the universe then is a synthesis of, on the one hand, the formative impulse of the creator and, on the other, the resistance of the material upon which that impulse is directed: it is, in other words, a mixture of Being and non-being, which, apart from the two poles of absolute Being and absolute non-being, means that every actual being exists as having a greater or a lesser share in Being – and the greater the share in Being, the closer the resemblance to the creator and to the Good. Moreover, bearing in mind the originary generosity of the creator to have as many beings as possible resembling himself, this means that he will also will into being even those creatures that have only the remotest resemblance to himself, only the most residual share in Being, since this is, after all, still a kind of resemblance, a kind of approximation to Being, however imperfect.

In the Platonic scheme the creator has no choice: if there is to be a world at all in which his Being and goodness are shared as widely as possible, then he can bring it into being only as a synthesis of the greatest possible manifold of polarities, of which those between Being and non-being, good and evil, are the pre-eminent and determinative examples. This element of necessity is acknowledged by such Platonists as Plotinus, who asks whether 'the All necessarily comports the existence of matter?' and answers 'Yes: for necessarily this All is made up of contraries; it could not exist if matter did not'.[3] Non-being – evil – is therefore a necessary condition of the existence of the universe as a whole but the good that is constituted by there being just such a universe is greater than the good of the solitary existence of 'the untroubled, the blissful life of divine beings'.[4]

Augustine and other Platonizing Christian theologians rework the same essential point in such a way as to allow for a less restricted view of the divine freedom in creating.

God, writes Augustine,

is existence in a supreme degree – he supremely *is* – and he is therefore immutable. Hence he gave existence to the creatures he made out of nothing; but it was not his own supreme existence. To some he gave existence in a higher degree, to some in a lower, and thus he arranged a scale of existences of various natures . . . Thus to this highest existence, from which all things that are derive their existence the only contrary nature is the non-existent. Non-existence is obviously contrary to the existent. It follows that no existence is contrary to God, that is to the supreme existence and the author of all existence whatsoever.[5]

Whatever is, therefore, is by virtue of the mere fact that it 'is' at all is in accord with God's creative intention.

As for those defects, in things of this earth, which are neither voluntary nor punishable; if we observe them closely we shall find that, on the same principle as before, they attest the goodness of the natures themselves, every one of which has God as its sole author and creator . . . Therefore it is the nature of things considered in itself, without regard to our convenience or inconvenience, that gives glory to the Creator . . . And so all nature's substances are good, because they exist and therefore have their own mode and kind of Being, and, in their fashion, a peace and harmony among themselves . . . [Even] the process of destruction, which results in the disappearance of mutable and mortal natures, brings what existed to non-existence in such a way as to allow the consequent production of what is destined to come into being.[6]

This is the essence of what John Hick has called the aesthetic theme within Augustinian theodicy,[7] which he criticizes for its detachment from the reality of our actual human experiences of suffering and other evils. It is a theme that was also, famously, to re-emerge in the great eighteenth-century debates concerning theodicy, as in Voltaire's satirical refutation of Leibnizian and Popean optimism in *Candide*, where the eponymous hero's encounter with just about every conceivable form of evil, natural and moral, casts the claim that all is for the best in the best of all possible worlds into a virtually ridiculous light.

But the argument in favour of the necessity of lesser evils for the sake of a greater good is not the only outcome of applying the definition of evil as non-being. According to Augustine this definition suggests a further thought: that we simply cannot explain evil, since what is not, what has no existence, offers no point of contact for the understanding. It is, ultimately, simply inexplicable. 'No one therefore,' Augustine remarks, 'must try to get to know from me what I know that I do not know, unless, it may be, in order to learn not to know what must be known to be incapable of being known!'[8] In evil reason encounters a limit that, though opposite to the limit it encounters in respect of God (the limit that is the focus of negative theology), has a kind of inverted mirror-image relation to it.

Platonism was, obviously, only one source of Augustine's and other ancient theologians' thinking about this question. More important (in principle, at least) was Scripture, and the story of the Fall (and its remedy) found there – although, as we have seen, theologians such as Athanasius could interpret the Fall story in thoroughly Platonic terms that most modern scholars of the Hebrew Bible would regard as involving an utter distortion of the text.

For the new world religion of Christianity the whole question involved a twofold innovation concerning the role of freedom. On the one hand, the sovereign freedom of God in bringing the world as a whole into existence was asserted as never before. Creation was not the ordering of a primal chaos (although the Genesis text itself might well suggest just that), but creation out of nothing (*ex nihilo*) in such a way that nothing could impede, distort or thwart God's exercise of his creative powers. The presence of evil in the universe could not be a necessary condition of there being a universe at all, since that would imply an unacceptable constraint upon divine almightiness. But if talking up God's freedom in this way thus compounded the problem of evil, Christian doctrine compensated with a no less marked talking up of the role of human freedom. Here was the source and origin of evil in the universe, namely, 'our first disobedience' – a matter not of ontology but will. The evil we suffer is the punishment that fits the evil of the crime of our disobedient will. Ambitiously this explanation embraced not only the evils that human beings inflict upon each other but what would come to be called natural evils such as the sufferings of animals or the sufferings that befall us as a result of natural processes (earthquakes, diseases and all manner of accidents). Whatever disorder there is in the cosmos is the product of our Fall, the story now ran. Above all this included our own death, now seen not as an ineluctable part of our finite, creaturely condition (as, e.g. in both Homer and the Hebrew Bible), but as the punishment for sin.

It would be a mistake to imply that there is simply 'a' Christian view of the question of evil. In all periods of its history Christianity has conducted a vigorous internal debate as to the scope and detailed implications of the broad picture. Questions that have recurred again and again include those that reflect both the general issues arising for any form of theism as well as those rooted in the particular interpretation of the biblical evidence. Such issues include the extent and nature of human freedom prior to the Fall, as well as the implications for the goodness of God's creative action of his having brought into existence a world in which so privileged a place would be given to creatures capable of working such havoc. Did God have complete foreknowledge of the Fall? If so did he in some way predestine Adam and Eve to err? How complete was the Fall? Did it bring about the complete obliteration of the image of God in human beings to such a degree that, while free prior to the Fall, we have now lost all power of ourselves to help ourselves? Or do we retain a residual rationality and freedom sufficient to understand our predicament and to seek liberation from it (even if we may not be able to accomplish such liberation without the additional help of divine aid)? Generally, the former of these positions is characteristic of Protestantism (and certainly for Luther and Calvin themselves the human predicament is so desperate that we have virtually no say in the matter of our own salvation: *all* is of grace, hidden in the inscrutable mystery of divine election), whilst the latter represents a Catholic view (shared with liberal Protestantism) – but, of course, in each case with many gradations and variations. Questions further extend to how it is that subsequent generations too are implicated in the Fall, and whether God acts justly in sentencing the whole human race to death for the crime of one or two individuals, as well as to the nature and justice of the mechanism of God's subsequent scheme of salvation. Debates have raged as to whether the Incarnation would have happened anyway as part of God's original plan for consummating his fellowship with the human race, or whether it was his response, as it were, to the situation brought about by human mismanagement of the cosmos. An important underlying theme in both Jewish and Christian accounts is the weight that the biblical story places not only upon human action in general but also upon the historical responsibility of Israel and/or the church and the setting of the story of creation and Fall in a narrative that hinges upon the triumphant consummation of history and the eschatological fulfilment of all God's purposes.

If Christianity opened up a whole new dimension in the discussion of evil, it is no less true that pre-Christian perspectives continued to affect the discussion. The introduction of the themes of freedom and history did not of themselves alter the basic impulse of theodicy: to argue that, seen as a whole, the existence of the world as it is, with all its imperfection, is part of a greater good than any alternative. It is better, it is said, to have a universe in which free, self-conscious and rational beings exist, even if they abuse or lose those defining characteristics, than one in which no such beings ever emerged. The good of the creature's freely chosen fellowship with God is a good so great that nothing can weigh in the balance against it. Even if the event of human sin is seen as opposed to God's original plan for creation, it is argued that God's way of responding to this is to bring about a still greater good than would have existed without it – what Hick calls the '*O felix culpa*' theme in theodicy, drawing on a Latin liturgical antiphon translatable as 'O happy fault, that merited such and so great a redemption'.[9] And even if, as has increasingly been the case since the scientific revolution, it is acknowledged that the existence of a physical universe is inseparable from a law-bound complex of physical processes that must inevitably lead to inconvenience and pain for animate beings such as ourselves (and, probably, other animals), this too is seen as inseparable from the greater good. Such inconvenience and pain do not constrain God's creativity (as chaotic matter constrained the Platonic world-maker), but were foreseen and willed by God for the sake of his final purposes. As Leibniz bravely argued – although his argument is best known in the form of its caricature in *Candide* – this is the best of all possible worlds, and the apparent inflexibility of the laws of nature, extending to the pre-determination of our own actions and mental processes, is simultaneously the external expression of a still more fundamental order of freedom. It is in this order of freedom that we may speak of the origin and direction of the world as the product of divine goodness and of its end as involving the reward of human virtue.

Whilst some of these questions and issues (such as the details of the various theories of atonement) are of an almost exclusively theological interest, others, however, are also of interest to philosophy. Indeed, one might say that a philosophy that has no interest in or ability to deal with what is called evil is itself going to be of little service to human beings inhabiting a world in which it comes so easily to speak of evil, and to help them think their way through to the best possible self-understanding. Especially, the centuries of debate have played a crucial role in developing the whole Western discourse about the nature and functioning of freedom, and the possibility of radical freedom in a world governed by a seamless web of natural (if also, as theists argue, divinely ordained) laws. However, it is not my intention here to go into the detail of the debates about, e.g. the relationship between divine foreknowledge and human freedom, but, whilst acknowledging that many of the traditional questions of theodicy continue to be the focus of extensive discussion, to see how the modern situation has at many points transformed the context of discussion and how, looked at philosophically, this requires us to reflect on just what it is that is being looked for in any attempt to justify belief in the face of evil.

In previous chapters I have identified the rise of the historical consciousness, the turn to the subject, and the linguistic turn as defining features of the modern philosophy of religion, along with the challenge of reductionism and the summons to hermeneutical reflection. Let us now see, then, how the question of theodicy is transformed as it is filtered through these movements in the history of ideas.

I have already indicated here that, as with the rise of historical consciousness in general, the biblical story of creation, Fall and redemption played a crucial long-term role in stimulating the historicizing of the question of evil. Throughout the Christian era in the

West, the question of evil still often started out as (or took the form of) a question about the essence or nature of evil. At the same time the fact that the biblical and doctrinal 'explanation' of evil took the form of a historical narrative centred on the free actions of human persons meant that a purely metaphysical account of evil was progressively moved into the background. Evil was primarily to be understood within the horizon not of Being but of history. This also points immediately to the closely-associated turn to the subject, and the reciprocal roles of the human subject in determining the character and consequences of evil and of evil in revealing the distinctive historical being of humankind. Evil and history are intertwined in such a way that it is precisely as beings that 'have a history' (a phrase that still has a negative moral ring to it) we are the beings that bring evil into the world, whilst, conversely, evil itself, as that which both marks our actions hitherto and as that in us which is to be overcome, is the constant lure to historical action. And if this seems, on the one hand, to be a distinctively modern perspective, it also, as Mircea Eliade pointed out, corresponds to archaic, pre-modern and traditional humanity's view of history as a sphere of terror and guilt, of exclusion from the eternally recurring world of ritually repeated archetypes.[10]

Before coming back to a closer investigation of the relationship between evil and subjectivity, however, it will be helpful to make a number of more general observations about the historicization of consciousness for the understanding of evil.

The first is that although the biblical narrative and its interpretation by the religious communities of Israel and the church did much to stimulate the rise of history there is an important sense in which history has retroactively undercut some of the basic assumptions of the Judaeo-Christian schema. Already by the eighteenth century a keener historical-critical sense was piling up problems for the traditional reading of the Genesis narrative, and the nineteenth century was to see the demolition of some of its basic premisses. This was especially the case when the very conception of human origins was itself historicized under the influence of Darwin. It was no longer possible to imagine the original state of human beings as having been that of the complete and utter perfection described in traditional doctrinal treatises. On the contrary, the first human beings were now seen to have evolved out of a preceding animal state. In comparison with them it was increasingly implausible to regard 'ourselves' as a fallen or degenerate brood. If anything our individual and collective state might seem to represent progress over that primitive state. At any rate, there was no paradise back there in the immemorial past, but only nature red in tooth and claw, a struggle for survival in which the process of hominization itself was inseparable not only from our ancestors' violent competition with other species, but also with their own intraspecific violence.[11] Not that it needed Darwin to make the fundamental point. Hegel was already able to assume a model of human history in which the Fall was understood as a breaking-away from a primal state of unity with nature and, as such, 'a successful climb'. Kierkegaard, for all his polemics against Hegel, poured similar scorn on the dogmatic tendency to elevate Adam to impossibly perfect heights as the original perfect man. Instead the emergence of consciousness was – though still, for Kierkegaard, a fall – a leap from ignorant innocence into freedom. Freedom, as he understood it, was not our state preceding the Fall, but coincided with it. If a certain nostalgia continued to imbue the urban animals of the nineteenth century, this was not a nostalgia for the perfections of the Adam of earlier Christian doctrine but for the womb of nature: a longing to renounce the terror and the challenge of history.

The eighteenth century already understood the general point regarding the need for universal physical laws as a necessary condition of there being a world at all and of human life in it, even though these same laws could, on occasion, restrict, frustrate or overthrow human aspirations. Hume's cool irony and Voltaire's outrage made clear the problems this raised for theodicists. Darwin, however, showed the extraordinary degree to which competition, struggle and violence permeated the basic mechanisms of animal and human evolution. The realm of animate beings was drenched in blood long before the first Cain laid violent hands upon his brother. Moreover, as the detail of the scientific picture of the world became filled in, it became ever harder to see how freedom could count as a significant cause in any chain of cosmic events. If history meant a domain in which human beings could indeed act and bring their intentions to fruition through conflict – as, for example (once more), in Hegel – this could only be because historical action was not seen as causative in the same sense as causes in the physical world (a distinction that became institutionalized in the modern period in the distinction between the natural and human sciences). Human actions, such as the disobedience of Adam and Eve, could no longer be plausibly represented as causally responsible for those laws of nature that made conflict, violence and death a necessary concomitant of all life-processes.

The modern experience of history also raised a very different kind of problem for theodicy, though whether this problem is all it seems is something we shall return to at a later point. This has to do with the sheer scale of cruelty, terror, misery and horror that humanity has brought upon itself in the modern period. The traumas of the slave trade, of industrialization and urbanization were rapidly followed by the nightmare of total mechanized warfare, marked by battles such as the Somme and Verdun in which literally millions of combatants perished, and by the destruction of civilian populations, most horrifically in the Holocaust and the bombing of Hiroshima and Nagasaki. For several generations the world lived with the ever-present fear of an all-out nuclear exchange that would very possibly end all civilized human life on earth and since that fear has receded international affairs have been dominated by a succession of genocidal wars marked by sickening cruelty, even if rarely on the scale of the blood-letting of 1914–45. The cumulative force of such events has been to put a serious question mark against any attempt to rewrite in historical terms the view that the dark side of life is a necessary but acceptable condition of a larger overall good. What happiness is worth such faults as these? What good, we ask, could possibly be justified by Auschwitz?

Certainly, if there is nothing beyond history, if, with Hegel, we adopt Schiller's line that 'World history is the Last Judgement' as meaning that the only possible justification for the evil experienced in history is in the outcome of the historical process itself, it would seem difficult to maintain a steady optimism. The fate of a historicist understanding of life devoid of any supra-historical dimension is powerfully, and tragically, demonstrated in the history of Marxism. Without entering too closely into the debate as to how far Marxism ever really was a scientific theory of history (as Marx and many Marxists claimed) or how far it was a resurgence on modern soil of the spirit of Hebrew prophecy (as religious apologists have often suggested), it is clear that, seen from a certain angle, Marxism as a phenomenon of the nineteenth and twentieth centuries appealed to a historicization of Jewish-Christian hopes for a Kingdom of God, in which the present sufferings of the proletariat would, in some sense, be overcome in the end-state of communism towards which history was inexorably moving. Overcome, but hardly redeemed. For Marxism offered little to those whose lives would come to an end before the advent of communism other than the opportunity of sharing in the historical task of bringing it to pass and the prospect of being remembered as a hero of the revolution. In the apocalyptic climate of much modern history, it is clear that, for many, this was a sufficient incentive and a large enough hope. For the citizens of communist states, however, it soon seemed like the endless sacrifice of the present generation for the sake of a nebulous future good whose arrival seemed to be being continually deferred as five-year plan after five-year plan failed to deliver the final victory of communism. The same catastrophic violence that made traditional theological responses to the question of evil also impacted upon the realizability of the Marxist hope. What signs did history really offer that things were getting better? The burden weighed particularly heavily on those who belonged to generations that had not themselves chosen this path of historical development. The uncertainty of the promised future coupled with the limitations of individual finitude and mortality thus conspired to drain Marxism of its power to provide a sustaining hope, outside the extraordinary atmosphere of moments of great historical convulsion. All of this was, of course, exacerbated for citizens of the Soviet Empire by experience of corruption, incompetence, deceit and terror, experiences that largely came to overshadow even the best efforts of sincere communists. However, it is likely that even without these accompaniments, the aspiration to do what one can to bring about a better future society will not be a final or adequate expression of the principle of hope. Even amongst the secular utopists there were those like the Russian N. Fedorev who saw 'raising the ancestors' as a necessary part of the utopistic project, so that they too could participate in the future utopia.[12] But this also means that the same essential criticism made of Marxism by religious believers will apply also to those versions of secular humanism that, without the specific Marxist conception of history, nevertheless look to the intra-historical self-fulfilment of the human community as the ultimate goal of free, rational activity and as the measure by which our actions should be judged and directed.

But if the historicization of thought undermined key aspects of the earlier Christian view, the historical element in that view itself facilitated a certain remapping of the question, turning it away from a theory of origins and towards a theory of historical action and the perfectibility, through history, of human (and, sometimes, cosmic) existence. Already in Kant the religious question had been formulated as 'What can I hope for?' In the twentieth century Ernst Bloch, though writing as an avowedly atheistic philosopher, posed the issue in terms that reflected a widespread shift in theology's own agenda. Taking the etymology of 'religion' as '*religio*' to imply a tying-back of humanity to its origins, and thus reflecting religion's function as a regressive power opposed to human progress, Bloch celebrated instead the 'principle of hope' that he found in the prophetic strand of the biblical witness and that could be seen there already in conflict with chthonic and cultic 'religion'. This 'principle of hope' was, in turn, reclaimed by such theologians as Tillich and Moltmann. In both Kant and Bloch, and, of course, to a much greater extent in more expressly believing thinkers, this hope is not exhausted in intra-historical tasks and outcomes but points, however enigmatically, towards some kind of supra-historical dimension that is indeed necessary if there is still to be talk of theodicy.

However, it is not at all obvious that the postulation of such a supra-historical realm can, of itself, avoid the objections brought against a purely secular justification of evil in the light of human progress. If the final good to be arrived at as the conclusion of history is understood purely supernaturally, i.e. as unconnected with the actual course of intra-historical processes, then the question of theodicy has not really been moved on at all, and the terms in which it is formulated will not engage with our thoroughly historicized self-understanding. Such an approach is characterized by a metaphysical detachment, an aesthetic lack of concern with the sheer actuality of lived historical experience. If, on the other hand, the evil perpetrated and suffered in the course of history is represented as somehow bound up with the fulfilment of God's purposes, as in some sense a necessary or essential aspect of such fulfilment, this, of itself, cannot escape the basic dilemma of classical theodicy, since it would seem that either God's goodness or his power are going to have to be surrendered or reinterpreted.

This is what many modern theodicies have done. The protest against God's almightiness (often in the name of the God of love) is already testified in radical Romanticism (as in William Blake) and, for all its theological unorthodoxy, at times became almost standard in twentieth-century theology. It was succinctly, if crudely, expressed by Geoffrey Studdert-Kennedy ('Woodbine Willy'), a well-known padre in the British Army in the First World War, in many of his popular writings, including the poem 'High and Lifted Up' which parodies the language of conventional hymnody and exposes its emptiness and absurdity in the face of the horrors of the Western Front. At the climax of the poem Studdert-Kennedy declared:

And I hate the God of Power on His hellish heavenly throne,
Looking down on rape and murder, hearing little children moan.
Though a million angels hail Thee King of Kings, yet cannot I.
There is nought can break the silence of my sorrow save the cry,

'Thou who rul'st this world of sinners with Thy heavy iron rod,
Was there ever any sinner who has sinned the sin of God? . . .
Praise to God in Heaven's highest and in all the depths be praise,
Who in all His works is brutal, like a beast in all His ways.'[13]

The sentiment could be Shelley's – but what is remarkable is that such an expression of rebellion against divine almightiness is now being articulated within Christianity as an expression of Christian faith itself. Studdert-Kennedy's alternative to worshipping the God of power is to focus on the suffering Christ, stripped of power, but all the more purely revealing the divinity of love: 'For the God of Heaven is not Power, but Power of Love', as 'High and Lifted Up' concluded.[14] The turn to a 'kenotic Christology', the representation of Christ as the suffering, incarnate God emptied of power, proved a pervasive theme in twentieth-century theology, and there is no doubt that a significant part of its appeal was the way in which it enabled believers to confront the reality of that traumatic century. The issue was not often brought to a head in popular preaching or religious writing – and did not, of course, need to be in such contexts – but conceptually it was often unclear as to whether this self-emptying of divine power was final, defining for ever the nature and being of God, or whether it was, in some sense, merely provisional ('humbled for a season to receive a Name'). In the former case, the dilemma of theodicy has been resolved by dropping one of the terms (God's omnipotence), in the latter it has not been resolved but, as it were, deferred. Unfortunately, whether for reasons of ecclesiastical prudence or because of a sense that, for all the problems it brought in its train, almightiness could not simply be dropped from the divine nature if God was to remain God and if belief was not to open its doors to the spirit of reductionism, it is often not clear how far the proponents of such a kenotic Christology were really prepared to go in revising the basic concepts of classical Christian theism.

An alternative response that seems not only to surrender divine omnipotence but also, on occasion, divine goodness is that of process theology.

Although not generally classed as a 'process theologian' Teilhard de Chardin developed an extraordinary evolutionary theology that shares many features with process thought. As a convinced evolutionist (as well as being a Catholic priest he was also a palaeontologist), Teilhard recognized the inseparability of conflict and suffering from the basic processes of life itself, and was prepared to project the model of 'survival of the fittest' onto the plane of human history, dovetailing it into an understanding of the Eucharist as the participation of human beings in the divine suffering of Christ. Not only a priest and a Darwinian, Teilhard, like Studdert-Kennedy, experienced firsthand the horror of the First World War, serving as a stretcher-bearer through the battle of Verdun, perhaps the most intensive of all the killing grounds of the Western Front. In his notebooks written during the war he embraced the daily experience of horrific slaughter and suffering as offering the possibility of an evolutionary leap, the necessary anguish of a dynamic of crucifixion and resurrection from out of which a transformation of humanity was to be expected that would be simultaneously effective on the spiritual and material planes.

Teilhard's guiding principle in relation to the question of evil is simple: 'Physical and moral evil are produced by the process of becoming: everything that evolves has its own sufferings and commits its own faults. The Cross is the symbol of the arduous labour of evolution – rather than the symbol of expiation'.[15] The application of this to the specific circumstances of the war shines through the text of his meditation 'The Priest':

> Who shall describe, Lord, the violence suffered by the universe from the moment it falls under your sovereign power.
>
> Christ is the goad that urges creatures along the road of effort, of elevation, of development.
>
> He is the sword that mercilessly cuts away such of the body's members as are unworthy or decayed . . .
>
> The universe is rent asunder; it suffers a painful cleavage at the heart of each of its monads, as the flesh of Christ is born and grows. Like the work of creation which it succeeds and surpasses, the Incarnation, so desired of man, is an awe-inspiring operation. It is achieved through blood.[16]

The meditation ends with words to his fellow priests:

> Never have you been more priests than you are now, involved as you are and submerged in the tears and blood of a generation – never have you been more active never more fully in the line of your vocation.
>
> I thank you, my God, in that you have made me a priest – and a priest ordained for war . . .
>
> 'Happy are those among us who, in these decisive days of the creation and redemption, have been chosen for this supreme act,

the logical crowning of their priesthood: to be in communion, even unto death, with the Christ who is being born and suffering in the human race.'[17]

With such words Teilhard gives flesh (and blood!) to the aphoristic summary of a process approach to theodicy provided by A. N. Whitehead's statement concerning Christ, namely, that he is 'a fellow-sufferer who understands'. Teilhard's words are, of course, confessional, words of prayer, expressive of a deep and personal passion and not philosophical arguments. Nevertheless, they hang together with the overall shape of his theoretical works and help us to see just how the theoretical perspective of his evolutionized and historicized reinterpretation of Christian belief works out in its application to the experienced reality of physical and moral evil. Along with elements of the kenotic response – since Christ is figured here too as fully participant in the sufferings of creation – Teilhard so internalizes evil in the process of divine life itself that, analytically, we have to say that evil itself has become, if not an attribute, then a dimension of the divine being. God can only deliver us from evil to the extent that he delivers himself, but whether he can do so is probably the issue of a still unresolved historical process. At this point it seems that the gap between 'history' (in, e.g. a Hegelian or Marxist view) and divinity seems to have narrowed to vanishing point. What has God become other than the possibilities that we, through our historical action and suffering, seek to make actual in history?

And this can almost lead to a divinization, or quasi-divinization of evil itself. Perhaps the clearest example of this is in the provocative and, in many ways, courageous and brilliant fusion of Jungian psychology and process thought offered by Jim Garrison's *The Darkness of God: Theology after Hiroshima*. The Jungian element in Garrison's argument focuses on the idea that the aim of psychological development should not, as in traditional moral theology, be the elimination of suppression of the impulse to evil, but in the achievement of balance or harmony between the dark and light sides of our personality, 'wholeness', 'integration', 'homeostasis' being keywords of this Jungian project. Analogously, Garrison argues, it is a moralizing diminishment of the idea of God to equate God simply with goodness. God too has his dark side, as testified already by Isaiah: 'I make peace and I create evil' (Isa. 45.7). God's own nature is, as Garrison puts it, 'antinomial', containing contrasting or opposed laws. Just as individual life should be lived as a process of continuing self-integration, so history becomes, for Garrison, the process whereby God integrates and harmonizes his own light and dark aspects. However, as in the experience of analysis, a necessary part of this process is the discovery of and the confrontation with the darkness. Garrison's theoretical claim, then, is, in his words, 'that the impetus for the interaction of God with humanity is not so much due to an altruistic love of an impassible Being outside the human space/time who could just as easily not have acted as acted, as it is due to a God who is compelled to interact with the creation because the very anti-nomial nature of God demands it. God must interact with humanity because only through interacting can God be actualized'.[18]

Hiroshima, then (along with 'similar' events), is neither an event foreknown and predestined by God from before the foundations of the earth, nor is it the result of contingent human freedom that God has, somehow, to deal with. Rather it is the revelation of an aspect of God himself, that at the same time places a new level of responsibility upon us, which, if we accept it, can transform the 'crucifixion' of Hiroshima into a 'resurrection'. We ourselves can only grow or develop spiritually (indeed, since Garrison wrote in the 'heat' of the cold war, only *survive* physically) if we allow Hiroshima to teach us our own power and responsibility in face of the future.

There is much in Garrison's argument that is provocative rather than reasoned and obscure rather than enlightening, and it is not, finally, clear whether he is doing more than giving a rhetorically powerful expression to the urgency and magnitude of the historical responsibility imposed by the technology of nuclear weaponry. His study is, however, admirable in making clear the fundamental challenge posed by a thoroughly historicized view of life to traditional theodicy, or, we might say, the transformation undergone by the classical formulation of the dilemma of theodicy when this is passed through the filter of the historical consciousness. Here, it seems, either the power or the goodness of God must go. Not because evils did not occur in the ages before the advent of the historical consciousness, but because, in the light of that consciousness, we see the inseparability of evil from the actuality of history. Neither natural nor moral evil is something that befalls us, as it were, from without. It is, rather, part of what makes us what we are. It may give us something to struggle against, but if we were ever, finally, to be delivered from it, we would not know ourselves.

With or without the prospect of utopia waiting for us at the end of history, and with or without the accompanying presence of a divinity who shares in the processes of history, it seems, then, that, from the standpoint of religion, a thoroughly historicized understanding of ourselves must place narrow limits on what we can hope for, and, if we manage to resist cynicism or fatalism, deliver us into the hands of absurdity. Something like this was acknowledged by the revisionist Marxist philosopher Vitezslav Gardavsky when he concluded his study *God is Not Yet Dead* with the acceptance that the communist's non-belief in God was, in fact, absurd, because it took away from history the one sure basis for rationally justifying historical existence. Nevertheless, he insisted, this absurdity was the price to be paid for commitment to historical action and hope 'for a community offering a life worthy of man'.[19] Essentially this is the same claim as that of Camus in his retelling of the myth of Sisyphus, condemned by the gods to spend eternity rolling a massive stone to the top of a hill, only to have it roll down again, the perfect symbol of unending, purpose-less effort. But Camus concludes that, even at the foot of the mountain, faced with the prospect of one more tiring and pointless effort, Sisyphus is happy. 'One always finds one's burden again. But Sisyphus teaches the higher fidelity that negates the gods and raises rocks. He, too, concludes that all is well. This universe henceforth without a master seems to him neither sterile nor futile. Each atom of that stone, each mineral flake of that night-filled mountain, in itself forms a world. The struggle itself towards the heights is enough to fill a man's heart. One must imagine Sisyphus happy'.[20] To this, of course, must be added the proviso that Camus' 'happiness' has the same meaning as Sartre's despair, when the latter insists in his programmatic pamphlet *Existentialism and Humanism* that philoso-phy must from now on base itself on despair, renouncing the possi-bility of appealing either to transcendent values, or to a God or a future fulfilment whose existence is not in the gift of our own free action. Despair, Sartre says, means simply that 'we restrict ourselves to relying only on that which depends on our will, or on the ensemble of probabilities that make our action possible'.[21] Moreover, as Camus' novel *The Stranger* made clear, the human task, conceived from within this complex of thinking, is not to aspire to virtue, to the subjugation of passion or the realization of a value such as love. It is simply to accept the burden of being who we are, in spite of and perhaps in defiance of any pre-existing framework of moral or religious values. It is, at its simplest, just to be who we are, as the individuals we separately happen to be, each with our own particular mixture of good and evil.

It may be objected that the bleakness of the existentialist position evidenced by Sartre and Camus is by no means a necessary outcome of a historicized consciousness. It is obvious that there have been many philosophies of history produced in the last two hundred years that, in various ways, could be called 'optimistic', in the sense that they postulate a good outcome to the historical process, Hegel being only one outstanding example. However, such philosophies must face the difficulty generated by their own commitment to a historical point of view: that history itself challenges the possibility of attaining the kind of metaphysical overview of the whole realm of beings that would render judgments as to whether all is for the best intrinsically uncertain, not to say implausible. As long as history lasts, the outcome of history cannot itself be a factor in our judgments upon it. As we have seen, even Hegel conceded that if the philosophy of history is to claim the status of knowledge or science, then it can do so only with regard to those epochs of history that have come to an end. The owl of Minerva flies only at dusk, and even the Marxist 'belief' in a future state of communism turns out to be itself undermined by history. Since the era of existentialism, secular humanism has tended to edge away from defining too closely the, as it were, metaphysical implications of its own commitments and is likely to shy away from the admittedly histrionic language of absurdity, despair, etc. Nevertheless it seems that, if history is acknowledged to be open-ended and uncertain in its outcome, and if there is no available certainty regarding the fate of the individual who has to live and die before the arrival of the kingdom of God on earth, then, essentially, the existentialists articulate the assumptions of many who, for what-ever reason, would not wish to be associated with them. Indeed, even those religious responses to the modern, historicized experience of evil that have looked to God's self-emptying or to the divine presence within the travail of evolutionary and historical becoming might be seen simply as rhetorically embellishing the same fundamental insight as existentialism in such a way as to enable the existentialist struggle for historical authenticity to avail itself of the language, symbols and rituals of historic Christianity. That something like this is so is very nearly acknowledged in such existentialist theologies as those of Berdyaev and Tillich, both of whom have affinities with some of the approaches considered here.[22]

This is not intended as a condemnation. The obligation of truthful-ness to the realities of historical existence is a singularly challenging demand for religious thinking, and especially for a religious tradi-tion whose 'classical' formulations pre-date the rise of the historical consciousness. It is therefore all the more important for us to be clear as to the kind of status that is being claimed for any particular religious response to the question of evil. If religious writers themselves are under no obvious obligation to undertake such reflection, and may legitimately content themselves with being performers, as it were, of religious language, the philosopher of religion must, however painful this may be (and, if the philosopher is also a believer, it is likely to be extremely painful), look more closely at just what is being said here, how much, or how little.

But we may seem to have conceded too much too easily to existentialist despair. For even if it is the case that the experience of history shatters each and every attempt to gather reality into a single unified whole that can be thought metaphysically, thus rendering life in history uncertain in outcome and delivering us over to our finite and mortal present, does it necessarily follow that in saying what we have to say about history we have therewith exhausted all that is to be said about human destiny? If our absorption in historical becoming obscures the horizons of any metaphysical hope and thus leads us to abandon the project of theodicy in its classical form, are we thereby stripped of every possibility for personal, supra-historical hope?

The implications of the question of evil for religious belief, in other words, require us to confront the further questions of death and human identity. In doing so we move into the area of what we are taking as the second characteristic moment of the modern philosophy of religion: the turn to the subject.

9

Evil and Subjectivity

Outrage

Voltaire wrote graphically of the horrors of war and of the other evils that human beings perpetrate upon each other, yet at the same time his reflections on the question of evil seem finally to come to rest on the problem of natural evil as manifested by the Lisbon earthquake. It is indeed characteristic of the distance separating the early modern approach to the question from our own that whereas the earthquake served not only Voltaire but eighteenth-century Europe as a whole as a paradigm of evil, a test case for theodicy, *our* question centres on such human evils as the Holocaust and Hiroshima. Of course, the difficult questions posed for theology by natural evils have not gone away, but, in comparison with the questions forced upon religious thought by all that 'man has made of man' they seem to have grown less urgent.[1] At the same time, however, there appears in Voltaire a hint of what was to become a dominant motif of nineteenth- and twentieth-century renderings of the question of evil, a motif in which we can see the mark of the subjective turn in modern thought: outrage. For if the turn to the subject is often conceived primarily in epistemological terms, as in the Kantian reordering of the basic questions of metaphysics, this, as we have seen, is only one expression of a move that more fundamentally takes its point of departure from the lived experience of subjectivity, i.e. what it is to exist as a subject. It is on this basis that what I have called outrage is explicitly and sustainedly given its voice in discussions of evil. Rather than being seen – as previously by philosophers and religionists alike – as something needing to be quietened or silenced, outrage now came to be understood precisely as that which needed to be addressed and answered, as a fury and an anguish that would only go away when it had received satisfaction.

I have said that Voltaire provides an early example of this voice being given its due place. This may seem surprising insofar as *Candide* ends with the assertion that confronted by the world's evils all we can do is to cultivate our own garden. At first this looks like simple resignation – making the best of a bad job, as it were (a view strengthened by the conversation recorded in the final chapter between the Leibnizian Dr Pangloss and the dervish, a conversation in which the latter brushes aside all the theoretical questions Pangloss wants to discuss with the remark that when the Sultan despatches a ship to Egypt he does not, and does not need, to give thought to the effects of the journey on the mice in the hold). Nevertheless, there are many points in the text where the voice of outrage is unmistakable and, whatever else the enigmatic ending may mean (I personally take it to mean something not very different from Camus' retelling of the myth of Sisyphus), it clearly involves a repudiation of any philosophical or theological doctrine that all is for the best in the best of all possible worlds, a repudiation that is motivated by the hero's direct personal experience of natural and moral evils rather than by any kind of ordered argument.

However, the ancestry and the implications of this outrage are perhaps still more clearly reflected in Voltaire's poem on the Lisbon earthquake, written prior to the composition of *Candide* and very much reflecting the immediate and violent impact of the earthquake on his thinking. In one particularly forceful section he alludes to a biblical image often used in theological defences of God's justice, but does so in such a way as to turn it against any simple theodicy. The build-up to this point, however, already makes clear the pivotal role of simple, impassioned outrage.

> No, do not offer my agitated heart
> These immutable and necessary laws,
> This concatenation of bodies, spirits, and worlds.
> O dreams of savants! O profound chimeras!
> God holds the chain in his hand and is by no means unbound;
> All is determined by his benign choice:
> He is free, He is just, by no means implacable.
> Why then do we suffer under this fair master?
> Here is the fatal knot we must untie.
> Would you cure our ills by denying them?
> All the nations, trembling under this divine hand,
> Have sought the origin of this evil you deny.
> If the eternal law that moves the elements
> Causes rocks to fall under the impact of wind,
> If lightning sets branching oaks ablaze,
> They do not feel the blows that destroy them:

But I live, but I feel, but my oppressed heart
Demands assistance from the God who formed it.
Children of the Almighty, but born in misery
We stretch our hands towards our universal father,
The vase, we know, cannot say to the potter:
'Why am I so vile, so lowly, so unrefined?'
It has no speech, it has no thought;
This urn which falls from the potter's hand
And shatters in being made has received no heart
To desire any goods or to feel its misfortune . . .
Sad calculators of human miseries
Do not console me, lest you make my pains more bitter . . .
I am nothing but a weak part of the great whole
 Indeed; but animals condemned to life
 All sentient beings, born under the same law
Live in sorrow and die as I do.[2]

The image of the pot as not having the right to question the potter is deeply rooted in the monotheistic tradition. It is used by Paul to parry the question as to how those who reject Christ can be blamed, if faith itself is a gift of God, and Paul, in turn, is quoting back to Isaiah (Rom. 9. 19-21. Isa. 29.16, 45.9). But whereas it seems to be self-evident to Paul and Isaiah that the analogy fits closely the human condition and that we are as dependent for our being on God as the pot is dependent on the potter, Voltaire points decisively to the disanalogy, a disanalogy that has to do precisely with our existence as conscious and self-conscious beings, and, above all, as beings who are self-conscious in their suffering. Such beings, he is saying, may, indeed must, question their maker and cry out against a fate that condemns them to a life of so much suffering. We are not dumb artefacts but sentient beings, and it would be a denial of humanity itself to forbid us to protest or answer back. The ability to do just this is integral to our being the kind of beings we are. His implication, moreover, is that for all the philosophical sophistication of contemporary theories concerning the relationships between causes and effect, possible worlds and the pre-established harmony of freedom and necessity, Leibniz and his fellow theodicists are essentially pushed back to the dogmatic position that because we cannot know the whole picture we have no right to enquire about it and must simply accept the limitation on our knowledge and the existence of truths above our reason.

This repudiation of a time-hallowed appeal to human frailty in face of ultimate questions and the assertion of the rights of the outraged sensibility of an existing, suffering, and thinking being is also evidenced by the re-emergence of another biblical motif in the modern discussion of evil: the appeal to the exemplary suffering of Job. Here, however, the biblical paradigm, far from being repudiated, is reinstated and rescued from the falsification it had endured for centuries in ecclesiastical teaching. In the teaching of the church, Job had become 'patient Job', a prime example of patient submission to suffering and, as such, a type of Christ. A moment in the story favoured in iconographic representation is that of the exchange between Job and his wife, when she tells him to curse the God who has brought so many troubles upon his head, and so to die, and Job replies, 'You are talking like a foolish woman. Shall we accept good from God and not trouble?' (Job 2.10), on which the text comments, 'Job did not sin in what he said.' However, this incident and these verses are scarcely representative of *Job* as a whole. No less vivid, and far more likely to impress themselves on a modern reader, are the long passages in which Job effectively seems to be taking his wife's advice, as in his speeches in Chapters 3, 6, 9–10, 12–14, 16–17, 19, 21, 23–4, 26–31, in which he rejects the counsel of his friends, who urge him to see his punishment as somehow merited or part of God's plan, and, instead, bewails the sheer agony of his existence, the inexplicability and injustice of God's actions and his own desire for extinction.

> Let the day perish wherein I was born,
> and the night which said
> 'A man-child is conceived.'
> Let that day be darkness!
> May God above not seek it,
> nor light shine upon it.
> Let gloom and deep darkness claim it.
> Let clouds dwell upon it;
> let the blackness of the day terrify it.
> That night – let thick darkness seize it!
> Let it not rejoice among the days of the year,
> let it not come into the number of the months.
> Yea, let that night be barren;
> let no joyful cry be heard in it.
> Let those curse it who curse the day,
> who are skilled to rouse up Leviathan.
> Let the stars of its dawn be dark;
> let it hope for light, but have none,
> nor see the eyelids of the morning;

because it did not shut the doors of my mother's womb,
nor hide trouble from my eyes. (Job 3. 2-10)

Throughout these speeches Job not only insists on his own misery
and his right to express it honestly, he also brushes aside the arguments of his friends, theodicists to a man ('Your maxims are proverbs
of ashes; your defences are defences of clay' (Job 13.12)), and claims
that nothing short of a direct confrontation with God would give him
satisfaction, fearful and impossible as such a thing might be: '. . . let
the Almighty answer me' (Job 31.35) he concludes. Strangely, when
God finally does appear it is to say that it is Job, after all, who has
spoken well of him and not the friends.

The rediscovery of this angry, outraged Job, the Job who answers
God back and takes the Almighty to task for his maladministration of
the world, is already hinted at in measured tones by Kant, in his essay
'On the miscarriage of all philosophical trials in theodicy' in which he
contrasts the approaches of Job and his friends:

> Job speaks as he thinks, and with the courage with which he,
> as well as every human being in his position, can well afford;
> his friends, on the contrary, speak as if they were being secretly
> listened to by the mighty one, over whose cause they are passing
> judgement, and as if gaining his favour through their judgement
> were closer to their heart than the truth. Their malice in pretending
> to assert things into which they yet must admit they have no
> insight, and in simulating a conviction which they in fact do not
> have, contrasts with Job's frankness – so far removed from false
> flattery as to border almost on impudence . . .[3]

Kant therefore begins his concluding remarks with the comment
that 'in these matters [i.e. 'authentic theodicy'], less depends on
subtle reasoning than on sincerity in taking notice of the impotence of
our reason, and on honesty in not distorting our thoughts in what we
say, however pious our intention.'[4]

An essentially similar reinterpretation of Job is made more dramatically by Kierkegaard, in his philosophical novella *Repetition*. One of
the two central characters, a nameless young man who has suffered a
failed love affair, writes of what, in his own suffering, the figure of Job
has come to mean to him.

Rejecting the way in which the church limits the meaning of Job to
his submissive words 'The Lord gave, the Lord took away, blessed be
the name of the Lord', the young man addresses Job himself and asks:

Do you know nothing more to say than that? Do you dare say no more than what professional comforters scantily measure out to the individual . . . just as they say 'God bless you!' when one sneezes! No, you who in your prime were the sword of the oppressed, the stave of the old, and the staff of the brokenhearted, you did not disappoint men when everything went to pieces – then you became the voice of the suffering, the cry of the grief-stricken, the shriek of the terrified, and a relief to all who bore their torment in silence, a faithful witness to all the affliction and laceration there can be in a heart, an unfailing spokesman who dared to lament 'in bitterness of soul' and to strive with God . . . Woe to him . . . who would cunningly cheat the sorrowing of sorrow's temporary comfort in airing its sorrow and 'quarrelling with God.' Or is there so much fear of God today that the sorrowing do not need what was customary in those days of old? Perhaps we do not dare to complain to God? Has the fear of God then increased – or fear and cowardliness? In our time it is thought that genuine expressions of grief, the despairing language of passion, must be assigned to the poets, who then like attorneys in a lower court plead the cause of the suffering before the tribunal of human compassion. No one dares to go further than that. Speak up, then, unforgettable Job, repeat everything you said, you powerful spokesman who, fearless as a roaring lion, appears before the tribunal of the Most High! . . . Complain – the Lord is not afraid, he can certainly defend himself. But how is he to defend himself when no one dares to complain as befits a man. Speak up, raise your voice, speak loudly.[5]

Kierkegaard, then, wishes to reinstate the 'despairing language of passion' to the religious questioning of humanity's experience of evil, suggesting, with Job, that the task is not for us to become God's 'defenders', pleading the rightness or justice of God ('theodicy'), but by our questioning to create a situation in which God can, as it were – and whatever might be meant by such a thing – 'defend himself'. Such a strategy, of course, means that the believer is no longer obliged to come up with arguments or reasons for going on believing despite the fact of evil but must himself accept and embrace and make his own the voice of outrage, because anything less will fail to do justice to the human experience and the human need that the question of evil articulates.

Such an understanding of Job re-echoed through both religious and secular thought and literature in the culture of modernity. Margarete Susman sees in the figure of Job as refracted through the literary prism of Kafka's novels (of which she says 'No work bears more clearly the traits of Job's ancient dispute with God than Kafka's work'[6]) a symbol both of Israel itself and, vicariously, of the human condition in general. 'Since the earliest times and down to this day Israel has not ceased to quarrel with God, to take man's part in his dispute with God for His justice. This is the reverse side of life under the law that presupposes God's unconditional justice. And this demand for the unconditional purity of God's justice is intransigent precisely to the degree that God's demand on man is seen and accepted without condition.'[7] But, unlike the prophet (such as Jeremiah) who argues with God on the basis of a common and public covenant 'Job is all alone vis-à-vis this God. Neither his people nor humanity support him, and he does not support them; he argues only on his own behalf. His dispute is only between God and himself. He, this driven leaf, this dry stubble, this tiny, ephemeral, mortal being, abandoned by the whole world, is also unmistakably the one who confronts the infinitely distant God, who dares to lift his voice – the breath of a moment – in anguish and accusation against the Eternal One.'[8] But, paradoxically, this highly individualized confrontation with God makes Job, perhaps more than any of the other biblical prototypes, an exemplary figure for the modern Jew, of whom Susman writes '. . . the isolation and the abandonment of the Jew in exile has been completed with his assimilation into the occidental world. But the dispute with God cannot cease even now. The Jew cannot remain silent when God hides Himself now as He hid Himself before Job . . . [But] the process against God must assume a new shape; it must start anew and in a new version: a version in which God is all silence and man alone speaks. And yet, though His name is never mentioned, only He is addressed.'[9]

Susman's insights, though suggestive rather than argued and evocative rather than reasoned, point to the bridge that the Kierkegaardian reworking – or, better, rediscovery – of Job threw across from the world of biblical and religious thought to the culture of modernity, and shows how belief might, paradoxically, find itself again in the indictment of a silent God. As a culture of protest against the 'infernal machine' of a system of universal necessity that crushes individuals with wanton insouciance, artistic and literary modernism could find in the Job of Kierkegaard and Kafka a figure who embodied its own ambivalence in relation to religion – a comment that should alert us to the singular difficulty of deciding whether many of the key texts of modernism are to be read as protests against religion or as Job-like appeals for a more direct, more immediate confrontation with what Susman called 'the primordial fright' of religion, but also thereby all the more ready for the 'pure worship' and the 'pure Thou' of the encounter with God.

This ambivalence permeates one of the most influential texts in all modern discussions of the question of evil, Dostoevsky's *The Brothers Karamazov*, a text that also gave definitive expression to the voice of moral and religious outrage in face of humanly enacted evil. Although it is now reasonably clear that Dostoevsky's intentions were to write from a standpoint of faith, the text itself is seamed by such a network of fault-lines that belief is at continual risk of subsidence into unbelief, and those (many) early readers who interpreted Dostoevsky as a post-Christian and post-religious writer were, in their way, responding to a real possibility of the texts themselves.

I shall come back to other elements in *The Brothers Karamazov* that relate to the question of evil in the next section. Here I wish only to note the notorious 'rebellion' of Ivan Karamazov, declaimed by him to his younger brother, the novice-monk Alyosha. Here Ivan comes close to reversing the hypothesis he had propounded earlier in the novel: that if God does not exist, then everything is permitted, a word claimed by Sartre as anticipating the essential teaching of existentialism – precisely, perhaps, because of the implied reversal of the syllogism: that in a world in which, it seems, everything *is* permitted (because even the most unthinkable crimes do, in fact, occur), then God does not exist.

Ivan, however, does not claim that God does not exist. His argument is, rather, that the kind of evil that really is met with in our world is such as to render odious the belief in a final harmony or happy ending that could justify the course of world history. Even if there is a judgment and an eschatological fulfilment beyond history, world history itself can never be justified for having been the way it has, in fact, been. Interestingly, and importantly, although Ivan alludes to instances of large-scale massacres, his argument requires there to have been only one instance of innocent suffering, a point he makes in the following question to Alyosha: 'Imagine that you are creating a fabric of human destiny with the object of making men happy in the end, giving them peace and rest at last, but that it was essential and inevitable to torture to death only one tiny creature – that baby beating its breast with its fist, for instance – and to found that edifice on its unavenged tears, would you consent to be the architect on those conditions? Tell me, and tell the truth.'[10] To which Alyosha's answer is, as it must be, that no, he would not consent. This point is, inevitably, easily lost in the face of the mass suffering of, for example, the Holocaust, Hiroshima or the killing-fields of Cambodia. As we have seen, it was in large part the sheer scale of cumulative suffering in the twentieth century that, for many people, fatally undermined any optimistic interpretation of the principle that 'World history is the Last Judgment'. But each of these mass horrors is what it is because of each individual case that contributes to it. The fear and despair of a child in the death camps is not less because millions of others undergo a similar fear, and if only one child had thus suffered, Ivan would be right: that not only the policies of a government that allowed or caused such suffering, but, more fundamentally, the providence that is supposed to direct the course of history would also stand accused.

In leading up to this question, Ivan has given Alyosha several instances, culled from contemporary newspapers, of human cruelty to children. That they are children is important for Ivan's case precisely because, as he sees it (and the view is scarcely challenged in the book), children are essentially innocent. 'I understand solidarity in sin among men,' says Ivan, 'I understand solidarity in retribution too; but there can be no such solidarity with children. And if it really is true that they must share responsibility for all their fathers' crimes, such a truth is not of this world and beyond my comprehension.'[11] So, he gives the example of a five-year-old girl, locked up by her parents in the outside privy for a whole night having had her face smeared and mouth filled with excrement as a punishment for bedwetting (this is the baby beating its breast in his conclusion). But the climax comes in his account of a Russian landowner and general who discovers that his favourite hunting dog is lame, after a boy of eight had accidentally hit it with a stone he was throwing in play. The boy is locked up for the night and the next morning the general gathers his entire hunting-pack and, while the boy's mother looks on, has the boy stripped naked before setting the dogs on him, which, of course, tear him to pieces.

Having elicited from the saintly Alyosha the response that he too would shoot the man who could do such a thing, Ivan reaches his climactic conclusion, of which the following is only an extract.

You see, Alyosha, perhaps it really may happen that if I live to that moment [of the final harmony of all things], or rise again to see it, I, too, perhaps may cry aloud with the rest, looking at the mother embracing the child's torturer: 'Thou art just, O Lord!' but I don't want to cry aloud then. While there is still time I hasten to protect myself and so I renounce the higher harmony altogether. It's not worth the tears of that tortured child . . . It's not worth it, because those tears are unatoned for. They must be atoned for or there can be no harmony. But how? How are you going to atone for them? Is it possible? By their being avenged? But what do I care for avenging them? What do I care for a hell for oppressors? What good can hell do, since those children have already been tortured? . . . I don't want the mother to embrace the oppressor who threw her son to the dogs! She dare not forgive him! Let her forgive him for herself, if she will, let her forgive the torturer for the immeasurable suffering of her mother's heart. But the sufferings of her tortured child she has no right to forgive; she dare not forgive the torturer, even if the child were to forgive him! And if that is so, if they dare not forgive, what becomes of harmony? Is there in the whole world a being who would have the right to forgive and could forgive? I don't want harmony. From love for humanity I don't want it. I would rather be left with unavenged suffering. I would rather remain with my unavenged suffering and unsatisfied indignation, even *if I were wrong*. Besides, too high a price is asked for harmony; it's beyond our means to pay so much to enter on it. And so I hasten to give back my entrance ticket, and if I am an honest man I am bound to give it back as soon as possible. And that I am doing. It's not God that I don't accept, Alyosha, only I most respectfully return him the ticket.[12]

This is by no means a piece of reasoned argument, but what Kierkegaard called the 'despairing language of passion'. But that is precisely the point: that now, within the culture of modernity, just such despairing language is reclaimed, with help from the biblical (if not from the ecclesiastical) Job, and asserted not in ignorance but in defiance of the language of theodicy, as the most fitting way of speaking of the world's ills. In the case of Ivan, moreover, there is a mutually reinforcing twofold emphasis: on the one hand, as he acknowledges, he is prepared to hold on to his point even if he can be shown to be in the wrong: his outrage is its own justification and needs no rational defence; on the other hand (and this is his chief point), the tears of just one single infant are enough to call into question the whole edifice of cosmic harmony. Both these emphases, however, serve to emphasise the underlying point: that the immediate, existential, response to evil, 'the primordial fright' spoken of by Susman, has a legitimate and necessary place in any discussion of the subject, and any discussion that moves out of earshot of the anguished cry of such a response is inevitably going to lose its way and end as empty nonsense. In this matter, at least, the human subject, not the rational substance of Cartesian epistemology but the thinking reed of Pascal, demands, and has every right to demand, a hearing.

This, as I have already suggested, may not be Dostoevsky's own last word. But, I also suggest, it is a key to a central element of the modern response to evil. Should we seek to rise above it, to acknowledge its force as an immediate gut reaction but nevertheless resist its claim to decide the whole argument? The question is not so easy. But, we know, the aim of thinking about God is not to make religion easy, but to learn to think the questions of religion in their truth and therefore also in their difficulty. And that means, sometimes, thinking the question with total commitment and passion and continuing to think it even when no answer comes. The difficulty is not just finding 'the answer' but deciding the ground on which the question of evil is properly to be asked, and it is precisely this difficulty that the voice of outrage will not let us evade. Immediate and passionate as it may be (and thus far 'irrational') it is also philosophically important, since it compels us to ask all the more carefully just what it is we are trying to do here and just what kind of thinking the encounter with evil calls for.

Psychologies of evil

If the loss of inhibition regarding the right of moral outrage to enter into the debate about God's goodness in creation and world governance is one of the most striking expressions of the turn to the subject in the discussion of evil, it is only part of the picture.

Another aspect is the rise of what might be called psychologies of evil, that is, accounts of what it is in the human psyche that gives rise to the possibility of evil action. Rather than being seen simply as a brute fact, a *force majeure* confronting humankind – like the natural evil arising from the operation of the exceptionless laws of nature – the evil that rises from human beings themselves now becomes the centre of attention.

As in many other areas of the modern philosophy of religion, however, this move was not without precedent. Apart from the relevance of much biblical material, there were the analyses of Augustine, famously preoccupied not only with the question of evil as a metaphysical and theological problem but also as a mystery embedded in his own personal life and self-experience. In a simple but celebrated passage in the *Confessions* Augustine described how he participated as a teenager in robbing fruit from a pear tree in the neighbourhood. 'We took away an enormous quantity of pears,' he comments, 'not to eat them ourselves, but simply to throw them to the pigs. Perhaps we ate some of them, but our real pleasure consisted in doing something that was forbidden.'[13] 'The wrong itself', he added, was the only goal of such actions. The inexplicable perversion of the will away from the good and towards evil was a constant issue in Augustine's writing, corresponding psychologically to the metaphysical insistence on evil as non-being, a connection that he makes explicit at several points: 'It is not a matter of efficiency, but of deficiency; the evil will itself is not effective but defective. For to defect from him who is the Supreme Existence, to something of less reality, this is to begin to have an evil will.'[14] 'Consequently, although the will derives its existence, as a nature, from its creation by God, its falling away from its true being is due to its creation out of nothing.'[15] '. . . to abandon God and to exist in oneself, that is to please oneself, is not immediately to lose all being; but it is to come nearer to nothingness.'[16] At the same time, paradoxically, the very inexplicability of evil, an inexplicability that comes from its identification with the principle of nothingness, leads Augustine to trace the mystery of evil back to God's inscrutable choice to make of some of his creatures vessels of destruction, subject to wrath.

In the case of Augustine himself, the interconnection between the themes of nothingness, freedom and evil that such statements suggest continues to be thought within the general framework of a metaphysical and cosmological conception of Being. At the same time it is hard to avoid drawing an analogy – indeed, via Pascal, a line – from these Augustinian insights to the existentialist position of Sartre. Here, however, the human subject is no longer regarded as a 'nature' or 'essence' imbued with Being and, as it were, assaulted from without by nothingness. For Sartre, nothingness is inseparable from our very identity as centres of freedom in the midst of the otherwise impermeable viscosity of Being-in-itself. 'If nothingness can be given,' writes Sartre, ' it is neither before nor after being, nor in a general way outside of being. Nothingness lies coiled in the heart of being – like a worm'.[17] We ourselves, moreover, are that being 'by which nothingness comes to things'[18] and we are that by virtue of our freedom, our not-being-determined by the environing mass of Being-in-itself, or nature. Indeed, we are not determined by any nature, not even human nature, no matter whether that is conceived metaphysically, naturalistically or psychologically. Our existence precedes any essence. Sartre, committed to radical atheism, does not, of course, concede anything to Augustine's distinction between a good and an evil will. Sartre's will is beyond good and evil, it is the freedom in which and by means of which we decide what is to count as good, what as evil. It is pre-moral and, from the standpoint of conventional morality, amoral.

If Augustinianism was in such ways to remain a potent presence in twentieth-century existentialism, the Augustinian themes are dramatically transformed in their modernist reworking. Augustinianism alone is not decisive: Leibniz's writings on theodicy are themselves pervaded by Augustinian themes, and yet they strike a very different note from what we find in existentialism. For Leibniz the radical implications of the conjunction of freedom, evil and nothingness are still contained within an essentially theocentric and cosmological framework. The question is whether God's permission of evil by the human creature is compatible with the greater good of the universe as a whole, rather than what the conflux of freedom, evil and nothingness shows us about what it is to be a human being.

A watershed seems to be crossed at some point between Leibniz and Kant; the latter, as we have seen, also in his own way acknowledging the legitimacy of immediate moral passion in confronting the question of evil. Kant also gives added impetus to the psychologizing of the question of evil. In terms of these differences it is striking that Kant's study of *Religion within the Boundaries of Mere Reason* opens with a quotation from the Gospel of John, that 'the world lieth in evil', a reflection that moves Kant directly to the question concerning moral rather than natural evil and therefore to the question as to how the human being could be constituted in such a way as to affirm the original goodness of creation but also to allow for our becoming sources of evil. Kant's answer hinges on the distinction he draws between our 'predisposition' to good and our 'propensity' (or 'inclination') to evil. This is not to be understood in the Augustinian sense that having been created good and participating in goodness by virtue of our participation in Being we turned away towards the 'impossible nothingness' of evil by means of a free and unmotivated choice. For Kant our predisposition to good is not a 'nature' or 'essence' of goodness, a part of our original endowment, as it were. Strictly, it is morally neutral. Whatever can be explained 'naturally' (and Kant's proximity to Sartre – or, more precisely, Sartre's proximity to Kant – is evident here), that is, by reference to a predetermined nature, is simply a matter of natural causes and not a matter of freedom; therefore it is neither morally praiseworthy nor morally reprehensible. The bird of prey is not morally evil because its nature is such that it is preprogrammed to kill. If what is called 'sin' is simply an expression of natural drives for sexual gratification, power, etc., drives that our nature compels us to go along with, then, as Nietzsche was to point out, it is a misnomer, and there can be no real significance to our conventional distinctions between good and evil. That, however, is not Kant's position. For in addition to the determination of human behaviour by natural causes we find the no less important ground of determination by freedom. When it is said that human beings are good or bad 'by nature', Kant argues, what is really being said is that the human being, in acting according to freedom (for only in the light of freedom, of responsible choice, is it possible to speak of good or evil), is putting into effect a possibility that is his solely by virtue of his humanity. In this sense one can talk of the universality of sin, but Kant makes it quite clear that for this same reason it just doesn't make sense to speak of moral evil as an *'inheritance* from our first parents'[19] since that would mean that our evil action (yours and mine) would not be the outcome of our own free choice and therefore not evil. When we speak of 'causality' in connection with freedom, Kant avers, it is not a matter of seeking out its 'cause' in time but the reason for it, i.e. what it is that makes such an action the sort of action that it is.

Evil action is not simply a matter of an occasional lapse or breach of the moral law. It is, Kant says, a matter of adopting a strategy of evil, of freely incorporating maxims of evildoing ('Look out for number one', perhaps?) into our behaviour. Morality, or judgments concerning good and evil, can only be an issue of motivation, and this motivation itself cannot consistently be conceived as flowing from a predetermined nature but as something for which we ourselves are responsible. If we are really free in the choice of good or evil, that means that we choose our own motivations. This, essentially, is what Kant means by incorporating an incentive or motive into our maxims, i.e. taking it as a strategic principle of action. (Though, as Kant also says, it is in most cases impossible for us to be sure that wrong actions in others are more than occasional and, as it were, accidental breaches of the moral law since we cannot observe the internal free action of choosing moral maxims.)

The propensity to evil belongs to every human being. Within it, Kant distinguishes three grades. There is the frailty of human nature that is reflected in our failure to carry through the good maxims that we have consciously chosen. There is the impurity of the human heart, that is seen in the fact that although we often do the good or obey the moral law, we simultaneously seek personal gratification in so doing, e.g. as in doing the good for the sake of a reward – what

Kierkegaard was to call double-mindedness. Finally there is the stage of depravity or corruption in which there is a complete reversal of what should be the order of moral incentives.

But what is involved in this? Kant, as we have seen, distinguishes two levels or domains of being and causality, nature and freedom. All of us, as human beings, have natural needs and impulses. If our being was no more than an ensemble of such needs and impulses then we could not even talk of moral choices. However, at the same time, and in relation to every action we regard as 'human', we must also be counted as free agents, and therefore as responsible for what we are and do. The question then is as to the relation between these levels or domains. In a perfectly functioning moral universe the natural or animal impulses would not be eradicated. We would still feel hunger, the desire for sex, etc. But these impulses would all be directed and regulated by the requirements of morality, the will to the common good rather than to private gratification. As it is, however, we see, at best, a very mixed picture. For, in practice, human beings subvert the hierarchy of moral incentives and allow the natural impulses to direct their moral choices rather than vice versa. This, though, does not mean simply that we are naturally evil, evil by nature, and still less that we are irredeemably evil. For this subversion of the moral law is itself the freely chosen activation of the evil propensity. We are and remain free even in our adoption of evil maxims, for 'The human being must make or have made *himself* into whatever he is or should become in a moral sense, good or evil'.[20]

Yet, finally, and as for Augustine, there is a certain inscrutability or inexplicability concerning our fundamental choices. Because we are not dealing with an event in a chain of natural causes but with freedom there is a point at which the question 'why?' just cannot be answered. At the same time (unlike in Augustinian theories of humanity's total depravity and consequent incapacity for self-improvement) we remain open to the appeal of the moral law, we understand and, if we choose, can freely act on the obligation to seek and to do the good. In the essay 'On the miscarriage of all philosophical trials in theodicy' Kant is explicit that theodicy simply cannot be carried through as a theoretical endeavour, because theodicy would require the demonstration of the ultimate harmony or congruence between, on the one hand, the order of causality that binds all beings together in a seamless web of physical connectedness and, on the other, the order of freedom conceived in such a way as to require the coordination of divine and human freedom. This demonstration, however, would require a 'cognition of the supersensible (intelligible) world' that is not available to any mortal creature.[21] Anything that can be done in the direction of theodicy can be done only under the strict limitations that belong to a recognition of our own finitude and mortality. The argument of *Religion within the Boundaries of Mere Reason* is therefore not so much an exercise in theodicy in the strict sense of the term as a vindication in face of the prevalent moral evil of the world of the possibility of human freedom, and the continuing resonance in us and for us of the appeal to goodness. Despite it all, a freely chosen strategy of goodness remains meaningful and possible – but that possibility is not grounded in theological or metaphysical arguments but on an analysis of the subjective conditions of human action and what I have called a 'psychology of evil'.

Kant's 'high' doctrine of human freedom resonated throughout the succeeding generations of German idealist philosophy. This is also true of critics of that tradition such as Kierkegaard who, in some respects, marks a 'return to Kant' in opposition to Hegel. If Kierkegaard's 'image' in the history of religious thought is very much that of someone labouring under a deep sense of inherited guilt and giving voice to the darkest chord of Augustinian Christianity's obsession with sin, his study *The Concept of Anxiety* is, from a certain angle, a sustained destruction of the Augustinian idea of original – or, as Kierkegaard's Danish term emphasizes – inherited sin. For Kierkegaard as for Kant, we can become guilty of sin only in and by those free acts for which we are properly and fully responsible.

Sin is not the declared topic of *The Concept of Anxiety*. Indeed, defining his study as a strictly 'psychological' investigation, and declaring sin to belong exclusively to dogmatics, it would seem as if it is systematically excluded. At the same time, however, Kierkegaard emphasizes the concept of anxiety, understanding anxiety (or 'angst'[22]) as the psychological state that is the presupposition of sin. It is the state that makes any free action on the part of the human subject possible (and therefore, as for Kant, also makes sin possible) and is to that extent necessarily worked out in a certain proximity to what dogmatics has to say about sin. In keeping with this assertion Kierkegaard introduces the concept of anxiety by means of a reinterpretation of the Fall narrative of Genesis.

Repudiating the kind of dogmatic talking-up of Adam's prelapsarian perfections (which he describes as 'fantastic') that had characterized much of the Christian discussion in the past, Kierkegaard commits himself unequivocally to the view that the original state of the human being is ignorance. This, as he represents it, is an animal-like state in which 'The spirit in man is dreaming'.[23] As he goes on to describe this state it is one in which the human being exists as a synthesis of physical and psychic forces. 'Psychic' here, however, seems to mean no more than a kind of consciousness that goes with an awareness of emotional states but that does not have any freedom of action in relation to them, nor a conception of the self as being itself a centre or source of freedom. However, speaking of the human being as 'a synthesis of the physical and the psychical' Kierkegaard adds that 'a synthesis is unthinkable if the two are not united in a third'. And this 'third', he says, 'is Spirit', which, for Kierkegaard, means freedom.[24] The human being is first and only human when he takes over or 'owns' his factual givenness (what Heidegger would call his 'thrownness' into the world) as 'his': 'This is me!' However, it follows that the co-presence of the physical and psychical alone is not be enough for us to speak of *human* being. If we are to speak of an original state of *human* being, Spirit or freedom must already be there in some way. This way, according to Kierkegaard, is 'dreaming'.

> In this state there is peace and repose, but there is simultaneously something else that is not contention and strife, for there is indeed nothing against which to strive. What, then, is it? Nothing. But what effect does nothing have? It begets anxiety. This is the profound secret of innocence, that it is at the same time anxiety. Dreamily the spirit projects its own actuality, but this actuality is nothing, and innocence always sees this nothing outside itself.[25]

This is a powerful and very condensed passage, and it would involve an extensive diversion from our main course to give anything like an adequate exposition of it. What is important for our present purposes is that whilst *The Concept of Anxiety* in many ways remains within a Kantian paradigm, Kierkegaard is seeking to give a closer account than does Kant of the way in which freedom supervenes upon humanity's natural or animal constitution and he wants to do so by giving a genetic account of freedom's emergence; furthermore, in so doing he makes explicit the thematics of nothingness as marking precisely the boundary at which nature and freedom both touch and are separated.

The original state of the human being, then, is always already determined by its relation to a freedom that it does not yet understand or has not yet claimed as its own. Even the infant betrays an anxiety that stems from a premonition that its future is as an adult and not merely an eternal continuation of childhood. We know from the outset that we are going to have to be or to become beings of a different kind from what, in infancy, we know ourselves to be. Even though we have no real conception as to what it means or involves – it is, in Kierkegaard's terms, 'outside' us at this point – we sense that adult life is the goal towards which all our life-processes are tending (and even a two-year-old can speculate on 'When I grow up . . .'). In ignorance or innocence, then, we exist in a constant relation to a future and thus to possibilities that lie outside our immediate awareness. As Kierkegaard reinterprets the Genesis narrative this condition is brought to its extreme development in response to the divine prohibition concerning the fruit of the tree of the knowledge of good and evil. As merely 'possible', freedom in this stage of its development has not made any actual moral decisions and does not know what good or evil or right or wrong mean. The prohibition thus awakens or heightens a sense of 'being able' that was previously latent but unfocused or undirected. When the penalty ('If you eat from it you will die') is added to the prohibition, then '[t]he infinite possibility of being able that was awakened by the prohibition now draws closer, because this possibility points to a possibility as its sequence.'[26] In other words, our 'being able', our capacity for a future action or choice whose terms we do not as yet understand is intensified and compounded by the sense that this is no isolated occurrence but an action that will bring with it a whole set of inter-connected consequences that are determinative for our whole future. In this action that is still for us (for Adam, as for children) a possibility that we do not understand, we thus intuit what is to be the meaning of our very lives. This is the maximum point of anxiety. Everything hangs on a choice we do not understand and cannot understand until it is made, on what is, for us, incomprehensible, beyond our experience: nothing.

It is clear – or Kierkegaard wishes it to be clear – that the realization of freedom in action is not necessarily a fall. Sin is not an inevitable outcome of the way we were made. Sin, to be sin, must be attributed to a free choice. In principle, perhaps, it could go the other way. But the situation is somewhat different from the classical model of a perfect Adam who could in principle have continued in a state of free obedience. 'Freedom' is not an attribute of the human being apart from or prior to the realization of freedom in conscious choice or decision. It cannot be for Kierkegaard, as for Hegel, that the Fall is a successful climb, but, nevertheless, the Fall is somehow inseparable from our ascent to adulthood. In a passage that closely anticipates Sartre, Kierkegaard writes:

Anxiety may be compared with dizziness. He whose eye happens to look down into the yawning abyss becomes dizzy. But what is the reason for this? It is just as much in his own eye as in the abyss, for suppose he had not looked down. Hence anxiety is the dizziness of freedom, which emerges when the spirit wants to posit the synthesis and freedom looks down into its own possibility, laying hold of finiteness to support itself. Freedom succumbs in this dizziness. Further than this psychology cannot and will not go. In that very moment everything is changed, and freedom, when it again rises, sees that it is guilty. Between these two moments lies the leap, which no science has explained and no science can explain.[27]

Kierkegaard, then, neither explains nor gives a motivation for the Fall. That is something 'no science' can or should want to do. As for Augustine and for Kant, there is a final and definitive inexplicability. What he does appear to be doing is something like a proto-phenomenological account of the conditions that surround or accompany the emergence of freedom. It is an attempt to show us the kind of thing that freedom is, the kind of being that belongs to it. And the point is not that the inability to give an explanation is a result of failure on the part of the investigator, but that explanation is not what should be being looked for here. Freedom is not and can never be the kind of thing that can be 'explained', and, conversely, whatever can be explained is not and cannot be freedom.

At this point, perhaps, the philosopher hands over to the novelist – and it is scarcely coincidental that Kierkegaard himself often wrote more like a novelist than a philosopher nor that other philosophers in this existentialist tradition have likewise resorted to literary presentation: Sartre himself, Gabriel Marcel, Iris Murdoch and, from the literary side, novelists such as Dostoevsky, Kafka and Camus contributed immeasurably to shaping the existentialist outlook. Thus we can see in the works of Dostoevsky – who shares Kierkegaard's sense for the mystery of freedom – something of how those inexplicable and often almost unnoticed moments of anxiety between thought and action, between innocence and guilt, enter into our lives with a so often devastating effect (even when they do not, as so typically in Dostoevsky, culminate in murder). In this connection we may also remind ourselves of the distinctive modern awareness of language and of questions of representation and communication. As Kierkegaard himself put it: it is not just a matter of what is said but of *how* it is said.

It is perhaps time to try to pull together some of the threads of this necessarily tangled discussion, before we can move on to further aspects of the question of evil considered in the light of the modern turn to the subject.

Augustine saw evil in essentially Platonic terms as the manifestation of non-being, of what is without participation in the being and goodness of the Creator. This quality of nothingness, though conceived by Augustine within an overarchingly 'cosmic' account of evil, also fed into his description of the evil will's defection from God and its ungrounded indulgence in wrongdoing for its own sake. But, for Kierkegaard and, later, for Sartre, this same 'nothingness' is not simply a deficiency but the measure of the will's own freedom and of its distinctiveness, as free, from the order of natural causation. Nothingness becomes, as it were, the guarantor of the strong Kantian understanding of freedom, and the strong Kantian distinction between the realms of freedom and nature, together with the no less strong Kantian strictures on any attempt to speculate concerning the final harmony of these two orders. Does this, then, mean that the Augustinian aversion to nothingness has simply been abandoned? Perhaps not.

Let us look at it like this. For both Kierkegaard and Sartre (probably unlike Kant) freedom's 'groundedness' in nothing is inseparable from the situation that, as we actually encounter it in existence, freedom is characteristically manifested as sin (Kierkegaard) or in the 'bad faith' in which freedom flies from itself and evades the responsibility that belongs to its quality as freedom (Sartre). This does not mean that the human condition is one of the simple absence of freedom, but is rather seen as marked by the loss of freedom – something that both would see as very different from a life that never had the possibility of freedom in the first place. Freedom, truly to be itself, must be freely claimed and enacted by the existing subject. Such 'owning' of our own freedom is precisely what makes us 'subjects' in the strongest sense. Whether we own it or not, however, we cannot escape it, but it haunts as the nothingness of possibilities that are never realized, as the dim or buried knowledge that we are wasting our lives.

Let us take a concrete example. In her study *Eichmann in Jerusalem* Hannah Arendt coined the phrase 'the banality of evil' to summarize what she saw in Eichmann, the concentration camp commander who had been personally responsible for the deaths of at least hundreds of thousands of people, mostly Jews, in the most squalid and degrading circumstances. Like many others Arendt had expected to see in the man in the dock a terrifying moral monster, a larger than life incarnation of evil, inspiring fear and loathing. Instead, she saw a vacuous bureaucrat, whose telling of his own life story was not so much an apology for a programme of radical evil as a boring recitation of accidental and contingent acts and decisions that lacked any cohesive thread or purpose. Eichmann was not terrifying, he was banal. Interestingly, Arendt herself had early on been an Augustine scholar, and it is tempting to see in her account of Eichmann a modern re-writing, under the sign of the turn to the subject, of the Augustinian theme of evil as non-being. The evil of Eichmann was not that he had evil aims but that he had no real moral purpose or goal and, in other circumstances, would almost certainly have lived an uneventful, unnoticed and mediocre life. His evil was his failure to be the freedom that he was, as we are.[28]

Returning to the Kierkegaardian-Sartrean versions of freedom's failure, then, we could put it like this: that if freedom as the possi-bility to choose our own future and therewith our own selfhood is not realized, if it succumbs to anxiety in the moment of decision and congeals in bad faith and yet, as both Kierkegaard and Sartre empha-size, can never be shrugged off or discarded, then freedom remains as the simple nothingness of anxiety, a possibility that by not being realized perpetuates a kind of atrophy of personality, keeping us in but on the outer rim of the community of fully realized persons. Eichmann, as a figure of that half-light embodies just such an existen-tial atrophy. Yet the non-being manifested in his banal evil is at the same time that which makes possible our own self-choice in freedom. The possibility of being an Eichmann is the possibility every one of us has as a free being, as long as and to the degree that we do not realize that freedom.[29]

But what might move us to do such a thing? If freedom, as such, cannot be motivated or explained by anything in the natural order of causation, what can move us to want to be the freedom that we are? The first part of this chapter, I suggest, provides one possible answer, albeit in formal terms a negative one. Moral and personal outrage at the moral evil of the world as we experience it provokes us to want things to be otherwise. As Geoffrey Beaumont, the ingénu hero of David Lynch's film *Blue Velvet* cries out when confronted by the evil of Frank, a moral monster guilty of every kind of cruelty and deprav-ity, 'How can there be people like Frank in the world?' And we, confronted by Eichmann and his depressingly ubiquitous heirs, may similarly cry out, 'How can there be Eichmanns in the world? How can our human possibilities, so rich, so manifold, so creative, be squandered in such a way?' And our cry may move us to want things to be otherwise and to begin to will it that things indeed do become otherwise. Sharing the nothingness and the anxiety of empty possibility with the Eichmanns and the moral monsters, that same possibility gives us the hope of doing better.

Of course, moral outrage is cheap. It *may* move us to do otherwise. But it may exhaust itself in gesture politics. Yet even if it is acted upon, it – and the whole argument of this chapter – may fall short of what is required of a religious response to the question of evil. For, even if it is accepted, with Kant, that we must abandon any attempt at theodicy *à la* Leibniz, and turn instead to the concrete possibilities of historical action, to the realization of freedom in moral striving, this seems to say nothing of religion's characteristic concern for salvation. Religion, even in a historicized and subjective form would still, it seems, need to insist that it is not enough simply to join the fight against evil, we must also believe in deliverance from it and the making good of all that has been cast down, betrayed and ruined in the course of our unhappy history. But is this possible? Doesn't the outrage of an Ivan Karamazov, the cosmic humility of Kant and the existential focus of Kierkegaard undermine all but the most short-term and local optimism? Don't we find ourselves back once more at the bottom of the hill with Sisyphus, convinced only of our own courage and freedom to begin the long ascent all over again? What then has happened to the hope of salvation from evil in the modern philosophy of religion, and how can we articulate and understand such a hope from this far side of the experience of modernity?

10

Eternal Life?

Following such events in the history of ideas as the rise of the historical consciousness and the turn to the subject, but also (and no less
importantly) in the wake of the catastrophe of the twentieth century,
we ask: can our response to evil, realistically, be more than the heroic
moral resolve to try to do better, or, still more modestly, to take our
stand with Sisyphus and prepare once more to start rolling the rock
up the bleak mountainside confronting us? Such a reworking of
Voltaire's advice that we should be content to cultivate our gardens is
by no means contemptible, and if either moral teaching or religion
can move people towards such a preparedness and so help them from
sinking back into indifference or cynicism it is something at least. But
the rhetoric of religion surely promises more. Religion speaks not
merely of the possibility of historical action but of salvation, whether
as an alternative to this-worldly action or as its necessary condition.
'If only for this life we have hope in Christ, we are to be pitied more
than all men', wrote St Paul (1 Cor. 15.19). We may, for the purposes of
this study, leave it to theologians to argue over whether Christian
doctrine requires us to understand eschatological hope as salvation
from the world or as the spur to historical action in the world or how
exactly the relationship between this-worldly hope and otherworldly
hope should be configured, and how all these dimensions are affected
by the saving work of Christ – and the theologians will, as profes-
sionally they must, tell us that unless or until we have considered
such questions we are only touching the outer fringes of what really
matters. That may be. Nevertheless, we shall limit ourselves here to
asking about the question of a life beyond this present earthly life and
the implications of the prospect of such a life for this life in only the
most general terms. For whatever the specific doctrines of Christianity or other religions may teach in this area can make sense only
within the general horizon of expectation that is projected by the
question as that arises for us in our concrete historical circumstances.

The first point to make is, then, simply to remind ourselves that we
have been led to this question here and now by our reflections on the

question of evil. In many handbooks or introductions to the philosophy of religion 'the problem of evil' and 'immortality' are treated as distinct and separate topics. This is quite proper to the extent that there are certain issues peculiar to each that, from a certain angle of vision, do not overlap. The distinction between natural and moral evil, for example, has no obvious or direct connection to the key questions raised by the hypothesis of survival after death, and the question of the mind-body relationship and its implications for human identity, a question that is so often central to discussions of survival, is not immediately relevant to the question of evil. However, the filleting out of the topics peculiar to each of these areas should not lead us to overlook their fundamental unity. For whilst it might be possible in principle to be led to the question of survival by, e.g. reports of out-of-body experiences or visitations from the dead, there is a deep cultural, psychological and personal interconnection between the question of evil and the question of eternal life. This is especially the case if we look at it from the side of the question of evil. For, as we have been seeing, if our response to evil runs only as far as the boundaries of mortal, finite existence, this would seem to fall short of what is required of a religious response. For what, then, of the unrequited sufferings of those who die in their misery, who live to see neither a personal nor a collective fulfilment, who end in despair – as, the testimony suggests, so many of the concentration camp victims died and so many of the internal victims of Marxism's march towards communism?

Seeing the question like this, I suggest, is in fact integral to a historically-oriented conceptualization of the world. For seeing the world as a historical process immediately raises the question as to whether this process has a goal and, if so, whether that goal could be attained within the parameters of historical becoming or whether it involves postulating some trans- or supratemporal dimension of fulfilment if we are to talk at all of meaning in history. The concrete experience of evil, however, seems to militate against any idea of a purely intra-historical fulfilment, and we have seen the difficulties that belief in such fulfilment raised for Marxism and, by extension, other theories of historical progress. If we are to avoid the nihilism of radical existentialism, for which history is indeed going nowhere and 'means' only the endless Sisyphean labour of doing the best we can in the knowledge of our ultimate defeat, it would seem that either we must be able in some way to comprehend history as a whole, and so to understand the justification of the suffering of the part for the sake of the perfection of the whole, or we most posit some supra-historical resolution of the contradictions and frustrations that are left unfulfilled within history itself. Of these, the former seems to reflect a strategy that is thinkable in the context of a static cosmological world-view (though whether it can satisfactorily be achieved even within the assumptions of such a world-view is another matter again), where it might seem possible in principle to gain a vision of the whole. However, one outcome of the rise of the historical consciousness was precisely to blow such holism wide open. The historical vision is of a world that has been thoroughly temporalized, that is from beginning to end and from top to bottom in process towards an end that, because it is an end arrived at in and through time, is not completely given or present in any actual temporal experience and that cannot be separated from the uncertainties and multiple possibilities that belong to all historical becoming. Such an end is therefore unknown and unknowable. But if the end is missing, clearly no account of the whole is at all possible, for history only becomes a whole when its end is given.

The choice, then, seems to be narrowed down to the following: either Sisyphus – or a supra-historical fulfilment that gives meaning to time from beyond time: in other words, an eternal fulfilment that, as eternal, is not simply a matter of putting the final full stop to the process of historical becoming but is the possibility of fulfilment for each and every creature labouring in, with and under the conditions of historical time. This by no means requires us to disparage any effort towards the amelioration of the human condition within history or to turn away from history (though often the postulate of a supratemporal eternal fulfilment has gone along with such negligence of the actual historical task). On the contrary some presentations of supra-historical fulfilment (let us call it salvation) would argue that the postulate of salvation is the best of motives for intrahistorical action, and that it is belief in such salvation that first gives us the possibility of historical action, the only hope that can truly move us to do works of love.

Leaving such questions to one side, however, I should like to reflect further on what I take to be a necessary correlate of belief in a final, supra-historical salvation and which I take to be a primary motive for the rise of such belief: the recognition that without the postulate of eternal life, the question of evil will remain simply the scandal of evil.

Instructive in this respect is the trajectory of John Hick's thought in the period spanned by his books *Evil and the God of Love* (1966 – effectively the standard textbook on the topic for several theological generations in Britain) and his *Death and Eternal Life* (1976). Although these are, in a sense, two distinct studies, the connection between them and the progress from the one to the other is clear. In *Evil and the God of Love* Hick sets out systematically to reverse the terms of Augustinian theodicy. His criticisms of this tradition centre on what he sees as its 'sub-personal' approach, as reflected in its concern for metaphysical evil, the definition of evil in terms of ontological categories (i.e. non-being), its aesthetic attitude and the view of human suffering as a punishment for sin. In contrast to this Hick recommends what he calls the 'Irenaean type of Theodicy' and that he sees paradigmatically developed by Schleiermacher at the start of the modern period in theology. In line with some of the modern theodicies considered here, this dismisses the picture of Adam's original perfection as painted by earlier theologies and instead sees human life as a progressive development towards an ever-greater perfection. On this view the evil encountered in the world is not the punishment for sin, but part of an ongoing experience of 'soul-making'. 'And so man,' Hick writes, 'created as a personal being in the image of God, is only the raw material for a further and more difficult stage of God's creative work. This is the leading of men as relatively free and autonomous persons, through their own dealings with life in the world in which He has placed them, towards that quality of existence that is the finite likeness of God. The features of this likeness are revealed in the person of Christ, and the process of man's creation into it is the work of the Holy Spirit.'[1] This, as Hick takes it, is the sense of St Paul's words 'And we all, with unveiled faces, beholding the glory of the Lord, are being changed into his likeness from one degree of glory to another . . .' (2 Cor. 3.18). For all the evil in it, this world is 'a divinely-created sphere of soul-making'.[2] Finally, Hick's hope is for a universal salvation which, as he believes, alone does justice to the idea of God as love. However, it is clear that if this is to be so, and if, as Hick sees it, God's will is not about the execution of a cosmic master-plan but the engendering of relationships of free, autonomous, personal response, then a further dimension of existence will need to be postulated, since it seems clear that many finish their lives on this earth without having attained the point of being able to make such a response. In his earlier thought, Hick conceived this by means of analogy with the idea of purgatory. In the traditional view, souls deemed worthy of salvation but who were still far from perfection and could not therefore be translated directly from earth to heaven were sent to this intermediate state in order to work out the punishments due them – to serve their time, as it were – until they were sufficiently 'purged' to enter into the full splendour of heavenly existence. In Hick's view, the emphasis was not so much on punishment for past sins as growth in personal freedom and love. In *Death and Eternal Life*, however, he is led to postulate a state in which Christian ideas of purgatory and resurrection are combined with Eastern ideas of reincarnation and of a multilevelled universe. The result is what Hick calls 'pareschatologies', states of being that transcend our present experience, a sequence of 'progressively "higher" worlds', 'environments of ever more morally and spiritually perfect modes of existence'.[3] Only this, he suggests, can do justice, on the one hand, to the experienced limits of what is achievable in this world, and, on the other, to the freedom, depth and complexity of the final end towards which the religious vision points.

This is a brave exercise in inter-religious speculation, and such pluralism is, undoubtedly, integral to the horizon within which we must now attempt to think about God. However, its interest in the present context is the way in which, if one is to turn from a metaphysical to a historical posing of the question of theodicy, the question of death and of what lies beyond it become all the more pressing. For once history is grasped as such and not experienced simply as a mirror of eternal truths, it cannot but confront us with the questions 'Where is it all going?' 'What is it all *for*?', and if there is any such thing as meaning in history, it is tied up with being able to answer questions like these.

In turning to almost any text in this area produced in the period of the Enlightenment, as the historical consciousness gradually took hold of Western European thinking, it is immediately striking how central the role of personal immortality was in religious apologetics. It is with this question that Bishop Butler opened his *Analogy of Religion*, and he begins two 'dissertations' appended to that work with the remark that 'Whether we are to live in a future state . . . is the most important question which can possibly be asked . . .'[4] When, half a century later, in his *Critique of Practical Reason*, Kant offers his so-called moral argument for the existence of God it seems almost as if God's decisive function is to guarantee the personal immortality of the moral agent, an immortality that is necessary if there is to be a final coincidence of virtue and happiness. Kant does not argue for this on the grounds that we 'deserve' to be rewarded for our good works, since this would betray the moral impurity that Kant himself describes as the second level of operation of the propensity to evil, when we do what is right but for sub-moral reasons, i.e. fear of the law, or the desire for gratification. The sequence of Kant's argument is, rather, this: that the proper goal of moral striving is the realization of the highest good (the *summum bonum*); that the concept of the highest good itself requires the coincidence of virtue and happiness; and, since it is clear that no such coincidence is given on the plane of historical experience, then personal immortality and the postulate of a life beyond this life is the necessary condition of such a coincidence and, therefore, of the very possibility of moral striving. If the subtlety of this line of reasoning and the sophistication of its exposition put Kant in a different league from many of his Enlightenment contemporaries, the basic shape of his argument and the central claim that the resolution of the question of evil depends on the promise of a future life represents a widely shared view at the end of the eighteenth century. Religious apologists too laid great emphasis on such belief as one of the pillars – and one of the least dubitable elements – of religion.

Going forward a further half-century, Kierkegaard's *Concluding Unscientific Postscript* represents an early Christian response to the Hegelian conception of history. One of his principal complaints concerns the Hegelian appropriation of Christian terminology. As Kierkegaard saw it, Hegel's basic claim that the immanent processes of history can be thought of as a unitary whole in such a way as to justify the assertion that 'World history is the Last Judgment' would, if accepted, render Christian claims regarding the transcendence of God and the immortality of the individual redundant. Hegel's position is effectively a reductionist one, he is saying, and there is a clear either/or between Hegel and Christianity. The critical wing of twentieth-century philosophy readily endorsed Kierkegaard's critique of the system as flattening out the richness and diversity of values. Of less interest to modernist philosophy, however, was Kierkegaard's point that it was precisely the individual's concern for an eternal happiness (i.e. to paraphrase Kierkegaard, the question 'Will I find myself again in a future, conscious state after the death of my body and, if so, may I hope for a final and eternally continuing happiness as the content of that future state?'). My concern for my eternal happiness is not something that can be met or answered by the only prospect available to a Hegelian, namely, the general progress of the human race. Accepting Hegel's (or the Hegelians') claim that this position represented the outcome of a philosophical approach that was both rational and objective, Kierkegaard took the opposite tack of privileging the standpoint of subjectivity, and embracing existential passion, suffering and guilt as the defining characteristics of a subjective approach to truth. For, as he put the case, my concern for my eternal happiness – whatever the objective truth of the matter – can never be a matter of detached, neutral or disinterested observation or reflection. It makes all the difference to me, to how I feel about my life and to how I live it, whether I believe that 'the play is the tragedy "man" and the hero the Conquering Worm' (Poe) or that we were not made for dust. It cuts to the very heart of my sense of self. It is part of the logic of thinking about personal immortality that it should be addressed existentially and not logically, concretely and not in purely general terms, and this concreteness means that I cannot abstract my thinking about death and personal immortality from my own immediate interest in such questions.

> If . . . the uncertainty of death is merely something in general, then my own death is itself only something in general. Perhaps this is also the case for systematic philosophers, for absent-minded people . . . But the fact of my own death is not for me by any means such a something in general, although for others, the fact of my death may indeed be something of that sort.[5]

> I know that some have found immortality in Hegel, others have not; I know that I have not found it in the System, where indeed it is also unreasonable to seek it; for, in a fantastic sense, all systematic thinking is *sub specie aeterni*, and to that extent immortality is there in the sense of eternity, but this immortality is not at all the one about which the question is asked, since the question is about the immortality of a mortal, which is not answered by showing that the eternal is immortal, and the immortality of the eternal is a tautology and a misuse of words . . . A book raises the question of the immortality of the soul. The contents of the book constitute the answer. But the contents of the book, as the reader can convince himself by reading it through, are the opinions of the wisest and best men about immortality, all neatly strung on a thread . . . So then the question about immortality is a learned question. All honor to learning! All honor to him who can handle learnedly the learned question of immortality! But the question of immortality is essentially not a learned question, rather it is a question of inwardness, which the subject by becoming subjective must put to himself.[6]

As in Kierkegaard's rediscovery of Job, then, we have an acceptance of the necessarily partial, necessarily interested, necessarily passionate nature of the individual's own concern as an entirely fitting response to the question at issue. The key point here, however, is not simply to draw attention to the legitimacy (or to Kierkegaard's claim concerning the legitimacy) of such a subjective approach, but to see how it arises specifically as a response to a historicized understanding of the human situation and to a recognition of the limits of history in determining the final issue of human destiny and so, also, of the question of evil.

But, having raised the question, is it at all possible to give anything like a positive answer?

In the previous chapter *The Brothers Karamazov* was cited as one of the outstanding contributions to the modern theme of moral outrage in the face of evil. In terms of the often-quoted asseverations made by Ivan in the course of his 'rebellion' it would seem as if there is no way back from or though the fury of this outrage. Ivan is prepared to refuse the mother of the tortured child the right to embrace its murderer even if he is wrong. Nothing, it seems, no possible future state, could compensate for or make good the grievousness of such crimes perpetrated against innocent children. Similarly, both in *The Brothers Karamazov* and elsewhere, the ineluctable horror of death seems so to overwhelm Dostoevsky's characters, that any attempt on the part of the reader to hold on to any kind of hope in a future life is pitilessly beaten down.

As is well-known, Dostoevsky himself experienced the deep trauma of having been sentenced to death for his participation in a series of discussion groups that were regarded as subversive by the Czarist authorities, only to be reprieved minutes before the moment of execution. He pictured the scene in the early pages of the novel *The Idiot*, recalling how he spent what he believed were the last five minutes of his young life. From there on the novel recurs repeatedly to the question of death, often in still more brutal terms. A few pages on Prince Myshkin (the eponymous 'idiot' of the title) describes to the vivacious young daughters of General Epanchin an execution by guillotine which he attended and speculates on the thoughts of the man being guillotined.

It's strange that people rarely faint at these last moments. On the contrary the brain is extraordinarily lively and must be working at a tremendous rate – at a tremendous rate, like a machine at full speed. I fancy that there is a continual throbbing of ideas of all sorts, always unfinished and perhaps absurd too, quite irrelevant ideas: 'That man is looking at me. He has a wart on his forehead. One of the executioner's buttons is rusty' . . . and yet all the while one knows and remembers everything. There is one point which can never be forgotten, and one can't faint, and everything moves and turns about it, about that point. And only think it must be like that up to the last quarter of a second, when his head lies on the block and he waits and . . . *knows*, and suddenly hears above him the clang of the iron! He must hear that! If I were lying there, I should listen on purpose and hear. It may last only the tenth part of a second, but one would be sure to hear it. And only fancy, it's still disputed whether, when the head is cut off, it knows, for a second after that it's been cut off! What an idea! And what if it knows it for five seconds!

   Paint the scaffold so that only the last step can be distinctly seen in the foreground and the criminal having just stepped on it; his head, his face as white as paper; the priest holding up the cross, the man greedily putting forward his blue lips and looking – and aware of everything. The cross and the head – that's the picture.[7]

Plainly, for Myshkin, this is not just to be taken as a picture of an execution. It is a picture of human life, an anticipation of Beckett's line that we are born over a grave,[8] and what the condemned man experiences in those last moments is in some sense the truth of our common condition. The rationality and mechanical efficiency of the guillotine make it a particularly repulsive means of execution to Dostoevsky – but precisely these features help him to articulate the problematics of a Christian response to a view of the world in which the whole universe is nothing but a system of seamless cause-and-effect, mechanical, quantifiable and stripped of the pathetic fallacy that would invest life with sympathy, purpose or feeling.

This is brought out still more clearly in a later episode, and again in relation to a picture. This time it is Holbein's painting of the dead Christ in the tomb. The meaning of such a picture is expounded by the angry – and dying – young nihilist, Hyppolite Terentyev. In this picture, he says (very accurately):

. . . there's no trace of beauty. It is in every detail the corpse of a man who has endured infinite agony before the crucifixion; who has been wounded, tortured, beaten by the guards and the people when He carried the cross on His back and fell beneath its weight, and after that has undergone the agony of crucifixion, lasting for six hours at least (according to my reckoning) . . . It is simply nature, and the corpse of a man, whoever he might be, must really look like that after such suffering . . . In the picture the face is fearfully crushed by blows, swollen, covered with fearful, swollen and blood-stained bruises, the eyes are open and squinting: the great wide-open whites of the eyes glitter with a look of deathly, glassy light.[9]

Then the question arises, Hyppolite says, as to how the disciples and the women who followed Jesus must have felt when they saw him whom they had worshipped as no more than just such a corpse. Surely, he asks, 'if death is so awful and the laws of nature so mighty, how can they be overcome? How can they be overcome when even He did not conquer them, He who vanquished nature in His lifetime, who exclaimed, "Maiden, arise!" and the maiden arose – "Lazarus, come forth!" and the dead man came forth?'

More powerful than Christ, then, are the inexorable laws of nature, that, for just that reason, seem to Hyppolite to be more than merely mechanical or mathematically-determinate processes but offer instead a complete mockery of human beings' longing for a fuller, richer, more meaningful life.

Looking at such a picture, one conceives of nature in the shape of an immense, merciless, dumb beast, or more correctly, much more correctly, speaking, though it sounds strange, in the form of a huge machine of the most modern construction which, dull and insensible, has aimlessly clutched, crushed and swallowed up a great priceless Being, a being worth all nature and its laws, worth the whole earth, which was created perhaps solely for the sake of the advent of that being. This picture expresses and unconsciously suggests to one the conception of such a dark, insolent, unreasoning and eternal Power to which everything is in subjection.[10]

In *The Idiot* itself, there seems to be no answer to Terentyev's anguish in the face of death and its mockery of human values and aspirations. The novel ends in a brutal murder and the relapse of Prince Myshkin (the nearest thing in the novel to a Christ-figure) into a quasi-vegetative 'idiotic' state. But that is not the end of Dostoevsky's own questioning. He returns to the subject in other novels and stories, including *The Brothers Karamazov*. Here, as we have seen, it would seem as if Ivan's outrage draws a line that cannot be crossed. But Dostoevsky does not stop with Ivan. To Ivan's rebellion and 'Legend of the Grand Inquisitor' Dostoevsky counterposes the life of the saintly Father Zossima, which includes the narrative of the deathbed conversion of Zossima's brother Markel. Like Hyppolite, Markel has lost his childhood faith, and now finds himself confronting an early death from consumption. However, on the Tuesday of Holy Week, Markel begins to take the sacrament again and allows his mother to relight the candle under the icon in his bedroom. He urges his mother not to cry, since 'life is paradise, and we are all in paradise, but we won't see it, if we would, we should have heaven on earth the next day.'[11] He protests against being waited upon, as he believes himself to have sinned against all men, and deserves only to wait upon others. He tells his mother 'believe me, everyone is really responsible to all men for all men and for everything.'[12] He even prays to the birds outside his window for forgiveness: '"Yes," he said, "there was such a glory of God all about me; birds, trees, meadows, sky, only I lived in shame and dishonoured it all and did not notice the beauty and glory."'[13]

As it is set up in the novel, Markel's story, and the other stories collected in the life of Zossima, provide not exactly an 'answer' to Ivan – for there is no point-by-point correspondence – but a counterposition, and a reminder that Ivan's is only one view amongst others.

The question of death and its finality comes back into focus when Zossima himself dies. He has been a controversial figure in his monastery. Some regard him as a saint (this, most readers would assume, is the position of Dostoevsky), whilst others, led by the mad Father Ferrapont, accuse him of having been possessed – a situation, of course, that mirrors disputes recorded in the gospel accounts of Christ's own life. In the context of Orthodox spirituality, it is expected that if Zossima had been a true saint, his body would be preserved from decomposition and would give off the scent of sweet-smelling roses rather than that of dead flesh. However, it soon becomes evident that Zossima's body is rotting like anyone else's. Such sainthood as is attainable on earth, Dostoevsky implies, cannot be accompanied by any unambiguous signs or infallible marks. Sainthood, the life of virtue and love, cannot break or change the unalterable laws of nature. Whatever goodness there is in life exists only as veiled by the ambiguity of everyday reality.

Alyosha, Zossima's disciple, continues to sit by the body, however. As he does so he falls asleep during the reading of the gospel story of the wedding at Cana of Galilee at which Christ turned the water into wine, and in Alyosha's dream he sees the scene come to life, and, in the midst of it Zossima is present, and speaking to him. Zossima assures him of Christ's universal mercy and love, and, in terms recalling Markel's dying words, suggests that it is only Alyosha's fear that prevents him from seeing this. When Alyosha awakes, he rushes out into the monastery garden and falls on the ground, kissing it and watering the earth with his tears. In that moment he experiences perhaps the closest thing we find in Dostoevsky's novels to a positive mystical experience:

> There seemed to be threads from all those innumerable worlds of God [the stars], linking his soul to them, and it was trembling all over 'in contact with other worlds'. He longed to forgive everyone and for everything, and to beg forgiveness. Oh, not for himself but for all men, for all and for everything. 'And others are praying for me too,' echoed again in his soul. But with every instant he felt clearly and, as it were, tangibly that something firm and unshake-able as that vault of heaven had entered his soul. It was as though some idea had seized the sovereignty of his mind – and it was for all his life and for ever and ever . . . 'Someone visited my soul in that hour,' he used to say afterwards, with implicit faith in his words.[14]

Clearly this is an 'answer' for Alyosha himself in the face of the crisis brought on by the corruption of Zossima's body. But, even if we accept Kierkegaard's point about the legitimacy of a subjective approach when it is a matter of the individual's confrontation with their own death and the question of an eternal happiness, Alyosha's experience would indeed seem to be no more than an answer for himself alone. It comes to him as a dream, as what 'seems' to be, as what he 'longs' for. It is not the presentation of an argument or a fact. Like Zossima's sainthood, Alyosha's hope must accept the limita-tions and the ambiguity of earthly life. But, conversely, Dostoevsky is also suggesting that even the acceptance of these limitations and even the recognition of the irresistible universal power of the laws of nature need not and does not prevent us from making our own affirmations of faith. In the face of Hyppolite's ruthless cosmic machine, we have other options than despair; we can experience the world as paradise, as rich with the possibilities of spiritual com-munion.

But what of Ivan? Could he be talked round to such a view?

Ivan's own inner demons drive him relentlessly along a downward slope towards despair and mental breakdown. At his lowest point the devil himself appears to him, and they conduct an extended conver-sation. In the course of this the devil reminds Ivan of some of his own early ideas. One of these is the grotesque story of a Russian nihilist, who, in his life, 'rejected everything, laws, conscience, faith, and, above all, the future life.'[15] On dying he is deeply offended to wake up in a future life where, as a punishment for his unbelief, he is sentenced to walk a quadrillion kilometres. Russian anihilists, however, don't give up as easily as that, and so the man simply refused to budge and lay down on the road in protest. Nevertheless, after a thousand years of lying there, he finally got up and began to walk. Ivan at this point interrupts the devil and they have an absurd exchange concerning the meaning of spatial distance in the afterlife in the course of which the devil propounds his own nihilistic view of the cosmos as an eternally recurring and altogether pointless process.

> [O]ur present earth may have been repeated a billion times. Why, it's become extinct, been frozen; cracked, broken to bits, disintegrated into its elements, again 'the water above the firmament', then again a comet, again a sun, again from the sun it becomes earth – and the same sequence may have been repeated endlessly, and exactly the same to every detail, most unseemly and insufferably tedious . . . [16]

However, notwithstanding this melancholy vision of eternal recurrence, the devil continues the story to the end when, after walking for millions of years, the former nihilist finally arrives at paradise and

> . . . before he had been there two seconds, by his watch (though to my thinking his watch must have long dissolved into its elements on the way), he cried out that these two seconds were worth walking not a quadrillion kilometres, but a quadrillion of quadrillions, raised to the quadrillionth power! In fact he sang 'hosannah' and overdid it so, that some persons there of lofty ideas wouldn't shake hands with him at first – he'd become too rapidly reactionary, they said. [17]

The story is, of course, absurd, and is narrated by the devil, a figment of Ivan's imagination. Yet, for all this, it too, like the life of Zossima and the story of Markel, is a kind of response – albeit a very different kind of response – to Ivan's stated refusal in his 'rebellion' that no possible future state could compensate for the sufferings of this earth. This is no logical or cosmological proof of immortality, but, occurring in the context of Ivan's breakdown, it serves as an exercise in what I have called the psychology of evil to question whether the kind of refusal exemplified by Ivan's determination to return his ticket can really and consistently be carried through, whether hope is eliminable simply on the basis of conscious will. [18]

Putting it in terms of the previous discussion of the banality of evil as a modern reworking of the Platonic/Augustinian theme of evil as non-being, it suggests that even when a personality has been so reduced as almost to arrive at the point of self-dissolution – as we see happening in Ivan – it cannot, *qua* personality, escape the freedom that is the obverse of its fall towards nothingness, and since freedom means the possibility of historical action and therefore also of a relation to the future, comes the possibility of hope. This inextinguishability of hope is, it may be, precisely the force of the symbol of the final 'hosannah'.

That may seem a weak conclusion. However, for all the drama with which he presents the issues, Dostoevsky remains deeply aware of his own limitations *qua* novelist. Here, as at many other points in his writings, the most direct statements of Christian belief are placed in the mouths of drunkards, idiots and, as in this case, of a devil who is no more than a hallucination. These literary devices intentionally mark out the possibility of hope in a final and eternal happiness as necessarily enigmatic and uncertain for human beings suffering under the conditions of finite, mortal existence. Again, we note how, for us (still living through the situation of modernity), the 'answer' that most moves us is one that internalizes a self-reflecting under-standing of the problematics of language and communication. Religious populists may say that 'what people want' is clear, distinct and dogmatic teaching, but do the 'answers' such teaching offers do justice to the complexity of our actual experience?

That Dostoevsky compels us to ask such a question, and to ask it so sharply, indicates why his work had no less an impact on philoso-phers than it did in the field of literature. We are not dealing here simply with a literary illustration of philosophical problems, but with an attempt to tackle those problems in the form most suited to them. Dostoevsky's novelistic approach is not simply storytelling (though, as narrative theologians would argue, 'story' is an important dimen-sion of the religious response), but the creation of a space in and across which a dialogue of positions and counterpositions is devel-oped and that, on the analogy with a Platonic dialogue, may not issue in a result but nevertheless serves to clarify just what is at stake. In this respect the achievement of Dostoevsky's novels is to have consti-tuted just such a dialogical space as that which, in Chapter Seven, we described as the open space of contemporary philosophical enquiry and debate that is, at the same time, the space opened up by the hermeneutical movement in philosophy.[19]

We have allowed the discussion of evil and eternal life to be guided by the way in which the 'classical' questions of theodicy and immortality have been recast in the light of the historical consciousness and the turn to the subject. These last remarks about Dostoevsky, however, point to the inseparability of these dimensions of the question from the further characteristically modern emphasis on language and communication. If we are to understand what Dostoevsky is saying, we must do more than simply translate the unstable, shifting and ultimately enigmatic argument of the novel into a doctrine or proposition. Rather, we must allow the novel, as the distinctive linguistic construct that it is, to work upon us in its own novelistic way. Only so can we expect to feel not only the force of Dostoevsky's existential passion in posing these ultimate questions, but also the sharpness and the clarity with which he articulates them.

Still, it might be objected (from the standpoint of church doctrine, for example) that such a resort to literature merely demonstrates the weakness of any attempt to argue for faith on the ground of the modern turn to the subject. Mustn't such faith finally be condemned as 'merely' subjective? And, as such, doesn't it expose itself to the arguments of the reductionists? Isn't it perhaps itself an expression or acceptance of reductionism, in that it shows faith in the future life as no more than a subjective wish, a longing that it might be so?

With regard to Dostoevsky, such a conclusion would, to say the least, be weird. For his whole argument is developed in conscious and critical response to the reductionism of Feuerbach and his Russian disciples and a view of the cosmic situation which, as is made clear in the devil's evocation of eternal recurrence, has been stripped of all traces of the pathetic fallacy. What Dostoevsky is seeking is precisely a way of resisting the claims that the human person is reducible to the laws of nature, that society can be managed as if it were a machine, and that the aberrations and crimes of individuals can be treated as if they were diseases whose diagnosis and treatment were strictly quantifiable and without regard to the freedom and ultimate responsibility of the human subject. Of course, the model of reductionism that Dostoevsky was confronting was, from our standpoint one hundred and fifty years later, a relatively crude one. Our contemporary Darwinistic versions of reductionism, developed to an extraordinary degree of precision in the light of the expansion in knowledge of our genetic inheritance, seem to be on a different scale. But perhaps that is an illusion. For, whilst acknowledging the quantum leap between the Russian nihilists of the 1860s, with their dogmatic, mechanistic materialism, and the detailed mapping of human characteristics available to the human biologist of the twenty-first century, we should not miss an essential continuity and analogy between the two programmes, at least as regards their common stance vis-à-vis religion.

Dostoevsky's appeal to the prospect of eternal life – albeit under the veil of dreams, madness and the impenetrable omnipresence of human suffering – is, by intention, a countermove to such reductionism. It is an attempt to construct a discourse that allows for an appropriate valuing of the human person, and insists on the possibility of holding us responsible for our actions. Crucial to Dostoevsky's case, however, is the conviction that 'eternal life' is not just a cipher for moral accountability but that the hope of eternal life (Kierkegaard's 'expectation of an eternal happiness') is the sole horizon that could adequately ground a view of the person as a creative centre of inexhaustible mystery and integrity. Understood in this way it becomes the necessary presupposition of any discourse about purely moral acts and purposes. In his speech at the grave of Ilyusha, the schoolboy whose persecutors had been brought by Alyosha to be reconciled with him, Alyosha Karamazov exhorts the boys to carry forward the memory of this good act and the feeling of their companionship with them through life, as something that can inspire them to new deeds of kindness and compassion. If that were all, it might be taken (as many commentators have taken it) as recommending nothing more than any secular humanist might be prepared to sign up to. But, as the speech comes to an end and in the very closing lines of the novel, one of the boys asks:

'Karamazov . . . can it be true what's taught us in religion, that we shall rise from the dead and shall live and see each other again, all, Il[y]usha too?'

'Certainly we shall all rise again, certainly we shall see each other and shall tell each other with joy and gladness all that has happened!' Alyosha answered, half laughing, half enthusiastic.

'Ah, how splendid it will be!' broke from Kolya.

'Well, now we will finish talking and go to his funeral dinner. Don't be put out at our eating pancakes – it's a very old custom and there's something nice in that!' laughed Alyosha. 'Well, let us go! And now we go hand in hand.'[20]

Facing up to the situation that in an age in which the measure of knowledge is determined by natural science such a hope can never be an object of knowledge, but only what it is: a *hope*. Even though we can only speak about this hope 'half laughing' (and therefore not something we could ever prove or should ever attempt to prove in the face of the reductionist critique), Dostoevsky makes of it the defining measure of personal life. We are not moral agents onto whom eternal life might be added, but our being as persons is determined through and through by the fact that we are the beings capable of affirming such a hope. Nor is this hope simply a protest against the brute fact of death. On the contrary, having such a hope – or, more precisely, having the possibility of having such a hope – is what gives us the kind of claim on life that makes death problematic. If we expected nothing more, death would be no affront to human dignity. In any case, nothing that has been said implies that hope is any more than hope or constitutes an argument for immortal life as some kind of post-mortem state of affairs. This is not a last ditch plea on behalf of the kind of sentimental agnostic who – perhaps once a year on Christmas Eve – muses how much more pleasant life would be if only 'it' were all true. In the perspective adopted here the hope of immortality is not a matter of rationalizing the wishful thinking we all inevitably experience in some degree in contemplating the extinction of consciousness. It is instead a measure of the value we place upon human personhood.

The whole issue of reductionism – whether we are for it or against it – misses the hermeneutic point. At one level, the argument put forward here is what Don Cupitt would call 'non-realist', in that, as has just been stated, it is not a matter of speculating about some post-mortem state of affairs. However, such a categorization does not quite engage with the question being pursued here. If we have truly internalized the rise of the historical consciousness, the turn to the subject, and the linguistic turn, if we have become sensitive to the complex depth of all that is involved in being beings that live through their historically-transmitted self-representations, our question will become more a hermeneutic question concerning the meaning of what it is to hold to ultimate hope. In these terms the question is analogous to the question posed by Paul Ricoeur in his treatment of the symbolism of evil: it is a question as to what the phenomenon in question gives to thinking.[21] From this standpoint, the standpoint of thinking, the truly interesting phenomenon is not some future state (and therefore not the question as to whether such a state exists or not), but that we are beings who can hope for an eternal happiness – not only for ourselves as separate individuals but for one another, and, above all, for those Dostoevsky called the 'insulted and injured' of life. In relation to this the question, then, is what hope gives us to think about with regard to our understanding of God and, in connection with this, of the meaning and value that any specific discourse about God allows to the human subject.

Already from a Dostoevskian standpoint, the postulation of any post-mortem state of affairs that could be the subject of spiritualistic 'experiment' or 'evidence' would already betray an acceptance of a quantifying and reductionist approach to the mystery of the person. Even if such experimentation were to yield positive results, it would say nothing of the kind of quality of eternal life that could serve as an 'answer' to the question of evil – a point Dostoevsky makes by contrasting the 'quadrillions' of years the dead atheist takes in reaching paradise with the instantaneousness of his final 'hosannah'. Before deciding the issue one way or another – reductionist or anti-reductionist – we would need to have become clear as to what exactly it is we are looking for in posing the questions of evil and eternal life: Are we looking for a scientific picture of how things are, of what is the case? For all its one-sidedness, the kind of empiricist critique of religion reflected in the University Debate showed that that can scarcely be the case. Rather, religion seems to be articulating the commitment to or search for a way of representing our human way of being in the world – a word, an image, or meaning-event – that would enhance the possibility of historical action, in solidarity with and on behalf of others, and sustain the belief that our world, whatever else it may be, is a humanizable world, a potential home for beings such as ourselves.

Recalling what was said in Chapter Six regarding the political and cultural dimension of the hermeneutical task, we can see how the question of hope, as that has been developed here, points us towards the whole contemporary discourse concerning the meaning and value of the human person. As was also stated previously, this involves both an aesthetic dimension, in the sense of seeking, creating or affirming an image of the human that does justice to the best possibilities of human life (Alyosha's dream, perhaps), and also an ethical dimension, as we commit ourselves to defending and promoting those possibilities (Alyosha's ministry amongst the boys). This ethical dimension in turn requires engagement not only with affirmations and denials of hope in the lived singularity of the concrete individual life but also with the global political struggle for human flourishing (including, most urgently for our own time, the care of our planetary environment as a milieu for the sustaining of biological life as a necessary condition of spiritual life). Between these lies the task of philosophical enquiry narrowly understood: the labour of conceptual clarification that explicates and justifies the meaning of the image and of the ethical action that corresponds to it.[22] To sum up: the question of religion – the question of salvation and belief as focused through the struggle to maintain hope in the face of evil – is nothing other than the question as to who we ourselves are, the question of the human person. The non-reductive sense of this is epitomized in the words of Vladimir Soloviev (possibly the real-life model, at least in part, for Alyosha Karamazov) that 'belief in human personhood is at the same time implictly belief in God'.[23]

It might be objected that the attention given to the questions of evil and eternal life is quite disproportionate in relation to the whole field of the philosophical enquiry concerning religion. Nothing has been said here about such standard questions as the divine attributes or what would be involved in understanding God as Creator. This is true, and I do not at all intend to deny that there are other routes in to the key issues of the philosophy of religion, nor yet that, quantitatively speaking, what has been said here could not have been expanded tenfold. The point of philosophical questioning, however, is not exhaustiveness of that kind. It is not a matter of being able to write a 5,000-word essay on each of a specified number of set topics. It is, instead, a matter of asking the questions of religion in such a way as to bring into view something of the assumptions and presuppositions that have led to the posing of those questions in the first place and, consequently, whether on the basis of one single question or of a set of questions, being able to see something of the scope, meaning and implications of the matter of religion. My claim is that, by taking the question of evil as our worked example for the theoretical orientation adumbrated in the preceding chapters we have actually reached a point at which we can indeed think what it means for the religious person to appeal to belief in salvation in the context of the intellectual and cultural assumptions of modernity. For this is not in any way an isolated issue, but one that illuminates the wider field of religious ideas. This can, for example, be seen in relation to the doctrine of creation. Within a historicized and subjectively- and linguistically-turned world, the original created essence of the human being can no longer be seen as something that can be abstracted from its history, its self-consciousness, its hope. The role of the hope of an eternal happiness that has emerged through our reading of Dostoevsky, however, as pointing to the kind of beings we are, gives us the possibility of our own history in time as 'children of God'. In contrast to those theologies for which belief in an 'other' world or future life led to a denigrating of this world and this life, portraying it as a vale of tears through which we must pass but in which we have no abiding home, the 'other' world that is the focus of attention here is not a posthumous world or a parallel universe: it is the world that, through hope, makes this world humanly habitable, the paradise we could have today if we could embrace the doctrine of each being responsible for all. It is not the denial of time, but what gives us time, what gives us life, what creates community. Creation, for us, can only be understood from its end, not its beginning, but that end, as we have seen, exists only as the struggle between experienced evil and hope. That does not mean that we undertake the struggle against evil on behalf of some predetermined vision of how things could or should be. For we ourselves do not exist other than as this struggle, and our representations both of evil and of things hoped for reflect nothing other than ourselves in our own unending self-questioning, as we journey ever further into the mystery of personal, spiritual life.

This 'short course' began by characterizing philosophy as a questioning and elucidating of the presuppositions and assumptions underlying a given discourse. We may conclude that the assumption underlying and justifying the discourse of religion in our historical moment is that those engaged in this discourse are committed in the way just described both to the struggle and to the question. Since religion has no given or determinate field outside of or independent of these, it follows that without such commitment both the formal practice and the study of religion are finally vacuous. Where such commitment exists, however, religion may still prove to be a resource for the discovery of what is 'the best' for us to be and to do; a visionary expression of that 'best'; and a spur to its realization. It follows that when the issue is conceived in these terms there can be no great gain for humanity in excluding religion from the common social, cultural and intellectual task of deciding what is in fact the meaning of our short time under the sun.

Further Reading

Further reading will necessarily vary according to interest and intellectual orientation. Some will be more interested in exploring at greater length some of the particular thinkers discussed here, whilst others will be attracted to a more topic-based approach. In addition to sources already referenced in footnotes, both authors and topics can be pursued through standard reference works such as the excellent *Routledge Encyclopedia of Philosophy*, 10 vols., ed. Edward Craig, London: Routledge 1998, or series such as the Cambridge Companions (now available for most of the key thinkers in the history of the philosophy of religion) or the Routledge GuideBooks in Philosophy. There are also a number of Companions or general Introductions to the field that supplement or complement the approach taken here; see, e.g. Philip L. Quinn and Charles Taliaferro (eds), *Blackwell Companions to Philosophy: A Companion to Philosophy of Religion*, Oxford: Blackwell 1997, or Brian Davies, *Philosophy of Religion. A Guide and Anthology*, Oxford: Oxford University Press 2000. A good survey of philosophies of history is provided by the anthology: R. M. Burns and H. Rayment-Pickard (eds), *Philosophies of History. From Enlightenment to Postmodernity*, Oxford: Blackwell 2000. Autonomy, as a key aspect of the turn to the subject is covered in J. B. Schneewind, *The Invention of Autonomy*, Cambridge: Cambridge University Press 1998. For hermeneutics see P. Ricoeur, *Time and Narrative*, 3 vols., Chicago: University of Chicago Press 1984. The way in which the contemporary debate has been shaped by postmodernity is represented in several collections; see, e.g. P. Berry and A. Wernick (eds), *Shadow of Spirit: Postmodernism and Religion*, London: Routledge 1992, and P. Blond (ed.), *Post-Secular Philosophy. Between Philosophy and Theology*, London: Routledge 1998. On the problem of evil see K. Surin, *Theology and the Problem of Evil*, Oxford: Blackwell 1986, and O. Leaman, *Evil and Suffering in Jewish Philosophy*, Cambridge: Cambridge University Press 1995. For Russian religious philosophy see, e.g. F. Copleston, *Russian Religious Philosophy*, London: Burns and Oates 1988.

For other – diverse – approaches to the subject see:

W. Alston, *Perceiving God*, Ithaca: Cornell University Press 1991.

Don Cupitt, *The Religion of Being*, London: SCM Press 1998.

J. Derrida and G. Vattimo (eds), *Religion*, Cambridge: Polity Press 1998.

A. Flew, *God and Philosophy*, London: Hutchinson 1966.

J. Hick, *An Interpretation of Religion*, London: Macmillan, 1989.

F. Kerr, *Immortal Longings. Versions of Transcending Humanity*, London: SPCK 1997.

M. McGhee (ed.), *Philosophy, Religion and the Spiritual Life*, Cambridge: Cambridge University Press 1992.

Iris Murdoch, *Metaphysics as a Guide to Morals*, London: Penguin 1992.

K. Nishitani, *Religion and Nothingness*, Berkeley and Los Angeles: University of California Press 1982.

D. Z. Phillips, *Religion Without Explanation*, Oxford: Blackwell 1976.

A. Plantinga and N. Wolterstorff (eds), *Faith and Rationality. Reason and Belief in God*, Notre Dame, Indiana: Notre Dame University Press, 1983.

Notes

Introduction

1 See especially my *Kierkegaard: The Aesthetic and the Religious*, 2nd edn, London: SCM Press 1999; *Agnosis: Theology in the Void*, Basingstoke: Macmillan 1996; *Anxious Angels: A Retrospective View of Religious Existentialism*, Basingstoke: Macmillan 1999; and *Routledge GuideBooks in Philosophy: The Later Heidegger*, London: Routledge 2000.

2 See especially *Agnosis*, Chapter Four.

Chapter 1. What is Philosophy of Religion?

1 Rudolf Carnap, 'The Overcoming of Metaphysics through Logical Analysis', *Heidegger and Modern Philosophy. Critical Essays*, ed. M. Murray, New Haven and London: Yale University Press 1978, pp. 23–34.

2 Heidegger is one obvious exception, since he was, at least for a time, an active member of the Nazi Party.

3 Plato, *The Republic of Plato*, tr. F. M. Cornford, Oxford: The Clarendon Press 1941, p. 14.

4 Plato, *Republic*, p. 17.

5 S. Kierkegaard, *The Concept of Irony with Constant Reference to Socrates. Together with Notes on Schelling's Berlin Lectures*, tr. H. V. and E. H. Hong, Princeton: Princeton University Press 1989, pp. 259–71.

6 G. W. F. Hegel, *Phenomenology of Spirit*, tr. A. V. Miller, Oxford: The Clarendon Press 1979, p. 11.

7 Although, of course, in our present cultural situation crystals, aliens or Gaia are more likely candidates for non-scientific explanations than Zeus.

8 M. Heidegger, *Nietzsche, Vol.* III, tr. J. Stambaugh, D. F. Krell and F. A. Capuzzi, San Francisco: HarperSanFrancisco 1987, p. 6.

9 Justin Martyr, 'The First Apology', *The Writings of Justin Martyr and Athenagoras (The Ante-Nicene Christian Library, Vol.* II), tr. M. Dods, G. Reith and B. P. Pratten, Edinburgh: T. and T. Clark 1868, pp. 7–8.

10 Justin Martyr, 'First Apology', pp. 24–5.

11   Justin Martyr, 'First Apology', p. 80. Similar views might be found in, e.g. Clement of Alexandria, half a century on from Justin. See, for example, Clement of Alexandria, 'Exhortation to the Heathen', Chapter 6 'By Divine Inspiration Philosophers sometimes hit on the Truth' or Book I of 'The Miscellanies' in *The Writings of Clement of Alexandria, Vol.* I *(The Ante-Nicene Christian Library, Vol.* IV), tr. W. Wilson, Edinburgh: T. and T. Clark 1867. Both Justin and Clement, like other apologists, argue that the ultimate source of Greek philosophy is, via Egypt, Mosaic religion itself. Clement, in downplaying the originality of the Greeks, even goes as far afield as Hinduism and Buddhism for analogies to the truths found in Greek philosophy.

12   Thomas Aquinas, *The 'Summa Theologica' of St Thomas Aquinas, Part I, First Number*, tr. The Fathers of the English Dominican Province, London: R. and T. Washbourne 1911, pp. 13–14 (Q. 8, reply obj. 2).

13   See Frederick C. Beiser, *The Sovereignty of Reason The Defense of Rationality in the Early English Enlightenment*, Princeton: Princeton University Press 1996.

14   It is possible, for example, to see contemporary scientist-theologians such as John Polkinghorne as following in the Paley line, albeit at a much greater level of sophistication.

15   It is perhaps in the light of such systematic considerations as well as historical factors that Christopher Stead, whilst acknowledging the proximity of the apologists to pagan philosophy, finally refuses to allow the apologists to count as 'philosophers' in the same sense as, e.g. those of the contemporary Platonist schools. See Christopher Stead, *Philosophy in Christian Antiquity*, Cambridge: Cambridge University Press 1994, especially Chapter Eight 'The Debate about Christian Philosophy', pp. 79–94.

16   S. Kierkegaard, *Eighteen Upbuilding Discourses*, tr. H. V. and E. H. Hong, Princeton: Princeton University Press 1990, p. 86.

17   Some of the issues here relate to the kind of philosophical critique of technology found in the later Heidegger. See my *Routledge GuideBooks in Philosophy: The Later Heidegger*, London: Routledge 2000. However, see also the very different approach of Jürgen Habermas in, e.g. *Knowledge and Human Interests*, tr. J. J. Schapiro, Boston: Beacon Press 1971.

18   See Wilfred Cantwell Smith, *The Meaning and End of Religion A New Approach to the Religious Traditions of Mankind*, New York: Macmillan 1963.

Chapter 2. Modern Trends (i): History

1   It has been claimed that the term 'philosophy of religion' itself is first
     used in Ralph Cudworth's *The True Intellectual System of the Universe*
     (1678).

2   Of course, this is more than a matter of costume! It is a recurrent
     problem with many costume dramas in film and television that
     characters from the nineteenth century or earlier are shown speak-
     ing and acting as if they were our contemporaries. Like Holman
     Hunt, modern film producers usually take great pains to ensure the
     historical accuracy, the period detail, of their subject matter, say, an
     adaptation of Jane Austen or a tale of medieval knights. But again
     and again they overlook the differences in social and sexual
     behaviour, in figures and manner of speech, and we go away feeling
     that it wasn't quite right. Sometimes the harder they try, the more the
     difference stands out. At the level of popular culture perhaps, the
     historicality of the human situation has still not completely
     permeated our consciousness.

3   G. W. F. Hegel, *Early Theological Writings*, tr. T. M. Knox and
     R. Kroner, Philadelphia: University of Pennsylvania Press 1975.

4   Although Hegel equates positive religion with Judaism, this
     is probably not his main target. Hegel was brought up within a
     particular stream of rational Protestantism, and although there
     are many points in his life and work that are only questionably
     orthodox, he, like many other Protestants in the seventeenth and
     eighteenth centuries, connected Protestantism with the ideals of
     reason and political freedom. In other words, what he says
     about the Judaism of the time of Jesus is essentially an oblique
     comment on Catholicism as well as on a certain way of construing
     the role of the church within a Protestant state.

5   Hegel, *Phenomenology*, pp. 18–19.

6   G. W. F. Hegel, *The Philosophy of History*, tr. J. Sibree, New York:
     Oxford University Press 1956, p. 323.

7   G. W. F. Hegel, *Lectures on the Philosophy of Religion. One-Volume
     Edition. The Lectures of 1827*, tr. P. C. Hodgson, Berkeley, Los Angeles
     and London: University of California Press 1988, p. 75.

8   Hegel, *Philosophy of Religion*, p. 76.

9   It could be argued that this is, in fact, precisely what Aristotle's idea
     implies. However, there is a real – and clear – difference between
     Aristotle and Hegel at this point. Perhaps it could also be put like
     this: that Hegel's God not only moves, but is moved – albeit in the
     context of an infinite and reciprocal dynamic such that what is
     moved is also itself a (reciprocal) cause of motion in what moved it.

10   A partially analogous movement in Britain and America has been
     process philosophy (Whitehead) and process theology (Hartshorne),

and the promotion of panentheism: the idea that the world-process is a part of God's own life, God's self-discovery, as it were. Thus whilst one polarity of God is still metaphysical, eternal, etc., another is contingent, temporal and so on. On this view God himself is an incomplete, emerging, evolving being, whose life cannot be separated from his interactions with the world.

11 Michel Foucault, *The Archaeology of Knowledge*, tr. A. M. Sheridan Smith, London: Tavistock Press 1974, p. 10.

12 Foucault, *Archaeology of Knowledge*, p. 10.

13 Foucault, *Archaeology of Knowledge*, p. 7.

14 See Karl Jaspers, *The Origin and Goal of History*, tr. M. Bullock, New Haven and London: Yale University Press 1953.

15 Walter Benjamin, 'Theses on the Philosophy of History', *Illuminations*, tr. H. Zohn, London: Fontana/Collins 1973, pp. 259–60.

16 Benjamin, *Illuminations*, p. 265.

17 To this question see Michael Theunissen, *Negative Theologie der Zeit*, Frankfurt am Main: Suhrkamp 1992.

18 This comment applies just as much to the view, associated with Francis Fukuyama, that we have come to the 'end of history', i.e. that all the possibilities of human thought and activity have now been made known in principle and that all that remains is the application of them in the endlessly fluctuating circumstances of the future. For Fukuyama's view is nothing if not historical in the sense that it is only though history itself that we have arrived at the post-historical stage. See Francis Fukuyama, *The End of History and the Last Man*, London: Penguin 1992.

19 R. Bultmann, *History and Eschatology*, Edinburgh: Edinburgh University Press 1975.

Chapter 3. Modern Trends (ii): The Turn to the Subject

1 See Francesco Petrarca, 'The Ascent of Mount Ventoux', tr. H. Nachod, in *The Renaissance Philosophy of Man*, eds. E. Cassirer, P. O. Kristeller and J. H. Randall, jr., Chicago: University of Chicago Press 1948.

2 See, e.g. 'St Paul and Subjectivity' in Gabriel Josipovici, *The Book of God. A Response to the Bible*, New Haven and London: Yale University Press 1988.

3 See references in Theodore Kisiel, *The Genesis of Heidegger's Being and Time*, Berkeley and Los Angeles: University of California Press 1993, especially Part 1, Chapter 4, pp. 192ff.

4 Descartes, *Discourse on Method and the Meditations*, tr. F. E. Sutcliffe, Harmondsworth: Penguin 1968, p. 41.

5 Descartes, *Discourse on Method*, p. 55.

6   Pascal, *Pensées*, tr. A. J. Krailsheimer, Harmondsworth: Penguin 1966, p. 89.

7   Pascal, *Pensées*, p. 90.

8   Pascal, *Pensées*, p. 92.

9   F. D. E. Schleiermacher, *On Religion. Speeches to its Cultured Despisers*, tr. R. Crouter, Cambridge: Cambridge University Press 1988, p. 104.

10   Schleiermacher, *Speeches*, p. 110.

11   Schleiermacher, *Speeches*, pp. 111–12.

12   Schleiermacher, *Speeches*, p. 113.

13   S. Kierkegaard, *Concluding Unscientific Postscript*, tr. D. Swenson and W. Lowrie, Princeton: Princeton University Press 1968, p. 181.

14   Kierkegaard, *Concluding Unscientific Postscript*, p. 182.

15   Kierkegaard, *Concluding Unscientific Postscript*, p. 185.

16   'Paradoxically', because whilst Heidegger always seems to operate in a certain proximity to religious thought, Sartre is resolutely and from the beginning committed philosophically to consistent atheism. However, Heidegger himself draws a distinction between what he calls the merely ontic or *'existentiell'* approach of Kierkegaard, which is always directed towards illuminating the situation of a concretely existing individual, whereas his own analyses aim at what he calls a fundamental ontological analysis, i.e. an analysis of the underlying structures determinative for all individuals. Sartre, though seeking, like Heidegger, a general ontology, is also continually fascinated by and, perhaps, at his most insightful in giving an account of the actual ways in which the quest for and flight from freedom get worked out in the stuff of living.

17   F. Nietzsche, *Thus Spoke Zarathustra. A Book for Everyone and No One*, tr. R. J. Hollingdale, Harmondsworth: Penguin 1961, p. 174.

18   This, however, is only one reading of Nietzsche. There are other texts that could be read more as a critique of the ambition to self-assertion, and as sharply observant of the limits placed by chance and fate on any project of self-discovery and self-overcoming.

19   These are, of course, only a few examples, and reflect my own Protestant-existentialist orientation. However, it is no less true that the turn to the subject has been a powerful influence in Catholic thought, Karl Rahner being a striking example of how the classic Thomist model of the relationship between natural and super-natural is reworked within a philosophical situation shaped by Kant and Heidegger, so that the starting point is no longer reflection on such cosmological laws as causality or motion but 'Man in the Presence of Absolute Mystery'. See – amongst his voluminous output – Karl Rahner, *Foundations of Christian Faith. An Introduction to the Idea of Christianity*, tr. W. V. Dych, London: Darton, Longman and Todd 1978.

20 See M. Buber, *I and Thou*, tr. W. Kaufmann, Edinburgh: T. and T. Clark 1970. For the allusions to trees and cats see pp. 57–8 and pp. 144–5.

21 Even Kierkegaard may prove to be a more 'dialogical' thinker than he has generally been given credit for. See, e.g. George Pattison and Steven Shakespeare, 'Introduction' to *Kierkegaard: The Self in Society*, Basingstoke: Macmillan 1997. Also several recent studies including Pia Søltoft, *Svimmelhedens Etik – om forholdet mellem den enkelte og den anden hos Buber, Levinas og især Kierkegaard* [The Ethics of Vertigo – on the relation between the individual and the other in Buber, Levinas and, especially, Kierkegaard], Copenhagen: Gad 2000.

22 Bultmann, *History and Eschatology*, p. 150.

23 Bultmann, *History and Eschatology*, p. 150.

24 Bultmann, *History and Eschatology*, p. 150. The critical view taken here of the limits of what one can achieve on the basis of one's own will puts down a marker against the kind of existential heroism associated with a certain reading of *Being and Time*.

25 See, e.g. Alister Hardy, *The Living Stream. A Restatement of Evolution Theory and its Relation to the Spirit of Man*, London: Collins 1965. (Like James' *Varieties of Religious Experience* this is also the record of the author's Gifford lectures.)

Chapter 4. Modern Trends (iii): The Linguistic Turn

1 See Agnes Heller (ed.), *Lukács Reappraised*, New York: Columbia University Press 1983.

2 For the links between the Frankfurt School theorists and Paul Tillich see, e.g. Rolf Wiggershaus, *The Frankfurt School. Its History, Theories, and Political Significance*, tr. M. Robertson, Cambridge, MA: MIT Press 1994. Unfortunately most histories of the school have a secularist orientation that downplays the important connections between the agenda of the Frankfurt theorists and contemporary theology.

3 See, e.g. Gershom Scholem, *Kabbalah*, New York: Dorset Press 1974.

4 J. Milbank, *The World Made Strange. Theology, Language, Culture*, Oxford: Basil Blackwell 1987, p. 97.

5 See, e.g. Denys Turner, *The Darkness of God. Negativity in Christian Mysticism*, Cambridge: Cambridge University Press 1995; Michael A. Sells, *Mystical Languages of Unsaying*, Chicago: University of Chicago Press 1994.

6 J. G. Hamann, 'Des Ritters von Rosencreuz letzte Willensmeynung über den göttlichen und menschlichen Ursprung der Sprache (1772)' [The final opinion of the Rosicrucian Knight concerning the divine and human Origin of Language] in *Schriften zur Sprache*, ed. J. Simon, Frankfurt am Main: Suhrkamp 1967.

7   Hamann, *Schriften*, p. 223.

8   Hamann, *Schriften*, p. 224.

9   A point already made by Aristotle.

10   S. Kierkegaard, *Kjerlighedens Gjerninger* in *Samlede Værker*, 3rd edn, Vol. 12, Copenhagen: Glyldendal 1962, pp. 18–19.

11   Hamann, incidentally, was an important early influence on Kierkegaard. Nevertheless, Kierkegaard's insistence on the division between the 'spiritual' dimension of language and its sensuous embodiment in the spoken word marks a clear point of difference, since, for Hamann, the meaningfulness of language is inseparable from its corporeality.

12   See Charles L. Creegan, *Wittgenstein and Kierkegaard. Religion, Individuality and Philosophical Method*, London: Routledge 1989.

13   A formulation particularly favoured by Paul Tillich as, in his view, the one non-symbolic statement we can make about God.

14   John Wisdom, *Philosophy and Psycho-Analysis*, Oxford: Basil Blackwell 1969, pp. 154–5.

15   Wisdom, *Philosophy and Psycho-Analysis*, p. 156.

16   See A. Flew in the section 'Theology and Falsification', *New Essays in Philosophical Theology*, ed. A. Flew and A. MacIntyre, London: SCM Press 1955, pp. 96–9.

17   John Hick, 'Religious Statements as Factually Significant', *The Existence of God*, London: Macmillan 1964, pp. 252–74.

18   Flew and MacIntyre, *New Essays in Philosophical Theology*, pp. 99–103.

19   Flew and MacIntyre, *New Essays in Philosophical Theology*, pp. 103–5. There are parallels here to the theme of the divine 'incognito' in the incarnation, a theme developed by Kierkegaard in *Practice in Christianity* and, subsequently, by Bonhoeffer.

20   In Hick, *The Existence of God*, pp. 228–52.

21   '*Agape*' being the distinctive term for love used in the New Testament and often contrasted with '*eros*' to indicate a kind of love that is selfless and other-regarding, rather than a love that is driven by personal passion or need.

22   L. Wittgenstein, *Philosophical Investigations*, tr. G. E. M. Anscombe, Oxford: Basil Blackwell 1972, p. 3.

23   Wittgenstein, *Philosophical Investigations*, pp. 6–7.

24   See, for example, the way in which Dorothy Emmet discusses Kant's regulative ideals in D. Emmet, *The Role of the Unrealisable*, Basingstoke: Macmillan 1994.

25   See George A. Lindbeck, *The Nature of Doctrine. Religion and Theology in a Postliberal Age*, London: SPCK 1984.

26   See, e.g. Steven T. Katz, 'Language, Epistemology and Mysticism',

Mysticism and Philosophical Analysis, London: Sheldon Press 1978. The nub of Katz's argument is that 'there are no pure (i.e. unmediated) experiences' (p. 26) but that, on the contrary, experience itself is what and as it is because of our pre-experiential beliefs. These, however, are not understood *à la* Kant in terms of a priori conceptual structures but more in terms of our language and cultural conditioning. The influence of our personal and cultural mind-set on our experience is, of course, something that has long been familiar. But if remarking on this is to amount to a more than merely trivial observation it is necessary to consider the question as to how one might decide the boundary between what is and what isn't thus culturally variable and between what belongs to culture and what to biology. But this, it seems to me, is what Katz doesn't do – nor do most of those, like Lindbeck, who follow this line of argument: the exclusion of experience in favour of language and culture thus becomes an empty slogan of little real philosophical interest.

27 See F. Kerr, *Theology after Wittgenstein*, London: SPCK 1997, especially Part Two 'Changing the Subject' and Chapter Three 'The Solipsist in the Flyglass'.

28 Perhaps the best known of those who apply narrative theology to questions of ethics is Stanley Hauerwas – see any of his extensive publications.

29 See Nicholas Lash, 'How Large is a "Language Game"?', *Theology*, 87, January 1984, no. 715, pp. 19–28. Lash draws on Norman Malcolm to support the 'micro-' interpretation. Such an approach can – although Lash does not use it in this way – open up the possibility of a return to ideas of experience on Wittgensteinian soil in that it takes us back into the vicinity of the lived actuality of individual life.

30 See D. Z. Phillips, *Faith after Foundationalism*, London: Routledge 1988, especially Part Four 'Religion and Concept-Formation'.

31 For Heidegger's relation to Hölderlin see my *Routledge GuideBooks in Philosophy: The Later Heidegger*, London: Routledge 2000, especially Chapter Seven 'Hölderlin'.

32 J. Derrida, *Of Grammatology*, tr. G. C. Spivak, Baltimore: John Hopkins University Press 1976, p. 158.

33 Derrida, *Of Grammatology*, p. 69.

34 On the connection between Derrida and apophatic theology, see Kevin Hart, *The Trespass of the Sign. Deconstruction, Theology and Philosophy*, Cambridge: Cambridge University Press 1989; Harold Coward and Toby Foshay, *Derrida and Negative Theology*, Albany: State University of New York Press 1992 (this includes relevant selections from Derrida). See also John D. Caputo, *The Prayers and*

Tears of Jacques Derrida. Religion without Religion, Bloomington: Indiana University Press, 1998, especially Part One 'The Apophatic'. Nor is Derrida's impact limited to Judaeo-Christian traditions, cf. Robert Magliola, *On Deconstructing Life-worlds: Buddhism, Christianity, Culture*, Atlanta, GA: Scholars Press 1997.

Chapter 5. 'Nothing but ...'

1 See Paul M. van Buren, *The Secular Meaning of the Gospel based on an Analysis of its Language*, London: SCM Press 1963.

2 See Thomas J. J. Altizer and William Hamilton, *Radical Theology and the Death of God*, Harmondsworth: Penguin 1968.

3 This kind of interpretation of Bonhoeffer was developed, amongst others, by Ronald Gregor Smith. See, e.g. his *The New Man. Christianity and Man's Coming of Age*, London: SCM 1956, and *Secular Christianity*, London: Collins 1966.

4 J. A. T. Robinson, *Honest to God*, London: SCM Press 1963. This tradition of theological thinking has more recently been carried forward by Don Cupitt and the sequence of books beginning with *Taking Leave of God*, London: SCM Press 1980 – it is striking (and greatly to its credit) that SCM Press was particularly associated with this radical strand of modern theology.

5 G. W. F. Hegel, *Aesthetics*, tr. T. M. Knox, London: Oxford University Press 1975, pp. 9–10.

6 See G. W. F. Hegel, *Lectures on the Philosophy of Religion. One-Volume Edition*, tr. P. C. Hodgson, Berkeley, Los Angeles and London: University of California Press 1988, pp. 85–91.

7 L. Feuerbach, *Principles of the Philosophy of the Future*, tr. M. Vogel, Indianapolis: Hackett 1986, p. 30.

8 G. W. F. Hegel, *Philosophy of Right*, tr. T. M. Knox, Oxford: Oxford University Press 1967, pp. 12–13.

9 Hegel, *Philosophy of Religion*, pp. 75–6.

10 A steady trickle of commentators has taken Hegel's claim to count as a religious or Christian thinker seriously. For a recent contribution in this line see Rowan Williams, 'Logic and Spirit in Hegel', *Post-Secular Philosophy. Between Philosophy and Theology*, ed. P. Blond, London: Routledge 1988, pp. 116–30.

11 This described a Feuerbachian utopia – famously satirized by Dostoevsky in his *Notes from Underground*.

12 See L. Feuerbach, *The Essence of Christianity*, tr. G. Eliot, New York: Harper and Row 1957, Chapter One, pp. 1–32.

13 Feuerbach, *The Essence of Christianity*, pp. 275–6.

14 Feuerbach, *The Essence of Christianity*, p. 277.

15 Van A. Harvey, however, has argued that in his later works

Feuerbach moved towards a critique of religion that was closer to that of Freud, seeing religion more as an expression of humanity's infantile helplessness in the face of threatening and potentially overwhelming cosmic forces. See Van A. Harvey, *Feuerbach and the Interpretation of Religion*, Cambridge: Cambridge University Press 1995.

16 F. Nietzsche, *The Will to Power*, tr. W. Kaufmann, New York: Vintage 1968, pp. 12–13.

17 F. Nietzsche, *The Joyful Wisdom*, tr. T. Common, London: Foulis 1910, pp. 167–8. Kaufmann has translated this text with the title *The Gay Science*.

18 See F. Nietzsche, 'The Problem of Socrates', *Twilight of the Idols and the Anti-Christ*, tr. R. Hollingdale, Harmondsworth: Penguin 1968, pp. 29–34.

19 F. Nietzsche, 'First Essay: "God and Evil", "Good and Bad"', *The Birth of Tragedy and the Genealogy of Morals*, tr. F. Golffing, New York: Doubleday Anchor 1956.

20 Nietzsche, 'Second Essay: "Guilt", "Bad Conscience", and Related Matters', *The Birth of Tragedy and the Genealogy of Morals*, p. 218.

21 F. Nietzsche, *Selected Letters*, tr. A. N. Ludovico, London: Soho Books 1985, p. 363.

22 See E. Durkheim, *The Elementary Forms of the Religious Life*, tr. J. W. Swain, London: George Allen and Unwin 1976.

23 *Jung: Selected Writings*, ed. Anthony Storr, London: Collins Fontana 1983, pp. 239–40.

24 *Jung: Selected Writings*, p. 357.

25 See the various writings of Richard Dawkins and, with specific reference to the understanding of the brain as a system of networked computers developed in the context of the evolutionary process, Steven Pinker, *How the Mind Works*, London: Penguin 1997.

26 See Daniel C. Dennett, *Consciousness Explained*, London: Penguin 1991. In this connection we should note that when a consciousness-theorist such as David J. Chalmers sets out to promote an anti-reductive, dualist account of mind, he is nevertheless seeking a natural explanation and one that from a theological point of view is still essentially reductionistic in that it allows for an exhaustive explanation of the phenomenon of mind in terms of natural processes that do not require the hypothesis of any transcendent power – i.e. there is no 'other source' for the kinds of beings there are in the universe than the universe itself. See David J. Chalmers, *The Conscious Mind. In Search of a Fundamental Theory*, New York: Oxford University Press 1996. The point made in connection with Jung, that we must distinguish between rhetoric and substance, applies here too: it would be easy but mistaken for religious apologists to seize on

the anti-reductive rhetoric of Chalmers' work whilst overlooking its fundamentally naturalistic orientation.

27   A classic example of this – executed with extreme brilliance – is C. S. Lewis' *The Screwtape Letters*. A similar line of attack was also practised by both Dostoevsky and Kierkegaard.

28   It is for this reason that the central argument of John Milbank's *Theology and Social Theory: Beyond Secular Reason*, Oxford: Blackwell 1990 and the quest for a 'post-secular' paradigm of thought signalled by Milbank's associates in the 'radical orthodox' tendency is, finally, doomed to failure. Even if one admires the panache of this quixotic gesture, no one can really expect such theological flourishes to undo the global intellectual and cultural situation in which religion today finds itself. But worse – it is not entirely clear who might benefit from such gestures apart from those who make them.

Chapter 6. A Matter of Interpretation

1   See J. Derrida, *The Monolingualism of the Other, or, The Prosthesis of Origin*, tr. P. Mensah, Stanford: Stanford University Press 1998, p. 1.

2   F. D. E. Schleiermacher, *Hermeneutik und Kritik*, ed. M. Frank, Frankfurt am Main: Suhrkamp 1977, p. 101.

3   Schleiermacher, *Hermeneutik*, p. 116.

4   Schleiermacher, *Hermeneutik*, p. 167.

5   Schleiermacher, *Hermeneutik*, p. 169.

6   Schleiermacher, *Hermeneutik*, p. 169.

7   H.-G. Gadamer, *Truth and Method*, tr. J. Weinsheimer and D. G. Marshall, London: Sheed and Ward 1989, pp. 167–8.

8   See, e.g. W. Dilthey, *Selected Writings*, tr. and ed. H. P. Rickman, Cambridge: Cambridge University Press 1976. It is relevant that one of Dilthey's most ambitious works was a massive (and unfinished) life of Schleiermacher.

9   See H.-W. Bartsch, *Kerygma and Myth*, tr. R. H. Fuller, London: SPCK 1972. Perhaps the most succinct statement by Bultmann of the relationship between his own ideas and Heideggerian existentialism is in the article 'The Historicity of Man and Faith' in R. Bultmann, *Eschatology and Faith*, tr. S. M. Ogden, London: Collins Fontana 1974.

10   K. Barth, *The Epistle to the Romans*, tr. E. C. Hoskyns, Oxford: Oxford University Press 1968, p. 7.

11   See, e.g. Werner Jeanrond, *Theological Hermeneutics. Development and Significance*, London: SCM Press 1994. However, new titles in this area are constantly appearing.

12   See also Gadamer, *Truth and Method*, pp. 383ff.

13 M. Heidegger, *What is Called Thinking?*, tr. J. G. Gray and F. Wieck, New York: Harper and Row 1968, p. 17.
14 Benjamin, *Illuminations*, p. 265.

Chapter 7. Beyond Criticism

1 In the light of this comment we might, after all, suspect that Kierkegaard was, deep-down, more of a philosopher than the systematizers he attacked.

2 Sam Gill, 'The Academic Study of Religion', *Journal of the American Academy of Religion*, 72, 1994, pp. 995–6.

3 Milbank, *World Made Strange*, p. 50. The accusation of malice is, it should be said, a profoundly (and intentionally) anti-philosophical move, since the dialogical principle at the heart of philosophy can only function if all parties to the philosophical conversation are prepared to assume good-will on the part of the other interlocutors, unless or until some clear evidence to the contrary is offered. More broadly (and if taken seriously) such accusations undermine the core ethos of any common intellectual or academic life.

4 The point I am making here is analogous to one of the characteristic arguments of Paul Tillich, summed up in his comment that even '[t]he act of accepting meaninglessness is in itself a meaningful act' (P. Tillich, *The Courage to Be*, London: Collins Fontana 1962, p. 171).

5 For an account of how science has moved beyond simply giving us a view of the objective facts about the world to an all-embracing world-view that also provides imperatives for ethics and aesthetic practices see, e.g. Thomas Dixon, 'Theology, anti-theology and atheology: from Christian passions to secular emotions', *Modern Theology*, 15, 1999, especially pp. 320–5.

6 A classic exposition of such an anarchic approach to life is represented by the first part of Kierkegaard's *Either/Or*. The second part, it should be added, contains an equally classic response.

7 It may be objected that such a privileging of unity and consistency works against spontaneity and creativity and that the optimum position is one that achieves an open and evolving balance of creative chaos and purposive unity. It is, of course, not the task of a book like this to lecture individuals as to what this might mean for their intellectual, moral or psychological well-being. My point is simply to mark a boundary beyond which any kind of belief in personality is likely to suffer rapid and possibly irreversible corrosion.

8 The general shape of my argument here reflects that of Don Cupitt in

his recent book *Philosophy's Own Religion* (London: SCM Press 2000), where, for example, he writes of the present and future situation of religion that 'the philosophy of religion will lay out the possibility-conditions for religious writing. It will describe how post-modern philosophy sees language, the self, other selves and the world and this account will lead on to the constructive theology that shows in detail how religious writing can transform and redeem the world and human lives' (p. 30). In a different intellectual context something analogous was proposed in Paul Tillich's early essay 'Die Überwindung des religionsbegriffs in der Religionsphilosophie' ['The Overcoming of the Concept of Religion in the Philosophy of Religion'], P. Tillich, *Frühe Hauptwerke: Gesammelte Werke* Bd. I, Stuttgart: Evangelisches Verlagswerk 1959, pp. 367–88. In his later *Systematic Theology*, however, Tillich seems to have seen theology as more of an equal partner in the dialogue. It may be added that this is in fact how, in a secular society, many young people are now encountering the question of religion: through the study of philosophy at school level.

9   F. C. Baur, *Das Christlich des Platonismus oder Sokrates unde Christus. Eine religionsphilosophische Untersuchung*, Tübingen: 1837, p. 109.

10   Plato, '*Symposium or Banquet*', tr. Percy Bysshe Shelley, in *Five Dialogues of Plato on Poetic Inspiration,* ed. A. D. Lindsay, London: J. M. Dent 1910, p. 69.

11   Plato, '*Phaedo*', tr. H. Cary, *Five Dialogues*, p. 199.

12   As Shestov argued, the view that philosophy's ultimate concern is simply for the best, or what should matter most to human beings, a principle he finds articulated by Plotinus, undermines the very distinction between philosophy, religion and art. See L. Shestov, *In Job's Balances*, London: J. M. Dent 1932, p. 32.

13   Perhaps something like this is, for example, implicit in Kant's 'respect for the moral law'.

14   *Hölderlin*, tr. and ed. M. Hamburger, Harmondsworth: Penguin 1961, p. 134.

Chapter 8. Theodicy

1   David Hume, *Dialogues Concerning Natural Religion*, New York: Hafner 1948, p. 66.

2   Plato, *Timaeus*, tr. D. Warrington, London: J. M. Dent 1965, p. 19.

3   Plotinus, *The Enneads*, tr. S. Mackenna, ed. J. Dillon, Harmondsworth: Penguin 1991, p. 63.

4   Plotinus, *Enneads*, p. 57.

5   Augustine, *The City of God*, tr. H. Bettenson, ed. D. Knowles, Harmondsworth: Penguin 1972, p. 473.

6   Augustine, *City of God*, pp. 475–7.

7   See John Hick, *Evil and the God of Love*, London: Collins Fontana 1968, pp. 88ff. Hick is critical both of the aesthetic theme and of the definition of evil in terms of privation. However, the hermeneutical approach being pursued here means that even if we find these theoretically inadequate we do not simply discard them but attempt to seek out a meaning that can be hermeneutically clarified and, in the process of such clarification, brought into the space of our contemporary efforts to think about God.

8   Augustine, *City of God*, p. 480.

9   See Hick, *Evil and the God of Love*, pp. 182ff.

10   See M. Eliade, *The Myth of the Eternal Return or, Cosmos and History*, Princeton: Bollingen 1974, especially Chapter Four 'The Terror of History'.

11   For a highly influential account of how violence is embedded in the very processes of hominization, see the works of René Girard, especially, *Things Hidden Since the Foundation of the World*, tr. S. Bann and M. Metteer, London: Athlone 1987.

12   On Fedorev see, e.g. A. Walicki, *A History of Russian Thought from the Enlightenment to Marxism*, Stanford: Stanford University Press 1979, pp. 386–7.

13   G. A. Studdert-Kennedy, 'High and Lifted Up', *The Unutterable Beauty*, London: Hodder and Stoughton 1964, pp. 41–2.

14   Studdert-Kennedy, *Unutterable Beauty*, p. 43.

15   Teilhard de Chardin, *The Prayer of the Universe*, tr. R. Hague, London: Collins Fontana 1973, p. 105.

16   Teilhard, *Prayer of the Universe*, pp. 160–1.

17   Teilhard, *Prayer of the Universe*, p. 173.

18   Jim Garrison, *The Darkness of God: Theology after Hiroshima*, London: SCM Press 1982, p. 208.

19   V. Gardavsky, *God is Not Yet Dead*, tr. V. Menkes, Harmondsworth: Penguin, 1973, p. 218.

20   A. Camus, *The Myth of Sisyphus*, tr. J. O'Brien, Harmondsworth: Penguin 1975, p. 111.

21   J.-P. Sartre, *L'Existentialism est un Humanisme*, Paris: Nagel 1970, p. 49.

22   See the discussion of Berdyaev's and Tillich's view of history in my *Anxious Angels: A Retrospective View of Religious Existentialism*, Basingstoke: Macmillan 1999, pp. 183–5.

Chapter 9. Evil and Subjectivity

1   It is striking that even 'natural' disasters are today viewed through the lens of political and human factors: we ask why people were allowed to live in substandard housing in an earthquake zone, and what role our own abuse of the environment played in bringing about the conditions for, e.g. the catastrophic flooding of Bangladesh.

2   Voltaire, *Candide*, French text ed. J. H. Brumfitt, Oxford: Oxford University Press 1968, pp. 155–6 (my emphasis).

3   I. Kant, 'On the miscarriage of all philosophical trials in theodicy', *Religion and Rational Theology*, tr. and ed. A. Wood and G. Di Giovanni, Cambridge: Cambridge University Press 1996, p. 32.

4   Kant, *Religion and Rational Theology*, p. 34.

5   S. Kierkegaard, *Fear and Trembling* and *Repetition*, tr. H. and E. H. Hong, Princeton: Princeton University Press 1983, pp. 197–8.

6   M. Susman, 'God the Creator', *The Dimensions of Job. A Study and Selected Readings*, ed. Nahum Glatzer, New York: Schocken Books 1969, p. 86.

7   Susman, 'God the Creator', p. 86

8   Susman, 'God the Creator', p. 87.

9   Susman, 'God the Creator', p. 92.

10 F. M. Dostoevsky, *The Brothers Karamazov*, tr. C. Garnett, London: Heinemann 1912, p. 252.

11 Dostoevsky, *Brothers Karamazov*, p. 250. Even if Dostoevsky later shows that evil sets in at a relatively early age there is nothing in his work approaching the Augustinian view of original sin that each of us is conceived and born in sin prior to our committing any single sinful act, i.e., that ontological sin preconditions moral sin.

12 Dostoevsky, *Brothers Karamazov*, p. 251.

13 Augustine, *Confessions*, tr. R. S. Pine-Coffin, Harmondsworth: Penguin, 1961, p. 47.

14 Augustine, *City of God*, pp. 479–80.

15 Augustine, *City of God*, p. 572.

16 Augustine, *City of God*, p. 574.

17 J.-P. Sartre, *Being and Nothingness*, tr. H. Barnes, London: Methuen 1958, p. 21.

18 J.-P. Sartre, *Being and Nothingness*, p. 22.

19 Kant, *Religion and Rational Theology*, p. 86.

20 Kant, *Religion and Rational Theology*, p. 89.

21 Kant, *Religion and Rational Theology*, p. 31.

22 Earlier translations also use 'dread' for the Danish '*angest*'.

23 S. Kierkegaard, *The Concept of Anxiety*, tr. R. Thomte and A. B. Anderson, Princeton: Princeton University Press 1980, p. 41.

24 Kierkegaard, *Concept of Anxiety*, p. 43.

25 Kierkegaard, *Concept of Anxiety*, p. 41.

26 Kierkegaard, *Concept of Anxiety*, p. 45.

27 Kierkegaard, *Concept of Anxiety*, p. 61.

28 See H. Arendt, *Eichmann in Jerusalem. A Report on the Banality of Evil*, London: Penguin 1994.

29 These comments, it should be noted, suggest a way of hermeneutically retrieving a non-metaphysical understanding of the theme of evil as privation.

Chapter 10. Eternal Life?

1 Hick, *Evil and the God of Love*, p. 290.

2 Hick, *Evil and the God of Love*, p. 372.

3 J. Hick, *Death and Eternal Life*, London: Collins Fontana 1976, p. 463.

4 J. Butler, *The Analogy of Religion Natural and Revealed*, London: J. M. Dent 1906, p. 257.

5 Kierkegaard, *Concluding Unscientific Postscript*, p. 149.

6 Kierkegaard, *Concluding Unscientific Postscript*, pp. 153–4.

7 F. M. Dostoevsky, *The Idiot*, tr. C. Garnett, London: Heinemann 1913, pp. 61–2.

8 S. Beckett, *Waiting for Godot*, Act 2 (Vladimir).

9 Dostoevsky, *The Idiot*, pp. 399–400.

10 Ibid, p. 400.

11 Dostoevsky, *The Brothers Karamazov*, p. 296.

12 Ibid, p. 297.

13 Ibid, p. 298.

14 Ibid, p. 379.

15 Ibid, p. 682.

16 Ibid, p. 683.

17 Ibid, p. 683.

18 In connection with this we may note that a central strand in the novel concerns Ivan's culpability for the murder of his father, a question that hinges on the extent of his self-consciousness in prompting his half-brother Smerdyakov, the actual perpetrator of the murder. This part of the story strongly underscores Ivan's mental confusion prior to his breakdown, i.e., including the period of his 'rebellion', and his inability to understand his own motivations. In this context his refusal of hope and his readiness to give the nod to murder are, Dostoevsky hints, interdependent.

19 This understanding of Dostoevsky, of course, owes much to Bakhtin. See M. Bakhtin, *Problems of Dostoevsky's Poetics*, tr. C. Emerson, Minneapolis: University of Minnesota Press 1984.

20   Dostoevsky, *The Brothers Karamazov*, p. 821.
21   See P. Ricoeur, *The Symbolism of Evil*, tr. E. Buchanan, Boston: Beacon
     Press 1969, pp. 347ff. Ricoeur's study is a classic example of a
     hermeneutic approach that, as such, takes its starting point from the
     human and subjective phenomenon of confession and is worked
     through in the light of a historical contextualization of the issue.
22   That much of our reflection in these last chapters has been guided
     by references to literature might suggest that, in the context of
     modernity, 'philosophy' will not only be represented by what is
     taught under that title in universities, but operates through the
     medium of imaginative literature. This point corresponds to
     Bakhtin's remark that when the novel becomes the dominant form of
     literature we see also the novelization of other genres – including the
     writing of philosophy. It does not, of course, follow that each and
     every novel is thereby 'philosophical'. On the contrary, the philo-
     sophical element in a novel is likely to tear at its narrative and formal
     perfection – something that can be seen in the novels of Dostoevsky
     himself.
23   V. Soloviev, 'Lectures on God-Manhood', *Spor o Spravedliivost':
     Sochiineniia*, Moscow: Yeksmo Press 1999, p. 48.

Index